REA's Books

They have rescued lots of grades and more!

(a sample of the hundreds of letters REA receives each year)

"Your books are great! They are very helpful, and have upped my grade in every class. Thank you for such a great product."

Student, Seattle, WA

"Your book has really helped me sharpen my skills and improve my weak areas. Definitely will buy more."

Student, Buffalo, NY

"Compared to the other books that my fellow students had, your book was the most useful in helping me get a great score."

Student, North Hollywood, CA

"I really appreciate the help from your excellent book. Please keep up your great work."

Student, Albuquerque, NM

"Your book was such a better value and was so much more complete than anything your competition has produced (and I have them all)!"

Teacher, Virginia Beach, VA

(more on next page)

(continued from previous page)

"Your books have saved my GPA, and quite possibly my sanity. My course grade is now an 'A', and I couldn't be happier."

Student, Winchester, IN

"These books are the best review books on the market. They are fantastic!"

Student, New Orleans, LA

"Your book was responsible for my success on the exam. . . I will look for REA the next time I need help."

Student, Chesterfield, MO

"I think it is the greatest study guide I have ever used!"

Student, Anchorage, AK

"I encourage others to buy REA because of their superiority. Please continue to produce the best quality books on the market."

Student, San Jose, CA

"Just a short note to say thanks for the great support your book gave me in helping me pass the test . . . I'm on my way to a B.S. degree because of you !"

Student, Orlando, FL

JAPANESE GRAMMAR

with CD-ROM

William McGovern, Ph.D.
Professor of Japanese Studies

and the Staff of
Research & Education Association,
Carl Fuchs, Language Program Director

Research & Education Association
61 Ethel Road West
Piscataway, New Jersey 08854

Dr. M. Fogiel, Director

SUPER REVIEW®
OF JAPANESE GRAMMAR with CD-ROM

Printed in the United States of America

Library of Congress Control Number 2001096032

International Standard Book Number 0-87891-422-6

I-1

WHAT THIS Super Review WILL DO FOR YOU

This **Super Review** provides all that you need to know to do your homework effectively and succeed on exams and quizzes.

The book focuses on the core aspects of the subject, and helps you to grasp the important elements quickly and easily.

Outstanding **Super Review** features:

- Topics are covered in logical sequence

- Topics are reviewed in a concise and comprehensive manner

- The material is presented in student-friendly form that makes it easy to follow and understand

- Individual topics can be easily located

- Provides excellent preparation for midterms, finals and in-between quizzes

- Written by professionals and experts who function as your very own tutors

Dr. Max Fogiel, Director
Carl Fuchs, Language Program Director

CONTENTS

The Nature of the Japanese Language

Japanese is usually considered a difficult language, but its difficulty has been greatly exaggerated.

There are only two important obstacles in the path of the student. The first is the extraordinary variation between the written style, the spoken style, and the other forms of the language, and second the difference between Japanese and all other languages.

Notwithstanding the complexity of French, or German, or Latin, they are comparatively easy for the English student because of their similarity to his own language. Their grammar, their vocabulary, their underlying genius, all have points of contact. Nor, journeying still further Eastward, is Persian or Sanskrit entirely alien, since both come within the boundary of Indo-European culture.

Though this point is readily understood, many persons suppose that at least Japanese has some close similarity to Chinese; that they are in fact but different developments of the same linguistic stock. This is far from true for although, well within historic times, Japan has borrowed much from the richness of Chinese, in their essence Japanese and Chinese are almost as far apart as Japanese and English.

Chinese is monosyllabic. Japanese is polysyllabic. Chinese is terse, pithy, and to the point. Japanese is flowing, melodious, and vague. Chinese is highly difficult to pronounce, owing to the complex system of tones. Japanese has no tones and its pronunciation is unusually easy. Chinese has practically no grammar whatsoever. Its nouns have no number, gender, or case ; its verbs no tense. In fact there is no real distinction between a noun, a verb, and an adjective. The sense must be ascertained from the context. Japanese, especially in the written style, has an intricate grammatical system, and a large number of qualifying endings.

Though real Chinese and real Japanese have, therefore, nothing in common, modern Japanese has absorbed a great portion of Chinese idioms by a process of direct assimilation. When the Japanese came into contact with their Celestial neighbors, they were entirely ignorant of letters. They envied the Chinese their literature, their learning, and their culture, and for the Japanese to envy is to imitate. Accordingly before long the peculiar ideographs of China were employed to transcribe their own utterly alien tongue.

Chinese had no way of expressing tense or case endings, so that after a short time in addition to the symbolic characters taken wholesale from abroad, a set of fifty (with modifications seventy-five) phonetic letters were devised to supply the deficiency.

Quite apart from the ideographs a large number of Chinese words were likewise assimilated, for the native vernacular had terms for only concrete and familiar objects, and was urgently in need of the wealth and flexibility of vocabulary which its rival possessed.

Special Peculiarities

As instances of the peculiar structure of the language

the following points deserve attention, though no attempt should be made to memorize them :—

1.—Japanese nouns like those of China, have for the most part, neither article, number, nor gender.

2.—Case is indicated by means of prepositions, which, being placed after the word qualified are usually known as postpositions.

3.—Personal pronouns are very seldom used. " What doing ? " generally means " What are you doing ? " and " Reading," " I am reading." Even where employed, the so-called personal pronouns are really independent nouns, with a quite separate meaning. Such for example are the common words for " I "—*watakushi,* literally " selfishness," *boku*—" servant " ; *shōsei*—" junior " ; *sessha*—" awkward person." For the second person we find *anata*—" that direction " ; *kimi*—" lord," and *o mae* —" honorable in front."

4.—The Japanese adjective has one unique feature. Instead of being declined, and so correlated with the noun, it is a part of the verb, and can be conjugated in all of its tenses.

5.—The verb also is idiomatic and is built up on an entirely unfamiliar basis. In addition to the passive, there is a causative, a desiderative, an alternative, and other unusual verbal forms. The passive may be used in an active sense when speaking of the actions of a superior person.

6.—The structure of the sentence is quite unlike English, though both in syntax and in mode of expression, it resembles German. Long-winded sentences with the main verb at the end somewhat puzzle the beginner.

7.—More essential than any grammatical idiom or technical peculiarity, is the important difference between the mode of thought between Japan and the West. Exact translation is, in most cases, out of the question, since like circumstances do not call forth the same ideas. On meeting a person for the first time, an Englishman probably murmurs some platitude such as " I am glad to meet you." In most European languages the thought to be expressed would be more or less the same. In Japanese, however, the matter would be quite different. The stock phrase, *Hajimete o me ni kakarimasu* means literally " beginning-to august eyes to am-hanging," or more freely, " For the first time I have been able to catch your honorable eye."

Divisions of the Language

Unlike the scholars of the Middle Ages most European peoples now speak and write in more or less the same language, though, as far as English is concerned, the written style tends to an increase of words derived from Latin.

In the Orient there is usually a sharp line of contrast between the colloquial and literary forms, but in Japanese the situation is even more complicated, as there may be said to be at least four independent and two semi-independent styles. These are :—

I.—The Colloquial Style which is the medium for the ordinary exchange of ideas, and which is now more or less the same all throughout the country, though the Tōkyō or Kyōtō accent is considered the standard as opposed to various minor provincial dialects, the most important being those of Sendai in the North and Satsuma in the South. The grammar of the colloquial is entirely Japanese, and even in its vocabulary the native element greatly outweighs the Chinese element. Apart from postpositions, and other frequently used terms, the average educated person employs two Japanese words for every one Chinese word, making the average two-thirds to one-third.

2.—THE EPISTOLARY STYLE which is used almost exclusively for writing letters and postcards. Though it has now come to include in its vocabulary and idioms many Chinese expressions, in its grammar and general structure it closely resembles the spoken language of a few centuries ago. In fact in most books the dialogues are written in the epistolary style.

3.—THE LITERARY STYLE in which the books, magazines, and newspapers are written. The treatment of the nouns, pronouns, and prepositions (postpositions) is not essentially different from the colloquial, but the adjective and verb are built up on an entirely different system. An examination of the modern vocabulary would show about two-thirds of the words to be Chinese and one-third Japanese.

4.—THE CLASSICAL STYLE, which is in reality Classical Chinese, based on the language of the Confucian Canon. Prior to the Restoration this was employed in all serious and philosophical writing, the native literary language being used chiefly for romances, stories, and poems.

This state of things is not altogether without historical parallel in England. The language which Dr. Johnson spoke and the language which he wrote correspond in a general way to the difference between the colloquial and the literary style of Japan. Foreign elements, in one case Latin, in the other Chinese, characterize the latter. Had Dr. Johnson lived slightly earlier he would have undoubtedly written his serious works in Latin, just as Japanese scholars wrote in Chinese. Finally had he written his correspondence in the language of Chaucer, the analogy would have been complete.

In addition to the four distinct styles, there are several others which are mere modifications of these along certain lines. Notable among these are, first: the Court Language, which is closely related to the language spoken by the educated ladies, and second: the language of public speaking. The first is known by its preference for archaic Japanese forms in place of Chinese expressions, and also by its extraordinary euphemisms, *e.g.*, the common word for salt *shiwo* being replaced by *nami-no-hana*, "flower of the wave." The second is a combination of the literary and colloquial styles, since sermons, lectures, addresses, etc., are considered too serious to be delivered in the pure colloquial, and too ephemeral for the pure literary language.

Methods of Writing Japanese

Japanese epigraphy is a very interesting study since Japanese is one of the few living tongues which employs both phonetic and ideographic symbols in writing. Since there are three types of phonetic letters, Japanese writing may be divided in the following way:—

A.—Ideographic (*Honji*)
B.—Phonetic
  1.—Running Hand (*Hirakana*)
  2.—Stiff Hand (*Katakana*)
  3.—Roman Letters (*Rōmaji*)

Taking these up in their inverse order, we find that the whole of the Japanese language may be written with the ordinary English or Roman Letters, without recourse to any other symbols, whether phonetic or ideographic. The comparative simplicity of this scheme has won for it many adherents, and a number of books, and an occasional newspaper or magazine are published entirely in the *Rōmaji*, as it is called.

Up to the present the movement has not gone much farther than the simplified or phonetic spelling idea has done in England. This is due not only to the natural conservatism of the people but also to the fact that there are such large numbers of words pronounced alike and with widely differing meanings. This means, of course, that the adoption of any purely phonetic alphabet is laden with difficulty. Even when speaking, a Japanese must sometimes write an ideograph in the air with his finger before his auditors can comprehend him.

The stiff and running hands consist of approximately seventy-five letters devised for writing grammatical terminations. They are in reality nothing more than certain Chinese characters simplified and used phonetically. The whole of the language and not merely the tense endings and postpositions could be written in the *Kana*, but for the reason given previously no purely phonetic system has taken root. The stiff and running hands can be used almost interchangeably. Official documents usually employ the *Katakana*, all others the *Hirakana*, but even in the latter case, foreign names are transcribed in the stiff hand.

The *Honji* or *Kanji* consist of the ideographs taken over from China. Since they are symbolic rather than phonetic, a single ideograph may be pronounced in a number of different ways without changing the meaning. In almost all cases there are at least two pronunciations, one the old native word, and the other the Chinese term taken over with the character.

Thus for example the sign for man may be pronounced *hito* or *jin*, power *chikara* or *riki*, vehicle (literally wheel) *kuruma* or *sha*. In each case the former is the Japanese and the latter the Chinese sound. Generally speaking when the ideograph stands alone it is given the native rendering or *Kun*, and when compounded with other words the Chinese sound or *On*. Thus any one of the three words given above, if taken separately would be pronounced *hito*, or *chikara*, or *kuruma*, but we say *Jinrikisha* (the English rickshaw) for the old human-powered carriage.

Classical Japanese being pure Chinese, has no grammatical terminations, so the *kana* are not employed. In other cases, however, they are mixed with the *Honji* to indicate case, tense, etc. Thus for example in the following typical sentence the words in parenthesis would be written in *kana*, the others with the ideographs :—*Anata* (*wa*) *doko* (*ye*) *i*(*kimashita*) ?—" Where did you go ? "

The Japanese Alphabet

The native syllabary consists of five vowels, and nine consonants. The vowels are, of course, *a*, *i*, *u*, *e*, and *o* ; the consonants *k*, *s*, *t*, *n*, *h*, *m*, *y*, *r*, *w*. The consonants may not be employed alone, but must have a vowel attached to them. Thus the letters *ka*, *ki*, and *ko*, are all quite different in Japanese, and are conceived as separate letters. There being five vowel sounds for each consonant, there are forty-five compound letters, which with the five original vowels makes an alphabet of fifty in all.

The *Gojūon* or table of fifty sounds is sufficiently important to make memorization necessary :—

a	*ka*	*sa*	*ta*	*na*	*ha*	*ma*	*ya*	*ra*	*wa*
i	*ki*	*shi*	*chi*	*ni*	*hi*	*mi*	(*i*)	*ri*	*wi*
u	*ku*	*su*	*tsu*	*nu*	*fu*	*mu*	*yu*	*ru*	(*u*)
e	*ke*	*se*	*te*	*ne*	*he*	*me*	(*e*)	*re*	*we*
o	*ko*	*so*	*to*	*no*	*ho*	*mo*	*yo*	*ro*	*wo*

The four exceptions and the three missing letters should be carefully noted.

In addition to these so-called pure sounds there are a certain number of " modified " or *nigori* sounds. When preceded by other syllables, the *k* may change to *g*, the *s* to *z*, the *t* to *d*, the *h* to both *p* and *b*. In the *kana* this may be indicated by adding two dots to the original letter (*p* by adding a small circle). Thus *ka* with two dots is pronounced *ga*. This makes twenty-five additional sounds, with a nominal total of seventy-five in all.

ga	*za*	*da*	*ba*	*pa*
gi	*ji*	*ji*	*bi*	*pi*
gu	*zu*	*dzu*	*bu*	*pu*
ge	*ze*	*de*	*be*	*pe*
go	*zo*	*do*	*bo*	*po*

Actually the omission of *wi, wu,* and *we* brings the number down to seventy-two, and the addition of a final *n* makes a real total of seventy-three.

Pronunciation

The Japanese language is not at all difficult to pronounce, but the following points should be carefully considered :—

1.—Generally speaking there is only one sound for each letter. In English the words *pane, fat, father,* show that the letter *a* has a wide variation of sound, and so with the other letters. In Japanese though the vowels have a certain range of variation ; it is confined to narrow limits, and may be ignored.

2.—A very useful rule, and one which on the whole holds good, is that the vowels are to be pronounced as in Italian, and the consonants as in English. The five vowels have the following equivalents :—

a	varies	between	the	a	of	*cart*	and	*fast.*
i	,,	,,	,,	i	,,	*antique*	and	*stick.*
u	,,	,,	,,	oo	,,	*fool*	and	*foot.*
e	,,	,,	,,	e	,,	*grey*	and	*ten.*
o	,,	,,	,,	o	,,	*cone*	and	*cork.*

In each case the usual sound is nearer the first than the second example.

3.—In Japan there are practically no silent letters, even final *e* being pronounced. *Kuge* is not *kooj*, but *koogé*. The only possible exceptions to this rule are short *i* and *u*. Though not silent they are often so slurred over as to be almost inaudible. Thus *masu* sounds like *mas*, and *deshita* like *deshta*.

4.—In consequence of the preceding rule, double consonants must be distinguished. Thus *kitte* (stamp) must be pronounced *kit-te* to differentiate it from *kite* " coming "; *amma*, " shampooer," from *ama*, " nun "; and so on.

5.—The wide separation in sound between long and short vowels must be carefully studied. In *Rōmaji* long vowels have a stroke over them (*e.g.*, *ō*, *ū*, etc.) and have about the same quality but almost double the quantity of the ordinary vowels, *e.g.*, *ō* equals *o-o*, *ū* equals *u-u*, etc. Thus *toru* means " to take " and *tōru* " to pass by "; *o yama* " a small mountain," and *ō yama* " a large mountain "; *koko* means " here," and *kōkō* " filial piety." Long *ā* and *ē* very seldom occur, and long *i* is expressed by *ii*.

6.—In diphthongs each vowel retains its proper sound. Thus *ei* sounds almost like the English *a* in " wake," and *ae*, and *ai* are almost like the English " I."

7.—The pronunciation of the following sounds deserves especial attention. *F* is nothing but a modification of *h* and is sounded accordingly. The lower lip, instead of being placed on the teeth is thrust upward, outward, and forward. *R* has to take the place of *l* in Japanese, since the latter is entirely missing. Strictly speaking the Japanese *r* has a slight mixture of *l* and even *d* in it, but for ordinary purposes, to give it the English *r* sound is quite sufficient. *G* has always the hard sound as in "garden," the soft sound of "gem" being invariably expressed by *j*.

8.—In addition to these features the Tōkyō dialect has certain peculiarities of its own. Though in some ways less correct than the language spoken in Kyōto, it is rapidly becoming the standard for the whole nation, so that on most points the Tōkyō pronunciation should be followed. The letters which should be especially noted are *g*, *h*, *z* and *dz*, and *j*.

Initial *G* retains its hard sound but in the middle of a word it is much the same as the nasal *ng* of "singer" (not the *ng* of "finger"). Thus *kago*, "basket," is pronounced *kango*.

H becomes *sh* in vulgar Tōkyō dialect. In most cases this sound should be avoided but in certain cases the usage is universal. Thus *hito*, "person," is like *shito*, though the *sh* more closely resembles the *ch* in the German *ich*. The short *i* being almost inaudible *hito* becomes *shto*.

Z and *dz* are pronounced alike in Tōkyō, as are the two *j's* of *ji*. One is the modification of *shi* and should be sounded like the *z* in "azure." The other, the modification of *chi* is the *g* of "gem." In Tōkyō both have the latter sound.

9.—The following letters are missing in Japanese:—
c, *l*, *q*, *v*, *x*.

10.—Japanese, like French, has nothing like the strong tonic accent of English. Instead of *Yokohāma*, with the emphasis on the third syllable, each syllable should be stressed equally. In fact, though tonic accent is not entirely non-existent, it is so slight, and varies so much from place to place, that it may be entirely neglected by the average student.

CHAPTER 1
The Noun

Strictly speaking Japanese has no system of grammar at all. The large number of tense endings and postpositions are not codified, and may be arranged in any way that the student may find convenient. Foreign experts have devised more than twenty grammatical systems each widely differing from the other, and each equally correct. Each is pragmatic, and so long as it covers all the ground nothing can be said against it.

The one indigenous grammatical feature is the classification of all Japanese words into *Na*, *Hataraki-Kotoba*, and *Teniwoha*, which may be called uninflected words, inflected words, and postpositions.

The *Na* (literally "names") or uninflected words include the English Noun, Pronoun, and Numeral. They undergo no modification or inflection—case, etc., being expressed by means of postpositions.

The *Hataraki-Kotoba* (literally "working words") or the inflected words include the English Verb, Adjective, and Adverb. Instead of adding auxiliary words to indicate tense, etc., the word itself undergoes modification.

The *Teniwoha* correspond to the English Preposition, Conjunctions, and Interjections. They derive their name from the important postpositions, *de, ni, wo, wa.*

Article, Number, and Gender

In the vast majority of cases the ideas of article, number, and gender with regard to the *Na* remain unexpressed. Thus *ushi* means "the" or "a bull," or "the" or "a cow," or "bulls" or "cows"; *inu*, "dog" or "dogs," or "bitch" or "bitches"; *tori* "cock" or "cocks," "hen" or "hens." The exact meaning must be understood from the context.

This of course renders Japanese free from the artificial genders of most European languages, or even from the natural gender of English.

Case

Strictly speaking the Japanese nouns are also lacking in case, but to supply this deficiency there are a large number of postpositions to express case relationships. Of these postpositions only some nine or ten are of sufficient importance to require immediate attention. They may be arranged so as to correspond, more or less, to the Latin cases. They are:—

1.—Absolute	-	*wa*
2.—Nominative	-	*ga*
3.—Genitive	-	*no*
4.—Dative	-	*ni* or *ye*
5.—Accusative	-	*wo*
6.—Ablative	-	*de*, *to*, and *kara*

A few sentences easily illustrate their use. *Miru* is the Japanese word for *see*, so that *Ushi ga inu wo miru* signifies "The cow sees the dog," while *Inu ga ushi wo miru* means "The dog sees the cow."

Pronouns are treated as if they were nouns. *Watakushi* (pronounced *watákshi*) and *anata* being the most common words for "I" and "you." respectively. *Anata ga watakushi wo miru* means "You see me." *Hon* being "book," *hone* "bone," and *yaru* "give" (to an inferior) *Watakushi ga inu ni hone wo yaru* is "I give (to) the dog a bone."

No corresponds to the English "'s." *Tarō no hon* means "Taro's book," *inu no hone*, "the dog's bone," *anata no ushi,* your bull. *Watakushi ga inu ni Tarō no hone wo yaru,* "I give (to) the dog Taro's bone."

Both *ni* and *ye* are equivalent to the English "to," either expressed or understood, but *ni* is purely an indirect object, while *ye* has the sense of towards or in the direction of. *Tōkyō ye yuku,* "(I) go to Tōkyō" (note the omission of "I"); *Nihon kara Eikoku ye yuku,* "(I) go from Japan to England." (*Nihon or Nippon,* "Japan." *Eikoku,* "England." *Yuku,* "go.")

De and *to* present no great difficulty. *Watakushi ga anata to yuku,* "I go with you." *To* is like the English "with" or "and." *Anata ga kisha de yuku,* "You go by train" (*kisha* being "train") *Naifu de kiru,* "to cut with a knife" (*naifu* is the Japanese form of the English word "knife," while *kiru* is "cut.") *De* implies means or instrument.

Peculiar Case Formation

The only case particles which present any difficulty to the student are *wa,* the absolute; *ni* and *de* in the locative; and *de* in the predicative sense.

The subject, as we have seen, is often omitted in Japanese. *Hon wo yomu* means "I" or "You read a book." To express it fully, one must add *watakushi*, *anata* or whatever the pronoun may be, followed by *ga*. But between omitting the subject, and expressing it in full, there is a middle way. We may insert the subject half parenthetically to make sure that no mistake arises. Thus :—*Watakushi wa hon wo yomu* equals "(I) . . . read a book." In reality the *watakushi wa* is not a part of the sentence, but, to express the matter technically, is an independent and parenthetical clause standing in absolute relation to the sentence.

This absolute is very frequently used in Japanese, and generally it is almost indistinguishable in meaning from the nominative. In most cases we may say either *Anata ga inu wo miru* or *Anata wa inu wo miru* for "You see a dog." Strictly speaking, however, *wa* serves to emphasize the predicate, and *ga* the subject. Thus, for example, in answer to the question "Where are you going?" one should say *Watakushi wa Tōkyō ye yuku*, "I go *to Tōkyō*," the I, of course, being understood without special stress on it. In answer to the question "Who is going to Tōkyō?" the reply would be *Watakushi ga Tōkyō ye yuku.* "*I* go to Tōkyō."

Occasionally, however, the *wa* has an entirely opposite effect, and compares one subject with another. Thus *kore* means "this," *sore* "that," *umai* (pronounced *mmai*) "delicious," and *mazui* "distasteful." When we wish to contrast things and say, "This is nice but that is disagreeable," we have *kore wa umai, sore wa mazui*. Even in this case, however, it is chiefly the predicates which are contrasted, rather than the subjects, and in answer to which question "which is good?" *ga* would probably be substituted for *wa*.

Ni and *de* both have the additional meaning of " at " or " in." *Tōkyō ni* means " in Tōkyō." *Koko* means " this place," so that *koko ni* or *koko de* both signify " in " or " at this place," or " here." The difference between *ni* and *de* in this connection is somewhat subtle. *Ni* implies only existence at a specified place, *De* an action which is performed there. *Koko ni pen ga aru,* " Here a pen is " (" Pen " has been borrowed from English, while *aru* means " to be "), or as we should say in English, " There is a pen here." *Koko de watakushi wa hon wo yomu,* " I read a book here." Both *ni* and *de* may be placed in the absolute case by the addition of *wa,* when the locative phrase is unimportant, or when it is contrasted with something else.

The predicative use of *de* is even more important. In such a sentence as " This is a pen," the word " this " (*kore*) can be placed in either the nominative or the absolute case ; *aru* would signify " is," but what postposition would do after " pen " ? It is neither a direct nor an indirect object, so that neither *ni* nor *wo* will serve. The Japanese use *de* in such an instance. *Kore wa pen de aru,* and so in all other cases where the subject and the predicate refer to the same thing. This means, of course, that in the vast majority of cases where ever *aru* is found *de* is placed before it. Accordingly so frequent is the combination that *de aru* is usually contracted to *da,* while the more polite form of *aru, arimasu* coalesces with *de* into *desu.*

Finally, the distinction between *pen de aru* and *pen ga aru* should be carefully observed. The former means " (it) is a pen," and the latter " a pen is," or " there is a pen."

Other Parts of Speech

Before going further it is necessary to speak a word

regarding the other parts of speech, such as the pronoun, the verb, and the adjective.

The pronoun is considered, as we have seen, a sort of noun, and is treated accordingly. The same rules of number, gender and case apply to both, though pronouns more frequently make use of plural endings. Thus, *watakushi domo* equals " we "; *anatagata,* " you " (plural). The most common word for " he " or " she " is *ano hito* (literally " that person ") though we may also say *ano o kata,* " that lady " or " gentleman "; *ano otoko,* " that man," and *ano onna,* " that woman." *Sore* (literally " that ") is the most common word for " it."

All native Japanese verbs end either in *u* (*e.g. yomu, yuku,* etc.) or *ru* (*e.g. miru, taberu,* etc.). There is no infinitive, so that in mentioning a verb its familiar or impolite present is cited. Verbs are not affected by the person, number, or gender of their subjects. Thus *watakushi ga aru,* " I am "; *ano hito ga aru,* " he is "; *anatagata ga aru,* " you are."

All real adjectives end in *i* or, more correctly, in *oi, ui, ai,* or *ii.* All adjectives being quasi-verbs may be used either with or without a copula, *e.g., yoi* meaning " good "; for " the dog is good," we may say either *inu ga yoi* or *inu ga yoi desu.*

A familiar negative of verbs is formed by changing the *u* of *u* verbs to *a* and adding *nai, e.g., yomanai. Ru* verbs drop the *ru* and add *nai.* Adjectives change the final *i* to *ku* and add *nai, e.g., yoku nai.*

The Order of Words

The essential features of the Japanese arrangement of words in a sentence are comprehended in the following rules :—

1.—An ordinary sentence contains first the subject,

then the indirect object, the direct object, the means or instrument, and then the verb.

2.—Qualifying words precede the words which they qualify. In consequence, adjectives, as in English precede nouns (*e.g.*, " a good dog"—*yoi inu*) and, unlike English, adverbs precede verbs. Thus *yoku* meaning " well," and *hashiru*, " run," *yoku hashiru* means " to run well." In like manner, relative clauses are placed before their main word. For example, " the man who was rich," becomes " the rich was man." The only seeming exceptions to this rule are prepositions which become postpositions.

3.—An interrogation does not change the order of words in a sentence. The postposition *ka* is added to the usual arrangement. *Sore wa pen desu,* " That is a pen." *Sore wa pen desu ka ?* " Is that a pen ? " Should the sentence contain an interrogatory pronoun, the *ka* may be either omitted or retained. " Who ? " is *dare.* " Who are you ? " is either *Anata wa dare desu ?* or *Anata wa dare desu ka ?*

Vocabulary

kore, this (noun).
are, that (noun)—far things.
sono, that (adjective).
inu, dog.
iiye, no.
sō, so.
kodomo, child.
shimbun, newspaper.
nan or *nani*, what.
hana, flower.
tsukue, table-desk.
densha, tram.
chichi, father.
dare, who.
takusan, many, plenty.
otoko, man.
watakushi, I.
shiroi, white.
chiisai, small.
yoi, good.
taberu, eat.
miru, see.
iku or *yuku*, go.
no ue ni, on, upon.
sore, that (noun)—for near things.
kono, this (adjective).
ano, that (adjective).
neko, cat.
hai, yes.
tora, tiger.
hon, book.
niku, meat.

pen, pen.
empitsu, pencil.
Eikokujin, Englishman.
akindo, merchant.
doko, where, what place ?
san, Mr., Master, Mrs., Miss.
onna, woman.
anata, you.
kuroi, black.
ushi, cow.
aru, be.
yomu, read.
kaeru, return.
nai, is not.
oru, to be (for animate objects).

Exercise

1—*Kore wa inu desu.* 2—*Sore wa neko desu ka ?* 3—*Iiye, are wa tora desu.* 4—*Kono inu wa shiroi.* 5—*Sono neko wa kuroi.* 6—*Are wa ano chiisai kodomo no hon desu ka ?* 7—*Sō desu.* 8—*Watakushi wa hon wo yomu.* 9—*Anata wa shimbun wo yomanai.* 10—*Ushi wa niku wo tabenai.* 11—*Tarō wa hon wo minai.* 12—*Kore wa nan desu ka ?* 13—*Sore wa pen desu* (= *de arimasu*). 14—*Sore wa pen dewa nai.* 15—*Anata wa dare desu ka ?* 16—*Watakushi wa Sumisu desu.* 17—*Anata wa Fujita san desu ka ?* 18—*Hai, sō desu.* 19—*Kono hon wa yoku nai* 20—*Sono hana wa shiroku nai.* 21—*Empitsu wa doko ni aru ka ?* 22—*Empitsu wa tsukue no ue ni aru.* 23—*Tōkyō ni Eikokujin ga oru ka ?* 24—*Hai, takusan oru.* 25—*Densha de kaeru ka?* 26—*Anata no chichi wa akindo dewa nai.* 27—*Tōkyō kara Yokohama ye yuku.* 28—*Otoko to onna.* 29—*Watakushi no chichi wa akindo desu.*

Translation

1—This is a dog. 2—Is that a cat ? 3—No, that is a tiger. 4—This dog is white. 5—That cat is black. 6—Is that that small child's book ? 7—Yes (literally, it is so). 8—I read a book. 9—You do not read a newspaper. 10—Cows do not eat meat. 11—Tarō does not see the book. 12—What is this ? (literally, This thing as for, what is ?).

13—That is a pen. 14—That is not a pen. 15—Who are you ? (literally, You as for, who are ?). 16—I am Smith. 17—Are you Mr. Fujita ? (literally, You as for, Fujita Mr. are ?). 18—Yes, I am (literally, Yes, it is so). 19—This book is not good. 20—That flower is not white. 21—Where is the pencil ? (literally, Pencil as for, what place at is ?). 22—The pencil is on the table. 23—In Tōkyō are there Englishmen ? (more freely, Are there any Englishmen in Tōkyō ?). 24—Yes, there are many. 25—Will you return by tram ? 26—Your father is not a merchant. 27—I go from Tōkyō to Yokohama. 28—A man and a woman. 29—My father is a merchant.

Mount Fuji

Geisha

CHAPTER 2

The Verb

The Three Conjugations

Japanese is surprisingly lacking in irregular verbs, and practically all verbs are included in one of three conjugations: the Chinese Verbs, the Vowel Verbs, and the Consonant Verbs.

In China there are no real verbs, and what verbs there are have no tense inflection. The Japanese have an enormous number of these Chinese verbs in their language and to meet the necessity for inflection they have left the main word unchanged and added an auxiliary word *suru* (literally "to do") which is conjugated. Thus "to study" is *kenkyu suru;* "to promise," *yakusoku suru,* etc., and the past *yakusoku shita, kenkyu shita,* etc. This, of course, corresponds to our "*do* go," "*did* go," and "*shall* go." Accordingly, though there are innumerable Chinese verbs in the Japanese language their conjugation is simplicity itself, once the student has learned the various tenses of *suru.*

All vowel verbs end in *ru,* or more strictly in *iru* or *eru.* The *ru* being purely a suffix, the stem is either *i* or *e, e.g., miru* becomes *mi, taberu, tabe,* and so on. The stem ending in a vowel, all such verbs are called vowel verbs. Outside of some twenty exceptions (when the stem is *r*) all verbs ending in *iru* and *eru* belong to this class.

Consonant verbs end in *u*, *e.g.*, *kaku*, "to write," *aru*, "to be." *U* being the suffix, the stem is *kak* and *ar*. Consonant verbs are divided into the following six classes :—

1.—Those ending in *k*	such as *kaku*	and *yuku*.
2.— " " " *s*	" " *dasu*	and *hanasu*.
3.— " " " *t*	" " *matsu*	and *butsu*.
4.— " " " *b* or *m*	" " *yobu*	and *yomu*.
5.— " " " *r*	" " *aru*	and *naru*.
6.— " " " (*f*)	" " *kau*	and *iu*.

Two points deserve attention. In the third class the final *s* is purely phonetic, and not part of the stem, the Japanese being unable to pronounce *tu*. In the sixth class the words should be *kafu* and *ifu*, but as the *f* is silent it is usually omitted.

Though the stems are respectively *kak*, *das*, *mat*, *yob*, *yom*, *ar*, and *kaf*, etc., yet as consonants cannot stand alone in Japanese, they add an *i* to form the base which is most frequently used for conjugation, becoming, *kaki*, *dashi* (*shi* = *si*), *machi* (*chi* = *ti*), *yobi*, *yomi*, *ari*, and *kai*. This form is known as the second base, and should be carefully remembered.

The second base of vowel verbs is the same as the stem, *i.e.*, *mi* and *tabe*.

The Polite Conjugation

There are three ways of expressing every tense in Japanese. The first is the familiar, the second the polite, and the third the honorific. Since the polite form is not only the easiest but also the one most commonly used let us, for the time being, concern ourselves exclusively with it.

Politeness is expressed by the auxiliary suffix *masu* which may be conjugated through all the tenses. *Masu* itself refers to the present. It is invariably added to the second base of the verb. Thus we have the following table :—

Familiar Present	Second Base	Polite Present
I.—Vowel Verbs—		
1.—*miru*	*mi*	*mimasu*
2.—*taberu*	*tabe*	*tabemasu*
II.—Consonant Verbs—		
1.—*kaku*	*kaki*	*kakimasu*
2.—*dasu*	*dashi*	*dashimasu*
3.—*matsu*	*machi*	*machimasu*
4.—*yobu*	*yobi*	*yobimasu*
yomu	*yomi*	*yomimasu*
5.—*aru*	*ari*	*arimasu*
6.—*kau*	*kai*	*kaimasu*

Incidentally the polite forms refer not to the subject of the sentence but to the person spoken to. Thus one can use *masu* even when referring to oneself. *Watakushi wa Eikokujin de arimasu,* "I am an Englishman." *Tarō wa ōkii inu wo mimasu.* "Tarō sees a big dog."

The Positive Conjugation of Masu

Ordinarily *masu* has seven tenses, which are :—

1.—Present	- -	*masu*
2.—Past	- -	*mashita*
3.—First Future	-	*mashō*
4.—Second Future	-	*mashitarō*
5.—First Conditional	-	*masureba*
6.—Second Conditional	-	*mashitara*
7.—Gerund	- -	*mashite*

These are all, of course, added to the second base, *e.g.*, *kakimashita, dashimashitarō, machimashitara,* etc.

The use of each tense is somewhat peculiar and deserves special attention.

1.—The Present corresponds more or less to the English present, save that in Japanese it may also refer to a definite future. *Kyō watakushi wa Pari ye yukimasu,* "Today I go to Paris"; *Ashita anata wa Tōkyō ye yukimasu ka?* "Tomorrow will you go to Tōkyō?"

2.—THE PAST is like the English past, save that it includes the imperfect, the definitive past, and the perfect. Thus:—*Tegami wo kakimashita,* "(I) wrote a letter"; *Nihon ye yukimashita ka?* "Have (you) gone to Japan?" *Hai yukimashita,* "Yes, (I) went."

3.—THE FIRST FUTURE is something of a misnomer. More correctly it might be called the first probable, and refers to a probable or a possible present or future. *Tsukue no ue ni empitsu ga arimasu ka?* "On the table is there a pencil?"; *Hai arimashō,* "Yes (there) probably is"; *Kore wo kaimashō* "(I think I) shall buy this."

Quite often it is used very idiomatically. *Pen ga arimashō* (literally "there probably is a pen"), may mean "there is a pen, isn't there?" to which the answer would be, *Hai arimasu,* "Yes, there is." Again, it sometimes has the sense of "let us . . . ." *e.g., Sa yukimashō,* "Well then, let us go"; *Uchi ye kaerimashō,* "Let's go home"; *Hirumeshi wo tabemashō ka?* "Shall we eat lunch?"; *Hai tabemashō,* "Yes, let's."

Actually these idiomatic expressions have so monopolized the *mashō* form that now, in the majority of cases, the ordinary future probable is expressed periphrastically by adding *deshō* to the familiar present. *Ashita Tarō wa Tōkyō ye yuku deshō,* "Tarō is probably going to Tōkyō tomorrow"; *Itsu kaeru deshō,* "When will he probably return?"; *Raishū kaeru deshō,* "He will probably come back next week."

4.—THE SO-CALLED SECOND FUTURE has even less of the future in it, and refers almost exclusively to the probable past. *Tarō wa Eikoku ye yukimashita ka?* "Did Tarō go to England?"; *Hai yukimashitarō,* "Yes, he probably went," or, more freely, " Yes, I think so." Like the first future it may also be used interrogatively. *Hon wa tsukue no ue ni arimashitarō*, " The book was on the table, wasn't it ? " ; *Hai arimashita*, " Yes, it was." In place of *mashitarō* we sometimes find, *mashita deshō*.

5.—The First Conditional signifies *if* or *when* with regard to the present and the future. It can never be the final verb of the sentence. *Rondon ye yukimasureba hoteru ni tomaru deshō* " When (or if) you go to London, you will stay at a hotel, won't you ? " ; *Tsukue no ue ni empitsu ga arimasureba motte kite kudasai*, " If there is a pencil on the table, please bring it here " (*motte kite kudasai* is an idiom meaning " please bring it ").

6.—The Second Conditional signifies *if* or *when* with regard to the past. *Rondon ye yukimashitara Seinto Pōru wo mimashitarō ?* " When you went to London, you saw St. Paul's, didn't you ? " ; *Jirō wa Eikoku ye yukimashitara Eigo wo hanasu deshō*, " If Jirō went to England, he probably speaks English."

In practice no distinction is made between the first and second conditional. They are often used interchangeably.

7.—Although the gerund is in some ways the most important of the tenses the polite form is seldom employed so that we had best consider it separately.

The Negative Conjugation of Masu

Masu has a negative as well as a positive conjugation, but it is extremely simple. The present is *masen*, and the other tenses are formed by adding the contractions of *de arimasu* in the last six tenses. These are :—

Present	*de arimasu*	becomes	*desu.*
Past	*de arimashita*	,,	*deshita.*
First Future	*de arimashō*	,,	*deshō.*
Second Future	*de arimashitarō*	,,	*deshitarō.*

First Conditional	*de arimasureba*	becomes	*desureba.*
Second Conditional	*de arimashitara*	,,	*deshitara.*
Gerund	*de arimashite*	,,	*deshite* or *de.*

Accordingly the negative conjugation of *masu* is :—

1.—*masen*
2.—*masen deshita*
3.—*masen deshō*
4.—*masen deshitarō*
5.—*masenakereba*
6.—*masen deshitara*
7.—*masen de*

The two irregularities (the first conditional and the gerund) should be carefully noted. All the negative endings are added to the second base in the usual way, and the seven lents, *e.g.*, *kakimasen,* " do not write " ; *tabemasen deshita,* " did not eat " ; *yukimasen deshō,* " probably will not go," etc. When *de* comes before a negative it usually changes to *dewa. Kore wa pen dewa arimasen.*

Vocabulary

itsu, when.
kinō, yesterday.
cha or *o cha,* tea.
kome, rice.
asuko, there, that place.
soko, there, that place.
tonari, next-door, neighboring.
tokei, watch, clock.
hito, man, human being.
nezumi, mouse, rat.
Seiyōjin, an Occidental.
heya, room.
shippo, tail.
sei, stature.
hikui, low.
tsuku, arrive.
naru, become.
oi, an exclamation calling attention.
mada, still, as yet.
sumu, reside.
kyonen, last year.
motte kite kudasai, please bring.
kyō, today.
ashita, tomorrow.
tenki or *o tenki,* weather.
ku, ward (of a town).
koko, here, this place.
yūbinkyoku, post office.
mura, village.
otō san, father (honorific).
ano hito, that man, he she.

Nihonjin, Japanese man, woman, etc.
isshūkan, one week.
warui, bad.
un, luck.
takai, high, dear.
nagai, long.
kuru (second base, *ki*), come.
tomaru, stop, remain.
au, meet.
tabitabi, often.
osoi (with the dative in front of a verb, *osoku*), late.
nē san, elder sister, waitress.
Seiyō, the Occident.

Eibun no hon, a book written in English.

Note also the complex adjectives:—

un ga yoi, lucky. *un ga warui*, unlucky. *shippo ga nagai*, long-tailed. *sei ga takai*, tall. *sei ga hikui*, short statured.

Exercise

1—*Anata wa itsu kimashita ka?* 2—*Kinō tsukimashita.* 3—*Itsu kaerimasu ka?* 4—*Ashita kaerimashō.* 5—*Osoku narimasureba Rondon ni tomarimasu.* 6—*Oi, nē san—o cha ga aru ka?* 7—*Arimasu deshō.* 8—*Arimashitara motte kite kudasai.* 9—*Suzuki san ni aimashita ka?* 10—*Mada aimasen deshita.* 11—*Kome wo tabemashitarō.* 12—*Hai, tabitabi tabemashita.* 13—*Sasaki san wa doko ni sumimasu ka?* 14—*Kanda ku ni oru deshō.* 15—*Neko wa doko ni orimasu ka?* 16—*Koko ni orimashita ga, ima asuko ni oru deshō.* 17—*Koko ni yūbinkyoku ga arimasu ka?* 18—*Koko ni wa arimasen ga tonari no mura ni arimasu.* 19—*Anata wa tokei ga arimasu ka?* 20—*Iiye, watakushi wa tokei ga arimasen.* 21—*Otō san wa Eibun no hon ga arimasu ka?* 22—*Hai, arimasu.* 23—*Ano hito wa un ga ii, kono hito wa un ga warui.* 24—*Nezumi wa shippo ga nagai.* 25—*Kyonen Seiyo ni orimashitara Okusuhorudo ye yukimashitarō.* 26—*Hai, Okusuhorudo ni isshūkwan tomarimashita.* 27—*Kore wa anata no heya de arimasu ka?* 28—*Iiye, sore wa watakushi no heya desu.* 29—*Kyō wa ii o tenki desu.*

Translation

1—When did you come? (literally, You as for, when came?). 2—I arrived yesterday. 3—When will you return? 4—I shall probably return tomorrow. 5—If I be (literally, become) late I shall stop in London. 6—Hi! there, waitress—Have you any tea? (literally, tea exists?). 7—There probably is some. 8—If there is please bring some. 9—Have you met Mr. Suzuki? 10—As yet I have not met him. 11—You have eaten rice, haven't you? 12—Yes, I have often eaten it. 13—Where does Mr. Sasaki live? 14—I think he lives in Kanda Ward. 15—Where is the cat? 16—She was here, but now she is probably over there. 17—Is there a post office here? 18—There is none here but there is one in the next village. 19—Have you a watch? (literally, You as for, a watch exists?). 20—No, I have not a watch. 21—Has your father an English book? 22—Yes, he has. 23—That man is lucky; this man is unlucky. 24—Rats have long tails, *or* Rats are long tailed. 25—Last year when you were in the Occident I suppose you went to Oxford. 26—Yes, we stayed in Oxford for one week. 27—Is this your room? 28—No, that is my room. 29—Today the weather is good (literally, Today as for, good weather is).

CHAPTER 3

The Verb (cont.)

The Five Verbal Bases

We have now reached a point where we may enquire more fully into the structure of the verb. We have already spoken of the second base. In all there are five, one for each of the vowels.

With the consonant verbs, each base ends in a vowel arranged in the alphabetical order, *a, i, u, e, o*. Thus :—

(*a.*)—Consonant Verbs

	1.	2.	3.	4.	5.
(*kaku*)	*kaka*	*kaki*	*kaku*	*kake*	*kakō*
(*dasu*)	*dasa*	*dashi*	*dasu*	*dase*	*dasō*
(*matsu*)	*mata*	*machi*	*matsu*	*mate*	*matō*
(*yobu*)	*yoba*	*yobi*	*yobu*	*yobe*	*yobō*
(*yomu*)	*yoma*	*yomi*	*yomu*	*yome*	*yomō*
(*aru*)	*ara*	*ari*	*aru*	*are*	*arō*
(*kau*)	*kawa*	*kai*	*kau*	*kae*	*kaō*

The vowel verbs have also five bases, but they are formed in a different way, and three of them are identical :—

(*b.*)—Vowel Verbs

	1.	2.	3.	4.	5.
(*miru*)	*mi*	*mi*	*miru*	*mire*	*mi*
(*taberu*)	*tabe*	*tabe*	*taberu*	*tabere*	*tabe*

To these five bases there are added various suffixes indicating special tenses, moods, and relationships. Thus, for example, the third base alone expresses the familiar present, and *masu* is added to the second base to form the polite conjugation. *Nai* (the irregular negative form of *aru*) added to the first base indicates the familiar negative, *e.g.*, *kakanai,* " do not write " ; *tabenai,* " do not eat " ; *kawanai,* " do not buy." *Ba* added to the fourth base gives the first conditional.

Additions to the Second Base

In addition to *masu* there are three other second base suffixes which are of sufficient importance to require immediate consideration. These are *tai, sō,* and *ni.*

Tai is called the desiderative suffix. Added to the second base it expresses " wish to . . ." or " want to . . ." Thus *kakitai,* " wish to write " ; *mitai,* " wish to see," etc. Both *nai* and *tai* are adjectives and like other adjectives may be conjugated through all the seven tenses. *Tai* however, has also a periphrastic conjugation by the addition of the various tenses of *desu, e.g., kakitai desu, kakitai deshita, kakitai deshō,* etc. *Tarō san! asobimashō ka?* " O Tarō, let us play." *Ima wa hon wo yomitai desu,* " No I want to read a book now." *Kinō tegami wo kakitai deshita ga kami ga arimasen deshita,* " (I) wanted to write a letter yesterday, but there was no paper."

Sō is called the apparitional suffix, and indicates appearance or likelihood with regard to the future. Like *tai, sō* may be used with *desu. Ima wa ame ga furisō desu,* " Now rain seems likely to fall."

Ni is called the purposive suffix, and followed by another verb of motion (chiefly *yuku*) indicates intention. *Masao wa doko desu ka?* " Where is Masao ? " *Hon wo kai ni ikimashita,* " (He) has gone (in order) to buy a book." *Momiji wo mi ni ikimashō,* "Let us go and (literally 'in order to ') see the maples."

The Gerund and Assimilated Second Base

Most important of all, however, is the formation of the Gerund from a modification of the second base, known as the assimilated second base.

We have already seen from the gerund of *masu* (*mashite*) that *te* is the sign of the gerund, as *ing* (*e.g.*, " rowing," " going ") is in English. Originally this *te* was added directly to the second base, *e.g., kakite,* " writing " ; *arite,* " being," etc. This is still the case in the written language and with the vowel verbs in all cases. Thus even in the spoken language the gerund of the vowel verbs is as follows :—

	SECOND BASE	GERUND
miru	*mi*	*mite*
taberu	*tabe*	*tabete*

The consonant verbs have now acquired a contracted form of the second base to which they add the *te*. These forms are irregular, and differ in each of the six classes, but fortunately all verbs in each class are conjugated exactly alike. The following table should be carefully mastered :—

PRESENT	SECOND BASE—GERUND ENDING	ASS. BASE—GERUND
*kaku**	*kaki-te*	*kai te*
dasu	*dashi-te*	*dashi te*
matsu	*machi-te*	*mat te*
yobu	*yobi-te*	*yon de*
yomu	*yomi-te*	*yon de*
aru	*ari-te*	*at te*
kau	*kai-te*	*kat te*

Accordingly all *k* verbs form the assimilated second base by dropping the *k, e.g., saku* becoming *sai*. The *s* verbs

*There are a few *g* verbs, *e.g., kagu,* " to smell." Its second base is of course *gi,* and its assimilated second base *kai,* the *te* changing to *de*. Thus the gerund is *kaide.*

alone have the second base and the assimilated second base the same. The *b* and *m* verbs change the *bi* and *mi* to *n* and the *te* to *de*, while the *r*, *t*, and *f* verbs change their *chi*, *ri*, and (*h*)*i* to *t*. It follows that occasionally the gerund of several different verbs are the same and the sense can only be told by the context. Thus the gerunds of *katsu*, "to be victorious," *karu* "to hunt," and *kau* "to buy," are all *katte*.

It should be remembered that there is a marked difference in the pronunciation of *te* and *tte*. Double *t* should almost be pronounced as in *cat town*.

The Use of the Gerund

The gerund is frequently employed and it has many different meanings. Its idiomatic usages we shall examine hereafter, but let us at present consider how it corresponds to and differs from the English present participle.

As in English the gerund is frequently used with the verb "to be," though in Japanese the gerund precedes rather than follows it. In addition to *aru* (or *arimasu*) there are *oru* (or *orimasu*) and *iru* (or *imasu*). *Aru* refers chiefly to an inanimate subject; *oru* and *iru* to animate subjects, *e.g.*, *Takeo san wa hon wo yonde imasu*, "Master Takeo is reading a book." *Danna san wa o uchi desu ka?* "Is (your) master at home?" (literally, "Mr. Master as for honorable house is it?"). *Ima gohan wo tabete orimasu*, "Now he is eating his meal."

As in English the periphrastic form may also apply to the past tense. *Kinō watakushi wa Fujita san ni tegami wo kaite orimashita*, "Yesterday I was writing a letter to Mr. Fujita."

The distinction in meaning between the simple and the periphrastic forms in Japanese differs on but one important point from English. In both languages the simple present refers to habitual or frequent action. (" (I) read the newspaper every morning "—*maiasa shimbun wo yomimasu*, etc.) to abstract action irrespective of time (" a bat flies "—*kōmori ga tobimasu*) or to present action irrespective of past or future. The periphrastic form has reference to a continuing action beginning in the past and continuing into the future. " What are you buying ? "—*Nani wo katte orimasu ka ?* In both languages the two forms have a similar meaning with regard to past action, but in English the present participle may have a future significance, *e.g.*, " I am going to France tomorrow." This is not allowed in Japanese. The gerund may never be used with a future sense, and the simple present must be used for definite future action. The occasional use of the gerund plus the first future signifies only a probable present. *Kami wo katte orimashō ?* —" You are buying paper, aren't you ? "

In Japanese the gerund is much more frequently used than the corresponding expression in English. Where we would say, " I went down town, bought a book, ate lunch and then returned home," the Japanese would say, " Going down town, buying a book, eating lunch, I came home." Japanese sentences are interminably long and all subordinate verbs in the direct line of thought are put into the gerund, only the final verb having a complete form.

Another idiom requires attention. A polite imperative is formed by the addition of *kudasai* to the gerund. *Pan wo katte kudasai*, " Please buy (some) bread." *Kore wo yonde kudasai*, " Please read this."

Vocabulary

motsu, hold, have.
maiasa, every morning.
kaku, write.
motte kuru, bring.

pan, bread.
nedan, price, cost.
uchi, house, home, inside.
otōto, younger brother.
ame, rain.
gwaikoku, foreign countries.
sakura, cherry tree.
Igirisu, England.
sashimi, a dish of raw fish.
morau, receive.
ototoi, day before yesterday.
byōki, ill, illness.
yoku, well.
kane-mochi, rich, a rich man.
iru, the same as *oru*.
suru, do.
tegami, letter.
mizu, water.
machi, town, street.
kau, buy.
harau, pay.
mise, shop.
go han, rice, food, meal.
furu, fall (of rain, snow, etc.
konogoro, recently.
Eikoku, England.
kore kara, henceforward, from now on.
hagaki, postcard.
kiku, hear, enquire.
iu, say, speak.
daibun, very much, rather.
bimbō, poor.
bōshi, hat.
mō, already ; *mo*, even, also.

Exercise

1—*Ano hito wa nani wo motte imasu ka?* 2—*Ano hito wa tokei wo motte imasu.* 3—*Anata wa nani wo shite orimasu ka?* 4—*Hon wo yonde imasu.* 5—*Watakushi wa maiasa shimbun wo yomimasu.* 6—*Jirō wa tegami wo kaite orimasu.* 7—*Ashita Nagasaki ye yukimasu ka?* 8—*Ikimasen.* 9—*Ikimasen deshō.* 10—*Sore wo yonde kudasai.* 11—*Mizu wo motte kite kudasai.* 12—*Machi ye itte pan wo katte nedan wo haratte uchi ye kaerimashita.* 13—*Mise ye itte pan wo kaimashō ka?* 14—*Otōto wa gohan wo tabete imasu.* 15—*Ame ga furisō desu ne.* 16—*Hamatake san wa gwaikoku ye yukisō desu.* 17—*Konogoro sakura wo mi ni ikimashita ka?* 18—*Eikoku ye kaeritai desu ka?* 19—*Iiye Igirisu ye kaeritaku nai.* 20—*Kore kara ano mise ye ikanai.* 21—*Watakushi wa sashimi wo tabenai.* 22—*Tanemoto san kara tegami ga kimashita ka?* 23—*Tegami mo hagaki mo moraimasen deshita.* 24—

Ano hito ni kiite kudasai. 25—*Dare ga sō iimashita ka?* 26—*Ototoi Tarō wa byōki ni narimashita ga kyō mō daibun yoku narimashita.* 27—*Chiisai toki ni bimbō deshita ga ima wa kanemochi ni narimashita.* 28—*Are wa dare no bōshi desu ka?* 29—*Sore wa anata no deshō.* 30—*Tenki ga waruku narimashita*

Translation

1—What has that man got? *or,* What is that man holding? 2—He is holding a watch. 3—What are you doing? 4—I am reading a book. 5—I read the newspaper every morning. 6—Jiro is writing a letter. 7—Will you go to Nagasaki tomorrow? 8—(No), I shall not go. 9—I probably shall not go. 10—Please read that. 11—Please bring some water. 12—Going down town, buying some bread, paying the price, I returned home (more freely, I went down town, bought some bread, paid for it, and then came home). 13—Shall I go to the shop and buy some bread? 14—My younger brother is eating his food. 15—It looks as though rain would fall, doesn't it? 16—It seems likely that Mr. Hamatake will go abroad. 17—Recently have you been to see the cherries? 18—Do you wish to go back to England? 19—No, I do not wish to return. 20—Henceforward I shall not go to that shop. 21—I do not eat raw fish. 22—Have you heard from Mr. Tanemoto? (literally, From Mr. Tanemoto, has a letter come). 23—I have received neither a letter nor a post-card. 24—Please ask that man. 25—Who said so? 26—Day before yesterday Tarō became ill, but today he is much better (literally, has become very well). 27—When he was small (*i.e.*, when young) he was poor, but now he is rich. 28—Whose hat is that? (literally, That as for, the hat of who is?). 29—It is probably yours. 30—The weather has become bad.

CHAPTER 4

The Verb (cont.)

The Formation of the Familiar Conjugation

Although in ordinary social intercourse the polite form is usual for the final or key verb, most of the subordinate and relative verbs are expressed by the familiar conjugation. In addition among intimate friends, members of the family, and when speaking to inferiors the familiar form is the only one employed, so that it is imperative to learn it.

Its acquisition is not difficult. The actual tense endings we may obtain from our knowledge of the conjugation of *masu*. These are, it will be remembered, *masu*, *mashita*, *mashō*, *mashitarō*, *masureba*, *mashitara*, and *mashite*. Eliminating the polite auxiliary, the endings are *u*, *ta*, *ō*, *tarō*, *eba*, *tara*, and *te*. In this manner two things come to light. One is that for the first six tenses every other form contains a *t*, and second that each of these three *t* forms has reference to the past. On tracing the history of the language we find that they were originally *te aru* =*ta* ; *te arō* =*tarō* ; *te ara*(*ba*) =*tara*, or in other words that each is the gerund plus the corresponding form of *aru*. Further we discover that the gerundial *te* is a contraction of *hateru*, " to complete," or " to finish."

Accordingly there were only three real tenses originally

—the present, the future, and the conditional, the three derived tenses being formed by *hateru* plus " to be."

In the familiar conjugation these three tense endings, being derived from the gerund, are attached to the assimilated second base. Thus the past, second future, and second conditional of *kaku* are *kaita*, *kaitarō*, and *kaitara*.

The other three tenses are formed by adding the endings *u*, *ō*, and *eba* to the stem (*e.g.*, *kak*, *das*, *mat*, etc.) of the consonant verbs.

Verbal Chart of the Familiar Forms

In this manner we obtain a complete verbal table of the familiar forms of all the consonant verbs, viz. :—

	K	*S*	*T*	*R*
(Present)	*kaku*	*dasu*	*matsu*	*aru*
(Past)	*kaita*	*dashita*	*matta*	*atta*
(1st Future)	*kakō*	*dasō*	*matō*	*arō*
(2nd Future)	*kaitarō*	*dashitarō*	*mattarō*	*attara*
(1st Con.)	*kakeba*	*daseba*	*mateba*	*areba*
(2nd Con.)	*kaitara*	*dashitara*	*mattara*	*attarō*
(Gerund)	*kaite*	*dashite*	*matte*	*atta*

B		*M*
yobu		*yomu*
	yonda	
yobō		*yomō*
	yondarō	
yobeba		*yomeba*
	yondara	
	yonde	

(*F*)	
kau	
	katta
kaō	
	kattarō
kaeba	
	kattara
	katte

The vowel verbs naturally differ slightly from this. In the first place, since there is no assimilated second base for them, the oblique tenses are added to the second base, and they acquire their future form by the addition of *yō* to their fifth base (which is the same as the first and second) and *ba* to the fourth base, thus :—

I	*E*
miru	*taberu*
mita	*tabeta*
miyō	*tabeyō*
mitarō	*tabetarō*
mireba	*tabereba*
mitara	*tabetara*
mite	*tabete*

Relative Clauses

In Japanese there are no relative pronouns—(" The man *who* comes," " *When* I come," etc.) and the Japanese are forced to use peculiar verbal constructions to take their place.

Even in English we can say " the ship-wrecked sailor " for " the sailor who was ship-wrecked " ; " the fluttering flag " for " the flag which is fluttering." In Japan this use of the verb attributively is very common and expresses all relative relations.

Yuku hito means " the man who goes " or " is going " ; *yaketa ie,* " the house which was burnt " ; *kinō kaita tegami,* " the letter which (I) wrote yesterday " ; *yukanai hito,* " those who don't go."

Two points deserve especial attention. In the written language any tense of the verb may be thus used. At present in the spoken language only the past and the present are so employed. The second point is the infrequent use of the passive in this connection. Japanese has a passive but it is very seldom used, and by some circumlocution the verb is kept active. Thus, " the ship-wrecked sailor " becomes *nansen ni atta suifu* (literally " ship-wreck to met sailor "). " The house which was bought by Mr. Sasaki," *Sasaki san no katta ie.* (Note the change of *ga* to *no*. This occurs in all such cases, for reasons which we shall see hereafter.)

Use of the active when the passive might be expected may cause ambiguity. *Shiranai hito* may signify either "a person who does not know" or "a person who is not known (to me)." The context generally indicates the way the phrase may be taken. For instance, *yonde shimatta hon* can not possibly mean "the book which has finished reading" . . . it can only mean "the book which (I, they, etc.) have finished reading." *Sumau tochi* can not mean "the locality which resides," but "the locality in which (so-and-so) resides."

The Irregular Verbs

Unlike most other languages, Japanese has almost no irregular verbs. The only words which depart from the usual are *suru, kuru, shinuru, inuru,* and *yuku.* In each case the irregularity consists merely in the formation of the five bases. Once these have been obtained their conjugation is the same as with the others.

Suru has the following five bases :—

1st Base	2nd Base	3rd Base	4th Base	5th Base
se or *shi*	*shi*	*suru*	*sure*	*shi* or *se*

Accordingly the polite conjugation is *shimasu, shimashita,* etc., and being a quasi-vowel verbs its impolite conjugation is :—

Present	-	*suru*
Past	-	*shita*
First Future	-	*shiyō* or *seyō*
Second Future	-	*shitarō*
First Conditional	-	*sureba*
Second Conditional	-	*shitara*
Gerund	-	*shite*
Familiar Negative	-	*shinai* or *senai*

Suru (literally " to do," " to make ") it will be remembered, is the auxiliary for the conjugation of the Chinese verbs.

Kuru, " to come," has for its five bases the following :—

1.	2.	3.	4.	5.
ko	*ki*	*kuru*	*kure*	*ko* or *ki*

In consequence its polite conjugation is *kimasu*, *kimashita*, etc., while the familiar forms are :—

Present	-	*kuru*
Past	-	*kita*
First Future	-	*koyō* or *kiyō*
Second Future	-	*kitarō*
First Conditional	-	*kureba*
Second Conditional	-	*kitara*
Gerund	-	*kite*
Familiar Negative	-	*konai*

Shinuru, " to die," is peculiar since it is half a consonant, and half a vowel verb. It has the additional present of *shinu*, while the five bases are :—

1.	2.	3.	4.	5.
shina	*shini*	*shinuru* or *shinu*	*shinure* or *shine*	*shinō*

(Ass. 2nd Base, *shin*)

The polite conjugation as *shinimasu*, *shinimashita*, etc., and the familiar is :—

Heian Jingu shrine

Confucian temple

Present	- -	*shinuru* or *shinu*
Past	- -	*shinda*
First Future	-	*shinō*
Second Future	-	*shindarō*
First Conditional	-	*shinureba*
Second Conditional	-	*shindara*
Gerund	- -	*shinde*
Familiar Negative	-	*shinanai*

Inuru, "to sleep," is conjugated like *shinuru,* and does not require special attention.

Yuku is irregular on only two points. The *yu* may be and in Tōkyō generally is replaced by *i, e.g., iku, ikimasu, ikanai,* etc. In the gerund the *i* is the only form allowable, and furthermore instead of being *iite* (from *ikite*) in accordance with the rule, it is *itte.* Thus the five bases are :—

1.	2.	3.	4.	5.
yuka	*yuki*	*yuku*	*yuke*	*yukō*
ika	*iki*	*iku*	*ike*	*iko*

The polite form is *yukimasu,* or *ikimasu,* etc., and the familiar forms are :—

Present	- -	*yuku* or *iku*
Past	- -	*itta*
First Future	-	*yukō* or *ikō*
Second Future	-	*ittarō*
First Conditional	-	*yukeba* or *ikeba*
Second Conditional	-	*ittara*
Gerund	- -	*itte*

Vocabulary

tokoro, place, residence.
imōto, younger sister.
henji, answer.
sa, well then, come now, I say.
dō, how ; *dō naru,* what becomes ?
oshieru, teach, tell.
mitsukeru, find, discover.
yadoya, hostel, inn.
okiru, get up, arise.
kesa, this morning.
ji, time, hour, o'clock.
han, half.

sugi, past, after.
yobu, call, send for.
Nihongo, Japanese language.
maiban, every night.
ani (*san*), elder brother.
konaida, the other day.
dasu, to take out, send.
butsu, beat.
shibai, theater, play, drama.
omoshiroi, interesting, amusing.
toru, take; *totte iku*, take away.
hayaku, early.
wakaru, understand.
nanji, what time? what o'clock?
ichi, one; *ni*, two; *san*, three; *shi*, four; *go*, five; *roku*, six; *shichi*, seven; *hachi*, eight; *ku*, nine; *jū*, ten. *jū ichi*, eleven; *jū ni*, twelve, etc.
fun, minute.
shiru (second base, *shiri*), know.
daikon, Japanese radish.
to, thus, that, " ".
neru, sleep, go to bed.
goro, about (with regard to time).

Exercise

1—*Kinō Kinoshita san no tokoro ye itta ka?* 2—*Ikimasen deshita.* 3—*Konaida imōto ni tegami wo dashita ga henji wa mada kimasen.* 4—*Sore wa daikon to iimasu.* 5—*Nani wo katta ka?* 6—*Kono hon wo katta.* 7—*Kinō kaita tegami wo mō dashita ka?* 8—*Mada dasanai.* 9—*Sa, ikō.* 10—*Ototoi atta hito wa dare desu ka?* 11—*Are wa Robinson san desu.* 12—*Kore wa Nihongo de nan to iimasu ka?* 13—*Ame ga fureba ikimasen.* 14—*Koko ni atta empitsu wa dō narimashita.* 15—*Ani ga mitsuketara totte ittarō.* 16—*Konogoro omoshiroi shibai wo mita ka?* 17—*Kyonen tomatta yadoya wa nan deshita ka?* 18—*Ashita no asa hayaku okite Kamakura ye ikō.* 19—*Wakatta ka? Hai, wakarimashita.* 20—*Kesa nanji ni okita ka?* 21—*Rokuji ni okimashita.* 22—*Anata wa maiban nanji ni nemasu ka?* 23—*Jūji goro nemasu.* 24—*Ichiji, niji, sanji, yoji, goji, rokuji, shichiji, hachiji, kuji, jūji, jūichiji, jū ni ji.* 25—*Jū ji han; san ji han; go ji go fun sugi; ni ji ku fun sugi.* 26—*Are wa anata no shitte iru hito desu ka?* 27—*Iiye are wa shiranai hito desu.* 28—*Gonsuke ga ottara koko ye yonde kudasai.*

Translation

1—Yesterday did you go to Mr. Kinoshita's place? 2—No, I did not go. 3—The other day I sent a letter to my younger sister, but as yet I have received no answer (literally, no answer has come). 4—They call that a (radish). 5—What did you buy? 6—I bought this book. 7—Have you already sent the letter which you wrote yesterday? 8—I have not sent it yet. 9—I say! let's go. 10—Who was the man I met yesterday? (literally, Yesterday met man who is?) 11—That is Mr. Robinson. 12—What do you call this in Japanese? 13—If the rain falls, I shall not go. 14—What has become of the pencil which was here? 15—If my elder brother saw it, he probably took it away. 16—Recently have you seen an interesting play? 17—What was the inn where we stayed last year? 18—Let us get up early tomorrow and go to Kamakura. 19—Do you understand? (literally, Have you understood?) Yes, I understand. 20—What time did you get up this morning? 21—I got up at six o'clock. 22—What time do you go to bed every night? 23—I go to bed about ten o'clock. 24—One o'clock, two o'clock, etc., to twelve o'clock. 25—10-30; 3-30; 5-05; 2-09. 26—Is that a man whom you know? (literally, That knowing-man is?) 27—No, that is a man whom I do not know. 28—If Gonsuke is (in) please call him here.

CHAPTER 5

The Adjective

The Three Forms of the Adjective

By a gradual process of contraction the present tense of the real adjective ends in *ai, ii, ui,* or *oi* (there being none in *ei*). This is called the *i* form and is used either predicatively (*e.g.*, "the child is good") or attributively (*e.g.*, "the good child").

There are also two other forms, viz., the so-called *ku* and *sa* forms. Theoretically *ku* is the adverbial form and any adjective may be made into an adverb by changing the *i* into *ku*. Thus *yoi*, "good," becomes *yoku*, "well"; *hayai*, "fast," becomes *hayaku*, "quickly." Actually, however, owing to a peculiar idiom, every adjective is considered by the Japanese to be an adverb if it immediately precedes the verb.

Accordingly it may be stated that by itself or in front of a noun, an adjective ends in *i*, and in front of a verb it ends in *ku*. *Kodomo ga ōkiku narimashita*, "The child has becomes big" (from *ōkii*, "big"). *Aoi desu ga kuroku miemasu nē*, "It is blue but it looks black, doesn't it?" (*nē*=the French "n'est ce pas," and sometimes the English "y'know"). Note that when *de* comes between the verb and the adjective the *i* form remains.

Sa is the sign of abstraction, and by changing the *i* to *sa*, the adjective is changed to a noun. Thus *takai*, "high," *takasa*, "height"; *hiroi*, "wide," *hirosa*, "width," etc. *Fuji san no takasa wa dono gurai desu ka?* "How high is Mount Fuji? (literally "Height of Mount Fuji as for about how much is?").

The Five Modes of Conjugation

The adjective, it will be remembered, is really a part of the verb and can be independently conjugated, though in polite conversation it is more usual to attach some form of *aru* as an auxiliary verb.

There are five ways of expressing the present tense of any adjective, *e.g.*, *samui*, "cold":—

1.—*samui*
2.—*samui desu*
3.—*samui n' desu*
4.—(*samuku arimasu*)
5.—*samū gozaimasu*

All five forms mean "(It) is cold," and there is little or no difference in meaning between them save politeness, the first being the least and the last the most polite. The fourth form is very seldom used in the positive, but *samuku arimasen* is the most common form for the negative.

Gozaimasu is the honorific form of *arimasu*, and when the adjective comes immediately before it, the *k* of the adverbial form is dropped, and the *u* left behind, making a diphthong. *Au* and *ou* are pronounced (and with the *Rōmaji* written) *ō*, *e.g.*, *takaku arimasu*=*takō gozaimasu*; *kuroku arimasu*=*kurō gozaimasu*. *Uu* becomes *ū* as in *samū gozaimasu* and *iu* either remains *iu* or becomes *ū*, *e.g.*, *ōkiku arimasu*=*ōkiu gozaimasu*; *yasashiku arimasu* =*yasashū gozaimasu*.

The Conjugation of the Adjective

Each one of these five forms may be conjugated through all of the seven tenses. The last four need cause no trouble, since the adjective proper remains the same, only the auxiliary verb being inflected, *e.g., samui deshita, samui n' deshita, samuku arimashita, samū gozaimashita,* and so on through the other tenses.

The negative is formed in the same way, as we have already seen :—*samui dewa arimasen deshita, samui n' dewa arimasen deshita, samuku arimasen deshita, samū gozaimasen deshita,* etc.

As a matter of fact, however, in the positive only the first and fifth, and in the negative the first, fourth and fifth are commonly conjugated.

The first form is more difficult and must be studied independently. Tenses are indicated by changing the *i* to *ku*, dropping the *u* and adding the familiar conjugation of *aru* :—

Present - -	*samui*
Past - -	*samukatta*
First Future -	*samukarō*
Second Future -	*samukattarō*
First Conditional -	*samukereba*
Second Conditional -	*samukattara*
Gerund - -	*samukute* or *samui de*

The irregularities of the first conditional and the gerund should be noticed.

The Conjugation of Tai and Nai

The desiderative and negative suffixes of the verb should not be forgotten. They are conjugated like all other adjectives, save that *nai* is chiefly used only in first mode and never in the fourth or fifth.

Owing to their frequent use their familiar tenses should be carefully learned.

	NAI	*TAI*
Present - -	*nai*	*tai*
Past - -	*nakatta*	*takatta*
First Future - -	*nakarō*	*takarō*
Second Future -	*nakattarō*	*takattarō*
First Conditional -	*nakereba*	*takereba*
Second Conditional -	*nakattara*	*takattara*
Gerund - -	*nakute* or *nai de*	*takute* or *tai de*

For example, *kakanakatta,* " did not write " ; *ikitakereba,* " if (you) wish to go."

Negative Conjugation of the Adjective

The negative of the first form of the adjective presents no great difficulty. The adjective is placed in the adverbial form and the various tenses of *nai* added.

Present - -	*samuku nai* (or *nai desu, nai n' desu*)
Past - -	*samuku nakatta*
First Future -	*samuku nakarō*
Second Future -	*samuku nakattarō*
First Conditional -	*samuku nakereba*
Second Conditional	*samuku nakattara*
Gerund - -	*samuku nakute* or *nai de*

In the same way *nai* may be added to the desiderative thus—*kakitaku nai,* " (I) don't want to write."

Present - -	*kakitaku nai*
Past - -	*kakitaku nakatta*
First Future -	*kakitaku nakarō*
Second Future -	*kakitaku nakattarō*
First Conditional -	*kakitaku nakereba*
Second Conditional -	*kakitaku nakattara*
Gerund - -	*kakitaku nakute* or *nai de*

In this connection one or two periphrastic forms of the verbal negative should be noted. *Mai* added to the third base of consonant verbs, or the first base of vowel verbs or to *masu* indicates a somewhat emphasized form of the negative first future, *e.g.*, *ashita Pari ye yuku ka?* "Will (you) go to Paris tomorrow?" *Iiye ikumai* or *ikimasumai*, "No I probably shall not go." For the same tense, *nai deshō* may also be used for *nakarō*. This especially is used to indicate an improbable present.

Finally, a very common negative gerund is formed by adding *zu* or *zu ni* to the first base, *e.g.*, *ikazu*, "not going" or "without going." *Kyō asameshi wo tabezu ni gakkō ye itta*, "Today I went to school without eating my breakfast."

Vocabulary

utsukushii, beautiful, clean.
ii = *yoi*, good.
kitanai, dirty, ugly.
yasui, cheap, easy.
ōkii, big.
kami, paper.
okoru, to be angry.
no mae ni, before, previous to.
gozaru (second base, *gozai*), to be.
iro, color.
katsudō shashin, cinematograph.
taiyō, the sun.
dōshite, why.
kwashi, cake.
dono gurai, how much.
mieru, look, seem, appear.
hayai, fast, early.
oishii, delicious, tasty.
nahanaka, very.
amari, too, too much (with negative verb, very).
yohodo, very.
akai, red.
sensō, war.
iru (second base, *iri*), want, need.
aruku, walk.
yube, last night.
tatemono, building.
omou, think.
anna, such a . . . .
e = *hai*, yes.
tadaima, just now.
san, Mount.

Exercise

1—*Kore wa takai; sore wa takaku nai.* 2—*Osokatta kara hayaku arukimashita.* 3—*Ano chiisai hana wa utsukushii.* 4—*Kono ōkii hana mo utsukushii.* 5—*Kinō tabeta kwashi wa oishikatta ka?* 6—*Hai oishiū gozaimashita.* 7—*Kono hon wa ii n' desu ka?* 8—*Hai nakanaka yoi n' desu.* 9—*Amari yoku arimasen.* 10—*Ano sakura no hana wa nani iro desu ka?* 11—*Are wa shirō gozaimasu.* 12—*Kono kami mo shirokatta ga mo kitanaku narimashita.* 13—*Yube katsudō shashin wo mi ni ikitakatta ka?* 14—*Amari ikitaku arimasen deshita.* 15—*Ikanakereba otō san ga okorimasu.* 16—*Sono ōkii mise wa takō gozaimasen.* 17—*Kono kami wa yasui n' desu ka?* 18—*E, yohodo yasū gozaimasu.* 19—*Sensō no mae ni yasukatta ga ima wa takaku narimashita.* 20—*Yasukereba katte kudasai, yasuku nakereba irimasen.* 21—*Kuroi empitsu wa gozaimasu ka?* 22—*Ano tatemono wa chiisō gozaimasu ne.* 23—*Sō desu ne. Amari ōkiu gozaimasen.* 24—*Tadaima taiyō ga akaku miemasu.* 25—*Anata wa dōshite anna warui koto wo shimashita ka?* 26—*Waruku nai to omoimashita.* 27—*Ittara yokatta.* 28—*Ashita ame ga furanakereba ii n' desu ga . . .* 29—*Kono pen wa yasukattarō.* 30—*Fuji san no takasa wa dono gurai desu ka?*

Translation

1—This is high; that is not high. 2—As I was late I walked fast. 3—That small flower is beautiful. 4—This big flower is also beautiful. 5—Was the cake which you ate yesterday nice? 6—Yes, it was delicious. 7—Is this book good? 8—Yes, it is very good. 9—No, it is not very good. 10—What is the color of that cherry flower? 11—That is white. 12—This paper was also white but it has become dirty. 13—Last night did you wish to go and see the movies? 14—I did not wish to go very much. 15—If you do not go, father will be angry. 16—That big shop is not pricey. 17—Is this paper cheap? 18—Yes, it is very cheap. 19—Before the war it was cheap but now it has become pricey. 20—If it is cheap please buy it. If it is not cheap I don't want it. 21—Is there a black pencil? *or* Have you a black pencil? 22—That building is small, isn't it? 23—That is so, isn't it ? It is not very big. 24—Just now the sun looks red. 25—Why did you do such a bad thing. 26—I thought that it was not bad (more freely, I did not know that it was bad) (literally, Bad not thus thought). 27—I wish we had gone, *or*, We should have gone (literally, Had we gone, it would have been good). 28—I hope the weather will be good tomorrow (literally, Tomorrow if the weather is nice, it would be good, but . . .). 29—This pen was cheap, wasn't it ? 30—How high is Mount Fuji ?

CHAPTER 6

The Adjective (cont.)

The Formation of Quasi-Adjectives

In addition to the real adjectives there are a large number of other words which may be used as adjectives. They are for the most part Chinese nouns which are provided with postpositions to indicate their qualifying relation.

There are three ways of forming a quasi-adjective from a noun. One is by compounding the qualifying noun with the main noun. Another is by adding *no* to the qualifying noun, and the third is by adding *na*.

The first is idiomatic and occurs only in certain specified instances. Just as the English say "a gold watch" instead of "golden watch," so in Japanese we may say literally "Buddha" (*butsu*), "temple" (*ji*) for "Buddhist temple," and *Nihongo*, literally "Japan language," meaning the "Japanese language."

Concrete and Abstract Quasi-Adjectives

These compounds cannot, of course, be made at will, and those in existence must simply be memorized.

For the other two classes there are certain fundamental rules whereby almost any noun may be changed into an adjective. *No* is added to concrete nouns, and *na* to abstract nouns. These terms are somewhat ambiguous, so that for the present concrete nouns may be defined as those which deal with time, place, country or material.

Thus, *kinu*, "silk," being material, we say, *kinu no kimono* for "silk clothes"; *Tetsu no fune* for "iron ship." The United States of America being a country, we say, *Amerika no hon* for "American book"; *Eikoku no fūzoku* for "English habits." Time and place adjectives are idiomatic and somewhat peculiar to Japanese. *Koko no hito* (literally "here's man") for "the man over here." *Rondon no kiri*, "a London fog." *Kyō no kwagyō*, "today's lesson."

"Beauty," on the other hand, being an abstract term, for "beautiful," we say *kirei na* (note that *kirei* though it ends in an *i* is not a real adjective, there being no *ei* forms). Again, *shizuka na*, "quiet"; *rikō na*, "clever"; *rippa na*, "splendid," and *baka na* "foolish"—from *baka*, "fool."

Inflection of Abstract Quasi-Adjectives

These quasi-adjectives being nouns cannot be conjugated, but abstract or *na* quasi-adjectives undergo certain changes according to their position in a sentence.

Just as real adjectives change their final *i* to *ku* when placed in front of a verb, so does the *na* change to *ni* in front of a verb. *Shōjiki na*, "honest," but *Ano hito wa shōjiki ni hatarakimasu*, "That man (he) works honestly." *Baka ni miemasu*, "(He) appears foolish."

There is also a separate predicate form. In modern colloquial Japanese the form of the real adjective remains the same whether used attributively (*yoi kodomo*) or predicatively (*kodomo ga yoi*). This is not the case in the written language, and the quasi-adjectives have retained traces of the earlier distinction. *Na* can only be used attributively, *i.e.*, in front of a noun. When the quasi-adjective is used predicatively, *i.e.*, placed after the noun, the *na* changes to *de*. Thus *kirei na hana*, "a pretty flower," but *hana ga kirei de arimasu*, "the flower is pretty." *Baka na kodomo*, "a foolish child," but *Ano kodomo wa baka desu*, "That child is foolish."

As in other cases, the *de* may combine with *arimasu* into *desu*, but unlike the real adjectives which may be used alone without a verb (*e.g.*, *yoi* = "is good") the quasi-adjectives always require a copula.

There are certain words which may be used either as quasi- or as real adjectives. Chief among these are :—

ōkii	or	*oki na*	for big.
chiisai	or	*chiisa na*	,, small.
okashii	or	*okashi na*	,, amusing.
atatakai	or	*atataka na*	,, warm.
yawarakai	or	*yawaraka na*	,, soft.
komakai	or	*komaka na*	,, infinitesimal.
kiiroi	or	*kiiro na*	,, yellow.
makkuroi	or	*makkuro na*	,, jet black, etc.

Vocabulary

tera, temple.
Amerika, America, U.S.A.
kin, gold.
kisha, train.
umi, sea, ocean.
sake, rice wine.
kata, person, gentleman, lady.
mukō, over there.
Hakurai, foreign make.
kodomorashii, child-like.
daiku, carpenter.
hontō ni, *jitsu ni*, really, truly.
taisō, very, much.
kōdai na, imposing, grand.
baka na, foolish.
rikō na, clever, wise.
shōjiki na, honest.
shinsetsu na, kind.
sakan na, prosperous, thriving.
jōzu na, skillful.
tassha, healthy.
you, to become drunk.
gwaimushō, foreign office.
gin, silver.
jidōsha, motor car.
dekiru, to be able, to make.

gakusha, scholar, learned person.
kao, face.
ikaga, how.
Wasei, Japanese make.
erai, great, famous.
mezurashii, rare.
murasaki, purple.
keredomo, but.
rippa na, splendid.
kirei na, beautiful, clean.
odayaka na, quiet, calm.
somatsu na, rude, rough, worthless.
fushōjiki na, dishonest.
benri na, convenient.
makka na, crimson.
heta na, unskillful.
suki na, pleasing, that which one likes.

Exercise

1—*Are wa rippa na tera desu.* 2—*Ano kōdai na tatemono wa nan desu ka?* 3—*Are wa gwaimushō desu.* 4—*Ano hana wa kirei desu.* 5—*Kono hana wa kirei de gozaimashita.* 6—*Amari kirei de wa gozaimasen.* 6—*Sono kodomo wa kirei na hana wo motte imasu.* 7—*Sore wa Amerika no hon desu ka, Igirisu no hon desu ka?* 8—*Mukō no jidōsha wa dare no desu ka?* 9—*Sono chiisa na kodomo wa baka desu ka?* 10—*Are wa baka de wa arimasen.* 11—*Ano inu wa rikō desu.* 12—*Kore wa gindokei desu ka?* 13—*Sore wa kindokei desu.* 14—*Sono hito wa Nihongo ga dekimasu ka?* 15—*Kore wa Wasei desu. Sore wa Hakurai desu.* 16—*Are wa murasaki no hana desu ka?* 17—*Murasaki no hana wa kirei de gozaimasu.* 18—*Kyō wa umi ga odayaka desu.* 19—*Ano hito wa erai gakusha desu keredomo hontō ni kodomorashiu gozaimasu.* 20—*Kore wa somatsu na mono desu ga . . .* 21—*Are wa rikō na hito desu ga fushōjiki desu.* 22—*Hontō ni shōjiki na hito wa mezurashii.* 23—*Sore wa anata no suki na mono desu ka?* 24—*Ano hito wa sake ni yotte kao ga makka ni natta.* 25—*Ano kata wa jitsu ni shinsetsu na hito desu.* 26—*Rondon wa taisō sakan na tokoro desu.* 27—*Kisha wa benri na mono desu.* 28—*Otō san wa ikaga de gozaimasu?* 29—*O kage san de tassha de gozaimasu.* 30—*Ano daiku wa jōzu desu ka heta desu ka?*

Translation

1—That is a splendid temple. 2—What is that imposing building? 3—That is the Foreign Office. 4—That flower is beautiful. 5—This flower was beautiful. 6—It is not very beautiful. 7—Is that an American book or an English book? 8—Whose is that motor over there? (literally, Over there's motor car as for, whose is?) 9—Is that small child a fool? 10—He is not a fool. 11—That dog is clever. 12—Is this a silver watch? 13—That is a gold watch. 14—Can that man speak (literally, Can he do) Japanese. 15—This is a Japanese article. That is an imported article. 16—Is that a purple flower? 17—Purple flowers are beautiful. 18—Today the sea is calm. 19—That man is a well-known scholar but he is really very childish. 20—This is a worthless thing but . . . (I beg of you to accept it). 21—That is a clever man but he is dishonest. 22—Really honest people are rare. 23—Is that a thing which you like? 24—That man being drunk on *sake* has a red face. 25—That gentleman is indeed a kind man. 26—London is a very thriving place. 27—Trains are convenient things. 28—How is your father? 29—He is very well, thanks (literally, By your favor, he is healthy). 30—Is that carpenter skillful or unskillful?

CHAPTER 7

The Adjective (cont.)

The Comparison of Adjectives

The comparison of adjectives is somewhat complicated in Japanese owing to the various periphrastic modes of comparison adopted which differ but slightly in meaning.

For the most part there is no expression of comparison whatever. *Empitsu to pen to wa dochira ga yasui?* "Which is cheaper, a pencil or a pen?" (literally "Pencil and pen and as for, which is cheap?"). *Empitsu ga yasui,* "The pencil is cheaper" (literally, "The pencil is cheap"). The same applies to the superlative. *Nashi to ringo to mikan to wa dore ga yasui?* "Which is the cheapest—a pear, an apple, or an orange?" Note that *dochira* is "which" when speaking of only two objects, and *dore* is "which" when speaking of more than two. *Nashi ga yasui,* "The pear is the cheapest."

When emphasis is needed there are several ways of indicating comparison, chief among which are the following :—

(*a.*)—By the use of *no hō ga* after nouns and *hō ga* after verbs and adjectives. *Fuji yama to Asama yama to wa dochira ga takai?* "Which is higher, Mount Fuji or Mount

Asama ?" *Fuji yama no hō ga takai,* "Mount Fuji is higher." *Sā kaerimashō,* "I say," or "Well then, let us go home" (*kaeru,* "to return"). *So desu nē. Kaeru hō ga ii,* "All right." (literally, "that is so, isn't it ?") "it is better to return." The superlative may also be expressed in this way. *Iroiro no kaki ga arimasu ga chiisai hō ga ii,* "There are various (kinds of) oysters, but the small (ones) are best."

(*b.*)—By the use of *yori.* Both *empitsu ga yasui* and *empitsu no hō ga yasui* mean "the pencil is cheaper," but we may also indicate the standard of comparison (*e.g.,* "The pencil is cheaper *than the pen*") by adding *yori* (literally, "than," "from"). *Nihongo wa Eigo yori mutsukashii desu,* or *Eigo yori Nihongo ga mutsukashii,* "Japanese is more difficult than English." *Anata wa watakushi yori wakai n' desu,* "You are younger than me."

(*c.*)—By the combined use of *yori* and (*no*) *hō ga.* This is but the emphasized form of the preceding. *Pen yori empitsu no hō ga yasui,* "A pencil is cheaper than a pen." *Sore yori kore wo katta hō ga ii,* "It would be better to buy this than that." *Tarō wa baka desu ga Tarō yori Jirō no hō ga baka desu,* "Tarō is foolish, but Jirō is even more foolish than Tarō."

(*d.*)—An even more emphasized comparative may be made by the use of *nao* or *motto,* both literally meaning "more." *Pen ga yasui keredomo empitsu ga nao yasui,* "A pen is cheap, but a pencil is even cheaper" (literally, "more cheap"). *Iku hō ga ii keredomo tomaru hō ga motto ii,* "It is all right to go but it is even better to stay."

(*e.*)—An emphasized superlative is formed by adding *mottomo,* or *ichiban. Kwagaku no uchi de rigaku ga ichiban mutsukashii,* "Among the sciences physics is the most difficult." *Pen ga yasui, empitsu ga nao yasui, fude ga mottomo yasui,* "Pens are cheap, pencils are cheaper, but *fude* (Japanese writing brushes) are the cheapest (of all)."

(*f.*)—By the use of *hodo*. *Hodo* means " as . . . as," or " as much as." *Kore wa sore hodo ii n' desu,* " This is as good as that." *Asama yama wa Fuji yama hodo takaku arimasen,* " Mount Asama is not as high as Mount Fuji." *Kyō wa kinō hodo samuku nai,* " Today is not as cold as yesterday."

(*g.*)—By the use of *hodo* plus the conditional. There are several extremely idiomatic expressions connected with *hodo*. The idea of " the . . . the," is rendered by the conditional of a verb or adjective plus the present plus *hodo*. Thus, *samukereba samui hodo ii,* " the colder the better " ; *atsukereba atsui hodo ii,* " the hotter the better." *Mireba miru hodo rippa desu,* " The more (one) looks (at it) the more beautiful it seems." *Hashireba hashiru hodo atsuku narimasu,* " The more one runs, the warmer one becomes."

Uses of the Gerund of Adjectives and Verbs

The general meaning of the gerund has already been discussed. We now come to a technical consideration of certain idiomatic usages. For both verbs and adjectives there may be said to be ten further meanings. These are :—

(*a.*)—CONJUNCTIVE, or serving to join two or more phrases. *Kawa ga semakute asai n' desu,* " The river is narrow *and* shallow." *Hon wo katte kaerimashita* " (I) bought a book *and* returned home." Sometimes in place of *and*, *but* is implied. *Hajime ga atte owari ga nai,* " There is a beginning, *but* no ending."

(*b.*)—CLAUSAL CONJUNCTIVE, or serving to join two or more clauses. *Kawa ga semakute yama ga takai,* " The river is narrow, *and* the mountain is high." *Takeo san wa asobi ni itte, Masao san wa uchi ni tomarimashita,*

"Master Takeo went out to play while Master Masao remained at home."

(*c.*)—CAUSAL. *Kinō ame ga futte ikanakatta,* "As it rained yesterday, I did not go." *Samukute yamemashō,* "Since it is cold let us stop." A more emphatic and usual way of expressing causality is by adding *kara* to the indicative. Thus, *Omoshiroi kara ikitai desu,* "As it is interesting I wish to go." *Kyō wa samui desu kara Fujita san wa konai deshō,* "As it is cold Mr. Fujita probably won't come today."

(*d.*)—INSTRUMENTAL. *Watakushi wa himo wo motte iwakimashita,* "I tied it up with some string" (literally, "I as for having string tied up").

(*e.*)—SEQUENTIAL. The gerund plus *kara* indicates temporal sequence. *Hirumeshi wo tabete kara ikimashita,* "I went after I ate lunch." *Are ga sunde kara kore wo sōji shite kudasai,* "After you have finished that, please clean this."

(*f.*)—CONCESSIVE. The gerund plus *mo* indicates *even, even though,* or *though. Itte mo yaku ni tachimasen,* "Even if you go it will be useless" (*yaku ni tatsu* is an idiom ="to be of use"). *Ame ga futte mo ikimasu,* "Even though it rains I shall go."

(*g.*)—PERMISSIVE. The gerund plus *mo* plus some form of *ii* ("good") expresses *may* or *can. Itte mo ii ka?* "May (I) go?" (literally, "Even though I go is it all right?"). *Hai itte mo yoi n' desu,* "Yes you may go." *Shirokute mo yō gozaimasu ka?* "Will a white (one) do?" The negative gerund plus *mo ii* means "need not," or in a question, "must (I)?" *Ikanakute mo ii ka?* "May I not go?" or "Must I go?" *Ikanakute mo ii,* "(You) need not go" (more literally, "Even though you do not go it is all right"). *Shirokunakute mo ii,* "It need not be white."

(*h.*)—Permissive Adverbial. The gerund of adjectives plus *mo* has also the peculiar idiomatic significance of "at the . . . est." *Osokute mo,* "At the latest"; *hayakute mo,* "at the earliest"; *ōkute mo,* "at the most," etc. *Osokute mo ni ji ni oide nasai,* "At the latest please come at 2 o'clock." Almost any adjective may be treated in this way.

(*i.*)—Emphatic. The gerund of adjectives plus either *shiyō ga nai, shikata ga nai,* or *tamarimasen* indicates emphatic assertion. *Atsukute shiyō ga nai,* "It is dreadfully hot"; *samukute tamarimasen,* "it is fearfully cold." *Tamarimasen* means "it cannot be endured," so more literally the sentence means, "It is so cold that (I) can't bear it." Both *shiyō ga nai* and *shikata ga nai* means "there is nothing to be done," or "(I) can do nothing" (literally, "doing-side is not"). They are often used independently in the sense of "never mind," or "there is no use crying over spilt milk."

(*j.*)—Absolute. The gerund of either verb or adjective plus the absolute particle, *wa,* is, among other things, almost equivalent to the present or the past conditional. Its chief use is when followed by *ikemasen* or *narimasen* (literally "it can't go," and "it won't become," and both are equal to the English "it won't do"). *Itte wa narimasen,* "If (you) go, it won't do," or "You must not go." *Shirokute wa ikimasen,* "If it is white it won't do," or "It must not be white." The negative gerund causes the expression to mean "must." *Ikanakute wa narimasen,* "If (you) don't go, it won't do," or "You must go." *Shirokunakute wa ikemasen,* "If it is not white it won't do," or "It must be white."

In all such cases the first or the second conditional may be used without changing the meaning, *Ittara* or *ikeba narimasen,* "You must not go." Incidentally it

Hokkaido

Shinto Shrine

should be noted that *te wa* is often contracted to *cha*. *Ame ga futcha komaru,* "If rain were to fall, it would be inconvenient." In like manner *de wa* contracts to *ja.*

All these forms have additional meanings, but they are less frequently used, and may be for the present omitted.

Vocabulary

dochira, which (of two).
dore, which (of more than two).
mikan, orange.
yori, more . . . than.
kumi, class, set.
kun, students' word for Mr. etc.
koe, voice.
tonikaku, in any case.
hai, fly (insect).
ryohi, travelling expenses.
yōkan, a sweet made from beans.
ate ni naru (to be) reliable.
yu, hot water.
tamaru, endure, to bear.
yōji, business.
yaku ni tatsu, to be of use.
samisen, a musical instrument like the mandolin, used by *geisha.*
ahō, fool.
umai, delicious.
samui, cold.
setsumei suru, explain.
kudamono, fruit.
no uchi de. among.
ringo, apple.
motto, more.
donata, polite form of *dare,* who
mottomo, most.
ichiban, most.
ka, mosquito.
urusai, troublesome, annoying.
zasshi, magazine.
namben, how many times (= many times).
rombun, article essay.
shitsurei, rudeness.
shikata ga nai, nothing can be done.
komaru, to be in trouble.
benkyō suru, to study diligently.
kurasu, to live (in economic sense).
aitsu, that fellow.
atsui, hot.
kore kara, henceforward.
made ni, by ; *made,* until.

Exercise

1—*Empitsu to pen (to) wa dochira ga yasui?* 2—*Pen ga yasui. Pen no hō ga yasui.* 3—*Pen yori empitsu no hō ga takai.* 4—*Kono kudamono no uchi de dore ga takai?* 5—*Mikan ga takai.* 6—*Mikan yori ringo no hō ga motto yasui deshō.* 7—*Kono kumi no uchi de donata ga ichiban wakō gozaimasu ?* 8—*Takeda kun wa mottomo wakai to omoimasu. Tonikaku Takeuchi kun yori wakai desu.* 9—*Ka wa hai yori urusai.* 10—*Koko ni tomaru yori kaeru hō ga ii.* 11—*Hayaku kuru yori osoi hō ga ii.* 12—*Kono kudamono wa yasukute yō gozaimasu.* 13—*Kono yu wa atsukute tamarimasen.* 14—*Kono hon wa takakutemo yokereba kaimasu.* 15—*Kyō wa samukute shikata ga nai.* 16—*Ashita Hagiwara san no tokoro ye itte mo yō gozaimasu ka ? Itte mo ii ga osokute mo san ji han made ni kaeranakereba narimasen.* 17—*Yōji ga arimasu kara itte wa ikemasen.* 18—*Kono sake wa warukute komarimasu.* 19—*Ano hito wa mainichi asa kara ban made benkyō shite gakusha ni naritai n' desu.* 20—*Oi ! Gonsuke. mise ye itte shimbun wo katte kite kure. Shimbun ga nakereba zasshi demo ii.* 21—*Nikkō ye ikitakatta ga ryohi ga takakute ikemasen deshita.* 22—*Ano hito wa baka de yaku ni tachimasen.* 23—*Sasaki san wa samisen wo oshiete kurashimasu.* 24—*Aitsu wa hontō ni ahō da. Namben setsumei shite mo wakaranakatta.* 25—*Yōkan ga umakatta kara takusan tabemashita.* 26—*Are wa ate ni naranai mise da kara kore kara asuko de kawanai hō ga ii.* 27—*Kono rombun wa mutsukashikute wakarimasen.* 28—*Bimbō demo shōjiki ni shinakereba narimasen.* 29—*Konaida wa shitsurei shimashita.*

Translation

1—Which is cheaper, a pencil or a pen ? 2—A pen is cheaper (two forms). 3—A pencil is dearer than a pen. 4—Among these fruits which is the dearest ? 5—The oranges are the dearest. 6—Apples are cheaper than oranges, I suppose. 7—Who is the youngest in this class ? 8—I think that Mr. Takeda is the youngest. In any case he is younger than Mr. Takeuchi. 9—Mosquitos are more troublesome than flies. 10—It is better to go back than to stay here. 11—It is better to go late than early. 12—This fruit is both cheap and good. 13—This water is so hot that I can't stand it. 14—Even though this book be dear, if it be good I shall buy it. 15—Today it is bitterly cold. 16—May I go to Master Hagiwara's house tomorrow? You may go but you must come back by half past three. 17—As there is some business, you must not go. 18—This *sake* is so bad I am in a mess. 19—He studies from morning till night and so hopes to become a scholar. 20—Here Gonsuke. Go to the shop and buy me a newspaper. If they haven't a newspaper a magazine will do. 21—I wanted to go to Nikko, but as the fare was so high I could not go. 22—He is a fool and quite worthless. 23—Mr. Sasaki gets a living by teaching the *samisen.* 24—That fellow is really an idiot. No matter how many times I explained to him, he did not understand. 25—As the *yokan* was nice I ate a lot. 26—As that is an unreliable shop it is better not to buy there any more. 27—This article is so difficult that I don't understand it. 28—Even though poor one should act honestly. 29—Excuse my rudeness of the other day (literally, The other day I did rudeness).

CHAPTER 8

Miscellaneous

Honorifics

Japanese, like other Asian languages, makes frequent use of honorific and humble expressions. In speaking to an inferior, ordinary forms are used, sometimes verging by contrast upon rudeness, but when speaking to an equal or superior (and these terms are interpreted rather broadly), one's own possessions and actions are deprecated and those of the person addressed elevated. Third persons are also so treated if present and even when absent if they are decidedly superior in rank. Things which *I* do to *you* and which *you* do to *me* have special forms. Even the relation of superiority or inferiority between *you* and some other person, or between two other persons are taken into consideration.

There are three ways of indicating honorifics: by the use of different words; by the use of *o* and *go*; and by the means of auxiliary verbs.

The change of words applies both to nouns and to verbs. In place of the plain word *miru*, to see, we have the humble word *haiken suru*, "(I) see," (literally, "Adoring glance do") and the honorific word is *goran nasaru*, "(You) see" or "(he) sees" (literally, "august glance deign"). Such words are comparatively frequent, but in most cases auxiliary forms are used for verbs, so that changes in nouns are more common. Words indicating relationship are especially subject to transformation. Among them are :—

	HUMBLE	PLAIN	HONORIFIC
Father	*chichi*	*chichi*	*o tō san* *go shimpu*
Mother	*haha*	*haha*	*okkasan* *o ka san*
Husband	*taku* *uchi* *shujin*	*teishu* (lower class) *danna* (upper class)	*danna san*
Wife	*kanai*	*o kami san* (lower class) *o ku san* (upper class)	*o kamisan* *o ku san*
Son	*musuko* *segare*	*musuko*	*musuko san* *go shisoku*
Daughter	*musume*	*musume*	*o jō san*
Elder brother	*ani*	*ani*	*nii san*
Elder sister	*ane*	*ane*	*nē san*

The second mode of forming the honorific is by the use of *o* and *go* and is even more frequent. *O* is generally prefixed to words (chiefly nouns and adjectives) of native origin, and *go* to words borrowed from China. Both literally mean " honorable," *e.g.*, *O tegami wo yomimashita,* " (I) read your letter " ; *o kuni,* " your country " ; *o taku,* " your house " ; *Kore wa anata no go hon de gozaimasu ka ?* " Is this your book ? " *O isogashū gozaimasu ka ?* " Are you busy ? " There are a certain number of words which have *o* and *go* so constantly prefixed to them as to have lost their honorific significance, *e.g.*, *o cha,* " tea " ; *o yu,* " hot water " ; *gohan* or *gozen,* " rice or food " ; *o kwashi* " cakes " ; *o tentō sama,* " the sun " ; *o tsuki sama,* " the moon."

The third method is the most important of all and consists in the addition of a number of auxiliary verbs. Chief among these are :—

(*a.*)—*Ageru,* which indicates an action done by the first person on behalf of the second or third person. In this as in most other cases the auxiliary verb is attached to the gerund. *Yonde agemashō ka?* " Shall I read to you ? " *Matsumoto san ni jū yen kashite agemashita,* " I lent Mr. Matsumoto ten yen."

(*b.*)—*Morau,* literally means " to receive," and as an auxiliary verb has a peculiar causative sense. *Takeda san ni yonde moraimashita,* " (I) got Mr. Takeda to read (to me)." *Fujita san ni jū yen kashite moraimashita.* " I got Mr. Fujita to lend me ten yen." *Morau* is a humble word and is chiefly used in connection with the first person. In this sense, of course, it indicates an action by the second or third person on behalf of the first person.

(*c.*)—*Kudasaru* (the irregular second base of which is *kudasai*) literally means " to condescend," and indicates a simple (*i.e.,* non-causative) action by the second or third person on behalf of the first person, or more generally, by a superior to an inferior. *Suzuki san ga yonde kudasaimashita,* " Mr. Suzuki kindly read (to me)." *Inouye san ga watakushi ni jū yen kashite kudasaimashita,* " Mr. Inouye kindly lent me ten yen." It will be remembered that the gerund plus *kudasai* expresses a polite imperative. *Tarō ye tegami wo kaite kudasai,* " Please write a letter to Tarō." Used alone, *kudasai* has the sense of " please give me . . ." *Oi! nēsan, mizu kudasai,* " Oh ! waitress (literally ' elder sister ') please give me some water." *Kureru* has exactly the same meaning as *kudasaru,* but it is not quite so polite. It is chiefly used as a polite mode of expression for the action of inferiors.

(*d.*)—*Nasaru* (of which the irregular second base is *nasai*) has two meanings. One is to express almost the same meaning as *kudasaru,* though usually it follows the second base preceded by *o* instead of the gerund, though occasionally it is attached to the gerund. *Takeuchi kun ga kono tegami wo o okuri nasaimashita.* "Mr. Takeuchi kindly sent me this letter." From (*koshi wo*) *kakeru* we have *o kake nasai,* "please sit down." Unlike *kudasaru* and *kureru,* however, *nasaru* cannot be used alone.

The second use is merely to indicate an action of any sort done by the second or third person, and without reference to the first person. *Rainen Nippon ye o ide nasaimasu ka?* "Are you going to Japan next year?" *Otōsan wa itsu o kaeri nasaimasu ka?* "When will (your) father return?"

(*e.*)—*Ni naru* is equivalent to the second use of *nasaru,* and is likewise used with the second base. *O kaeri nasaimasu* =*O kaeri ni narimasu.*

(*f.*)—*Gozaru* (of which the irregular second base is *gozai*) is the honorific form of *aru, oru,* etc., and may be used in their place when speaking to an equal or a superior and without reference to the quality of the subject. *Anata wa dare da?* "Who are you?" *Watakushi wa sendaku-ya de gozaimasu,* "I am the laundry-shop (man)."

(*g.*)—*Itasu, suru,* and *nasaru.* These three words are used as auxiliaries with Chinese verbs. They all have the same meaning, and vary only in politeness. *Itasu* is used in describing the actions of the first person, *nasaru* of the second or third person, and *suru* of either first, second, or third. *Ryokō itasu,* "I travel," *ryokō nasaru,* "you travel" or "he travels," *ryokō suru?* "I, you, they, travel."

Various Idiomatic Expressions

(*i.*)—*Honorific Phrases*

The following honorific phrases are sufficiently common and peculiar to require memorization :—

(*a.*)—*O kinodoku sama,* " I am very sorry for you " (literally, " hon. spirit of poison Mr.").
(*b.*)—*Go kurō sama,* " Thanks for your trouble " (literally, " honorable trouble Mr.").
(*c.*)—*O machidō sama,* " Pardon my keeping you waiting " (literally, " hon. waiting Mr.").
(*d.*)—*O kage de,* " By your kind influence " (literally, " hon. shade by ").
(*e.*)—*O jama itashimashita,* " Excuse my having interrupted you."
(*f.*)—*Go busata itashimashita,* " Excuse my remissness in calling (or writing)."
(*g.*)—*O itoma itashimashō,* " I am afraid that I must be leaving."
(*h.*)—*Go taikutsu de gozaimashitarō,* " I am afraid that you must have been bored."

(*ii.*)—*Honorfic Paraphrases*

The following list of words compiled by Rose-Innes consists of verbs which vary according to the subject spoken of, and will prove of great use to the student :—

	HUMBLE	PLAIN	HONORIFIC
Be	*iru* (*oru*)	*iru* (*oru*)	*o ide nasaru* *irassharu*
Come	*mairu* *agaru*	*kuru*	*o ide nasaru* *irassharu*
Drink	*itadaku* *chōdai suru*	*nomu*	*meshi agru* *agaru*
Do	*suru* *itasu*	*suru*	*nasaru*
Eat	*itadaku* *chōdai suru*	*taberu* *kuu*	*meshi agaru* *agaru*

Give	*ageru*	*yaru*	*kudasaru*
			kureru
			o yari nasaru
Go	*mairu*	*iku*	*o ide nasaru*
	agaru		*irassharu*
Inquire	*ukagau*	*tazuneru*	*o tazune nasaru*
		kiku	*o kiki nasaru*
Know	*zonjiru*	*shiru*	*go zonji de irassharu*
Look	*haiken suru*	*miru*	*goran nasaru*
Meet	*o me ni kakaru*	*au*	*o ai nasaru*
Receive	*itadaku*	*ukeru*	*o morai nasaru*
	chōdai suru	*morau*	
Show	*o me ni kakeru*	*miseru*	*o mise nasaru*
			o mise kudasaru
Speak	*mōshi ageru*	*iu, hanasu*	*ossharu*
Visit	*ukagau*	*tazuneru*	*o tazune nasaru*
	agaru		

(*iii.*)—*Peculiar Consonant Verbs*

The following are the principal verbs which though ending in *iru* and *eru* belong to the *r* class of consonant verbs and not to the vowel conjugation :—

(*a.*)—Eru Verbs

Kaeru,	return.	*Heru,*	diminish.
Suberu,	slip.	*Teru,*	shine.
Shaberu,	chatter.	*Neru,*	knead.
Shimeru,	to become moist.	*Aseru,*	hurry.
Fuseru,	lie down.	*Hoteru,*	tingle.

(*b.*)—Iru Verbs

Mairu,	go.	*Shiru,*	know.
Kiru,	cut.	*Soshiru,*	slander.
Negiru,	bargain.	*Iru,*	enter, need, parch.
Nigiru,	seize.	*Nonoshiru,*	revile.
Hashiru,	run.	*Majiru,*	mingle.
Chiru,	fall, scatter.	*Hairu,*	enter.
Ijiru,	meddle with.	*Hojiru,*	pick out.
Kagiru,	to be bounded.	*Kajiru,*	gnaw.
Kishiru,	grate.	*Magiru,*	tack.
Mushiru,	pluck.	*Najiru,*	rebuke.

(*iv.*)—*Idiomatic Expressions*

The uses of " . . . *to iu* . . ."; *koto ga; koto ga dekiru;* (*nai*) *koto wa nai,* and *mono ga* or *de* are both idiomatic and important.

1.—" . . . *to iu* . . ." *e.g., Taimusu to iu shimbun,* "A newspaper called the *Times*" (literally, "*Times* thus call newspaper"). *Tori to iu mono,* "Things called birds," or simply "birds" in a general sense. *Watakushi wa Sumisu to iu mono de gozaimasu,* "I am a thing called Smith"—"I am Mr. Smith." *Fujita san wa 'kyō Tarō ga kuru' to iimashita,* "Mr. Fujita said 'Tarō comes today'" (literally, "Mr. Fujita as for 'today Tarō comes' thus said"). There is no indirect quotation in Japanese.

2.—*Koto,* literally "thing" (in the abstract sense) may be used after the impolite form of any verb, which it changes into a noun. *Taberu koto,* "eating" or "the act of eating"; *nomu koto,* "drinking," etc. Its principal use, however, is to indicate a sort of perfect tense by means of the use of the past tense followed by *koto ga aru,* or a pluperfect by the past plus *koto ga atta. Anata wa Nippon ye itta koto ga arimasu ka?* "Did you ever go to Japan?" or "Have you been to Japan?" *Iiye itta koto ga arimasen,* "No, (I) Have never been." *Hai itta koto ga aru,* "Yes, (I) have been." *Kyonen made watakushi wa sake wo nonda koto ga arimasen deshita,* "Until last year I had never drunk *saké*."

3.—*Koto ga dekiru* (or *dekinai*), used after any verb expresses possibility (or with the negative, impossibility) and corresponds to the English "can . . ." *Anata wa aruku koto ga dekimasu ka? Hai aruku koto ga dekimasu.* "Can you walk? Yes, I can walk." *Iiye dekimasen,* "No (I) cannot." *Ima made watakushi wa Nihongo wo yomu koto ga dekinakatta ga rainen kara dekiru deshō.* "Up to the present I have not been able to read Japanese, but from next year I shall probably be able (to do so)."

4.—(*Nai*) *koto wa nai.* This is a very peculiar idiom and is an instance of a double negative making an emphasized positive. Literally *nai koto wa nai* signifies "it is not that it is not," "it *is*" or "there *are* some." *Kwashi ga aru ka?* "Is there any cake?" *Nai koto wa nai desu ga sukoshi dake desu,* "There is some, but only a little." The negative form of any verb may be used in place of *nai.* Thus *ikanai koto wa nai,* "(I) *am* going."

5.—*Mono ga* or *de.* This expression resembles *koto ga* but refers to concrete things. Its principal use is in such expressions as *taberu mono,* "a thing to eat" or "a thing fit to eat"; *suru mono,* "a thing to do" or "a thing fit to do." *Tako wa taberu mono desu ka?* "Is an octopus a thing fit to eat?" *Iiye taberu mono de wa arimasen,* "No it is not fit to eat." (Note, however, that the Japanese are fond of cuttle fish.) Such expressions as *Yotte iru mon' ka?* are quite common. This sentence means "Do you think I am drunk? Nonsense!" *Sore wa naku mon' ka?* "Do you imagine that is a thing to cry over? Bah!"

Vocabulary

(Include the lists of words found in the Lesson.)

kongetsu, this month.
raigetsu, next month.
sashi-ageru, to help to food.
kakaru, hang.
go zonji no tori, as you know.
bansankwai, a dinner-party.
sakujitsu, yesterday.
shiru, know.
yūbin, post, mail.
. . . ga suki, like.
kanji, ideographs.
hanahada, very.
sensei, teacher.
hazu, necessity (after a verb "ought.")
ka mo shiremasen, perhaps.
hajimeru, to begin.
kōen, park.
zonjiru, know.
enryo, to be diffident, stand on ceremony.
jibun de, alone, by one's self.
okuru, send.
. . . ga kirai, dislike.
dochira, whither? where?
dōzo, please.

Exercise

1—*Go shisoku wa itsu Eikoku kara o kaeri ni narimasu ka?* 2—*Kongetsu kaeru hazu desu ga, raigetsu ni naru ka mo shiremasen.* 3—*Hanahada gobusata itashimashita.* 4—*Kore ga wakaranai kara setsumei shite kudasaimasen ka?* 5—*Shite mo ii deshō ga senai hō ga ii.* 6—*Mō sukoshi sashi-agemashō.* 7—*Hajimete o me ni kakarimasu.* 8—*Ueno kōen wo mō goran nasaimashita ka?* 9—*Iiye mada mita koto ga arimasen.* 10—*Kinō shujin ga Yokohama ye irasshaimashite mada kaerimasen.* 11—*Itsu o kaeri desu ka?* 12—*Sō de gozaimasu ne. Go zonji no tōri de ashita bansankwai ga gozaimasu kara sore made ni kaerimasu deshō.* 13—*Dōzo enryo sezu ni o agari nasai.* 14—*Kono hon wo o me ni kakemashō ka?* 15—*Arigatō gozaimasu. Sakujitsu haiken itashimashita.* 16—*Konai koto wa nai desu ga itsu kuru ka shiran.* 17—*Kinō jibun de yuku koto ga dekimasen deshita kara yūbin de okurimashita.* 18—*Kore wo go ran nasai. Takeo san ga watashi ni kudasaimashita.* 19—*Sonna hon wo yonja ikan. Sore wa kodomo no yomu mon' ja nai. Anata wa pan ga suki desu ka?* 21—*Hai suki desu ga kwashi ga motto suki desu.* 22—*Kirai demo nai ga amari suki de wa gozaimasen.* 23—*Anata wa kanji wo yomu koto ga dekimasu ka?* 24—*Dekinai koto wa nai desu ga amari jōzu ja nai n' desu.* 25—*Kesa Murata san ga irasshaimashita ka?* 26—*Iiye mada o ide ni narimasen deshita.* 27—*Kono tokoro wa mutsukashikute wakaranakatta no ni Murai sensei ga setsumei shite kudasaimashita.* 28—*Ima wa dochira ye (o ide nasaimasu ka?).* 29—*Shiba kōen ye ikō to omotte orimasu.* 30—*Konaida Tanaka san kara tegami wo itadakimashita.*

Translation

1—When will your son return from England? 2—He ought to come back this month but perhaps it will be next month before he does (literally, Will it become next month ? I cannot know). 3—I have been very rude in not calling on you for a long time. 4—As I don't understand this, will you kindly explain it to me ? 5—It will be alright to do it, I think, but it would be better not to do it. 6—Can't I give you a little more (literally, A little more shall I help ?) 7—This is the first time that I have caught your eye (said on meeting a person for the first time). 8—Have you seen Ueno Park yet ? 9—No, I have never seen it. 10—Yesterday my husband went to Yokohama and has not yet returned. 11—When will he come back ? 12—Let me see. As you know he has a dinner party tomorrow night so he must come back before that. 13—Without standing on ceremony please eat (more freely, Please make yourself at home). 14—Shall I show you this book ? 15—Thank you. I saw it yesterday. 16—He *will* come, but I don't know when. 17—Yesterday I could not myself, so I sent it by mail. 18—Please look at this. 19—You must not read such books as that. That is not fit for children to read. 20—Do you like bread ? 21—Yes, I like it, but I like cake more. 22—I do not dislike it, but I am not particularly fond of it. 23—Can you read the Chinese ideographs ? 24—I *can* read them, but I am not very skillful. 25—Did Mr. Murata come this morning ? 26—No, he has not arrived yet. 27—As this part (literally, place) was so difficult that I could not understand it, Mr. Murai (literally, Teacher Murai) kindly explained it to me. 28—Where are you going ? 29—I am thinking of going to Shiba Park. 30—Recently I received a letter from Mr. Tanaka.

Analysis: Nouns

Declension

The Article

In Japanese there is neither definite nor indefinite article. Occasionally, however, we find forms which take their place. Such are *aru*, " some," or " a certain," for " a," *e.g.*, *Aru hito*, " some people," or " a certain person." *Kono*, *sono*, *ano*, " this, that, that," or relative clauses such as " letter just mentioned," " yesterday spoke to man," etc., are paraphrases of " the."

Number

For the most part number is also unexpressed, and no distinction is made between singular and plural. There are, however, a certain number of idioms which convey some numerical significance. Among these are :—

(*a.*)—Plural Suffixes. Occasionally when the distinction between singular and plural is to be emphasized, certain plural suffixes are added. They are taken from the written language, where their use is slightly more common. Such are :—

ra
domo (or *tomo*).
shu or *shū*.
dachi (or *tachi*).
gata.

There is no difference in meaning between them, except with reference to politeness, *ra* being the least, and *gata* the most polite. *Onna*, " woman," becomes *onnadomo* or *onnashu*, while *fujin*, " lady," becomes *fujindachi* or *fujin gata*. An official (*yakunin*) being a highly respected and much feared person the plural is naturally *yakuningata*. With nouns these suffixes are but rarely used but pronouns employ them more frequently, *e.g.*, *bokura* or *watakushidomo* for " we," *anatagata* or *anatatachi* for " you " (plural).

(*b.*)—Plural Prefixes. There are a few Chinese words which employ certain arbitrary plural prefixes, such as *ban*, " 10,000," *sho*, " all," and *sū*, " number." Thus *bankoku* (literally, " 10,000 country ") means " international "; *shokoku* (" all country ") " universal "; *shokun* (" all prince ") " ladies and gentlemen "; *sūnen* (" number year ") " a long time." Such words are for the most part purely arbitrary and had best be learned separately.

(*c.*)—Duplication of Words. There are a very few words which form a plural by complete reduplication. Thus *shima*, " island," becomes *shimajima*, " islands "; *kuni*, " country," becomes *kuniguni*, " countries "; *tokoro*, " place," *tokorodokoro*, " many places " or " here and there "; *toki*, " time," *tokidoki*, " sometimes." The initial letter of the duplicated word is usually softened. All such words, like those of the preceding form cannot be constructed at will, and should be individually committed to memory. In any case this method comes nearer to expressing the English " every " than the ordinary plural. Thus *kuniguni* is " every country " or " all countries," etc.

Numerical Expressions

Where a definite number is mentioned, numerals with or without numeral classifiers are employed. The latter are somewhat peculiar and must be considered more fully hereafter. Just as in English we say not " two teas," but " two cupfuls of tea," nor " two inks " but " two bottles of ink," so in Japanese we say not " two books " but " two volume of book " (*ni satsu no hon* or *hon ni satsu*) ; not " four pencils " but " four cylinder of pencil " (*shi hon no empitsu* or *empitsu shi hon*) ; not " five papers " but " five sheet of paper " (*go mai no kami* or *kami go mai*). Each sort of object has its own numeral classifier with which, generally, only the Chinese numerals are employed. Occasionally the numeral classifiers are dispensed with and the numeral (generally the Japanese numeral) used alone. Thus for " two boxes," *futatsu no hako* or *hako futatsu* ; " three oranges," *mitsu no mikan* or *mikan mitsu.*

Gender

As with number, no account is usually taken of gender either natural or artificial. At rare intervals where the sex of an object is to be emphasized, the following expressions are used :—

(*a.*)—*O* AND *Me* PREFIXED TO NOUNS.—*O* indicates a male and *me* a female. *Oushi*, " bull," *meushi*, " cow " ; *ouma*, " horse," *meuma*, " mare," etc. Before *t* or *d* *n* is added : *ondori*, " cock," *mendori*, " hen."

(*b.*)—*Osu* AND *Mesu*. These are the fuller forms of *o* and *me*, and instead of being prefixed are coordinated with the main word by means of *no*. *Inu no osu* or *osu no inu*, " dog," " *inu no mesu* or *mesu no inu*, " bitch."

(*c.*)—*Otoko* AND *Onna* (literally, " man and woman ") have the same use as *osu* and *mesu*, save that the latter are used only for animals and the former for either animals or human beings, though more especially the latter. *Otoko no ko desu ka onna no ko desu ka?* " Is it a boy or a girl? " *otoko no neko*, " a tom cat."

(*d.*)—Occasionally different words are used to indicate different sexes. For the most part, however, these refer only to relationships, such as *chichi*, " father," *haha*, " mother," *oji*, " uncle," *oba*, " aunt."

Case

In Japanese, nouns themselves have really no case, case relationships being indicated by postpositions. These must be reserved for especial consideration.

Classes of Nouns

Japanese has several classes of nouns and in order to gain a really adequate knowledge of the language it is necessary to be thoroughly acquainted with them. They are usually divided into three catagories—Simple, Derivative, and Compound Nouns.

Simple Nouns

Simple nouns consist chiefly of native words which have not been formed by changing or compounding simpler elements. Although this class is very numerous, it is not so much so as in other languages owing to the great use of Sinico-Japanese words, almost all of which are compound. Thus *kutsu*, " shoe," *hi*, " sun," *tsuki*, " moon." It should be noted that many words seemingly simple, and which are often so-called, are in reality compound.

Derivative Nouns

These also consist very largely of Japanese words though with a much greater proportion of Chinese words than in the preceding category. There are five divisions of derivative nouns, viz. :—

(*a.*)—Abstract Nouns, chiefly formed from the stem of the adjective plus *sa*, or from the full form of the adjective or verb plus *koto*. This corresponds in a general way to the English suffix " ness." *Takai*, " high," *takasa* or *takai koto*, " height " ; *akai*, " red," *akasa* or *akai koto*, " redness " ; *taberu koto*, " eating." There is a slight difference between the *sa* and the *koto* forms. The latter simply express quality, the former also indicate degree. *Takai koto*, " height," *takasa*, " the height of."

(*b.*)—Concrete Nouns, when formed by adding *mi* to the stems of adjectives give the sense of " ishness " or " a tinge of." *Akami*, " a tinge of red," or " something reddish." The full form of the adjective or verb plus *mono* indicates a concrete thing. *Takai mono*, " a high thing," *taberu mono*, " a thing to eat," or " a thing fit to eat." In certain specified instances the *mono* is added to the second base of verbs. *Kaimono*, " a purchase," *kimono*, " clothing," *yakimono*, " pottery," *tabemono*, " food."

(*c.*)—Augmentative Nouns are formed by adding *ō* in front of Japanese nouns. *Arashi*, " a storm," *ō-arashi*, " a tempest " ; *ō-baka*, " a big fool." Many Chinese words have *tai* or *dai* prefixed to them to indicate the same sense.

(*d.*)—Diminutive Nouns are formed by adding *ko* to Japanese nouns (rarely *o*). *Ko-inu*, " a small dog " (compare *inu no ko*, " a puppy ") ; *ko-gatana*, " a knife " (literally, " a small sword ") ; *o-yama*, " a small mountain " (compare *ō-yama*, " a big mountain "). Many Chinese words have *shō* prefixed to them to express the same meaning.

(*e.*)—VERBAL NOUNS. The second base of many verbs used by itself has the sense of a noun, somewhat as the gerund in English. *Warau,* " to laugh," *warai,* " laughter " ; *asobu,* " to play " ; *asobi,* " a game."

Compound Nouns

Under this category are found the greater part of Japanese nouns, for not only are many native words formed by compounding simpler elements, but practically all Chinese words consist of two or more elements. Compound nouns may also be divided into five categories :—

(*a.*)—NOUN PLUS A NOUN, or words formed by placing two nouns together. Most Chinese nouns come under this head, and it may accordingly be said to be the most common of all forms. *Furo,* " bath," *ba,* " place," *furoba,* " bath room " ; *den,* " electricity," *sha,* " carriage," *densha,* " tram " ; *te,* " hand," *fukuro,* " bag," *tebukuro,* " glove."

(*b.*)—ADJECTIVE PLUS A NOUN, or a noun formed by prefixing the stem of the adjective to a noun. This is also a very common form. *Kuromegane,* " black spectacles " ; *tōi,* " far," *tōmegane,* " telescope " ; *aomono,* " vegetables " (literally, " green thing "). In a few instances the adjective follows the noun. *Me,* " eye," *kurai,* " dark," *mekura,* " blind man."

(*c.*)—VERB PLUS A NOUN, or a noun formed by prefixing the second base of the verb to a noun. *Kakeru,* " to hang," *kakemono,* " a Japanese hanging scroll " ; *yakeru,* " burn," *ishi,* " stone," *yakeishi,* " lava."

(*d.*)—NOUN PLUS A VERB, or a noun formed by suffixing the second base of a verb to a noun. This is somewhat more frequent than the preceding. *Ki,* " spirit," *chigau,* " to change," *kichigai,* " lunatic " ; *ma,* " truth," *machigai,* "mistake"; *nuguu*, "to wipe," *tenugui*, "towel"; *hara* "abdomen," *kiru*, "to cut," *harakiri*, "suicide" (à la Japonaise).

(*e.*)—VERB PLUS A VERB, or a noun formed by compounding the second base of two or more verbs. *Hiku*, "to pull," *dasu*, "to take out," *hikidashi*, "a drawer"; *deru*, "to go out," *iru*, "to come in," *deiri*, "expenses," or "the coming in and going out." Occasionally, but not often we find the second base of an adjective plus a verb. *Nagai*, "long," *iku*, "to live," *nagaiki*, "a long life," or "longevity."

Common Compound Nouns

Owing to the number and importance of compound nouns the following notes, rules, and examples of common forms will be found useful.

(*a.*)—NOUNS PLUS NOUNS. The following are words so frequently used in compounds of this class as to merit special attention.

Ya, "shop" or "store"; *honya*, "bookshop." *Furudōgu*, "curio"; *furudōguya*, "curio-shop." In addition (sometimes with the addition of *san*) it has the following idiomatic meaning:—*honya-san*, "book seller"; *furudōguya-san*, "curio dealer."

Yama, "mountain," frequently met with in geographical expressions, as is also its Chinese equivalent *san*. *Fujiyama* or *Fujisan*, "Mount Fuji."

Shima, "island"; *Hiroshima*, literally "broad island," but now the name of an important coastal city. *Chishima*, "the thousand islands," *i.e.*, The Kurile Islands.

Kawa, "river." *Teimusugawa*, "The River Thames."

Hashi, "bridge." *Nihonbashi*, "The Bridge of Japan,' a famous bridge in Tōkyō. *In*, "place" or "institution"; *gaku*, "learning"; *gakuin*, "academy," etc.

"Narumi," Ando Hiroshige

Himeji castle

Wan, "bay." *Tōkyōwan,* "Tōkyō Bay." *Mura,* "village," and *machi,* "town"; *Akanamura,* "Akana village." *Machi* is sometimes called by its Chinese equivalent, *chō,* both may mean "district" or "block of houses," as well as "town." *Shi,* "city"; *Tōkyōshi,* "The City of Tōkyō"; *Rondonshi,* "The City of London."

Tōri, "street." *Nihonbashidōri,* "Bridge of Japan Street." *Ki,* "tree." *Sakura no ki,* or *sakuragi,* "cherry tree."

(*b.*)—VERBS AND ADJECTIVES PLUS *Te,* ETC. *Te* is often added to the second base of a verb to indicate a person, or the performer of an action. *Noru,* "to ride," *norite,* "rider"; *kaku,* "write," *kakite,* "writer"; *uru,* "to sell," *urite,* "a seller." More irregularly *do, to,* or *udo* are added to various forms of the verb or adjective to express the same thing. *Kariudo,* "a huntsman," from *kari,* "hunting"; *akindo,* "merchant," from *akinau,* "to trade"; *shirōto,* "an amateur," from *shiroi,* "white"; *kurōto,* "professional," from *kuroi,* "black"; *nakōdo,* "go-between," from *naka,* "middle." A "go-between" is an important and much employed person. Disputes are settled by means of intermediaries. *Te* is from "hand," and *udo* from *hito,* "man."

(*c.*)—COORDINATION. In certain compounds the nouns are coordinated, and the word *and* must be supplied between them, *e.g., kingin,* "gold and silver"; *kami hotoke ni inoru,* "to pray to the *kami* (Shinto deities) and the Buddhas"; *sōmoku,* "herbs and trees," or "plants"; *shōkō-kashi-sotsu,* "officers, non-commissioned officers, and men"; *ani ototo,* "elder brother and younger brother," *i.e.,* "brothers."

(*d.*)—COORDINATED OPPOSITES. This is a very peculiar idiom and consists of the combination of opposite terms which results in a neutral meaning. *Enkin* (literally,

" far-near ") " distance " ; *kandan* (literally, " cold-heat ") " temperature " ; *shimatsu* (literally, " beginning-end ") " the whole of an affair " ; *danjo* (literally, " man-woman ") " sex " ; *arunashi* (literally, " is-is-not ") " the question of the existence of a thing " ; *yoshi-ashi* (literally, " good-bad ") " quality."

Nouns as Other Parts of Speech

In certain cases nouns may be used as other parts of speech. Without change it can become a pronoun, and a numeral, as the Japanese regard these merely as two different kinds of nouns. A Chinese noun plus *suru*, etc., becomes a verb, and plus *no* or *na* an adjective. This *no* or *na* being changed to *ni*, the noun becomes an adverb. Their use in compound postpositions should also be noted. In such a case we have *no* plus a noun plus *ni*. Thus we have :—

> *No tame ni*, " for the sake of " ; *no ue ni*, " above," " on " (literally, " at top of ") ; *no shita ni*, " under," " below " ; *no kawari ni*, " instead " (literally, " in place of ") ; *no hoka ni*, " except for," " other than."

The postpositional use of *tokoro, toki*, etc., must be considered under the verb.

CHAPTER 10

Analysis: Pronouns

Personal Pronouns

As we have frequently had occasion to observe, personal pronouns are but rarely used in Japan, their meaning being understood from the context. In fact, strictly speaking, they do not exist at all, but in their place we find a number of nouns, etc., which have pronominal meanings. The more important are :—

(*a.*)—First Person (I)

1. *Watakushi*, *watashi*, or *washi* (literally, " selfishness ").
2. *Boku* (literally, " servant ") much used among students.
   These are the most common but there are also—
3. *Onore*, *ore*, or *ora* (literally, " self "), rather vulgar.
4. *Kono hō* (literally, " this side "), towards inferiors.
5. *Kochira* (" hither ") also towards inferiors.
6. *Shōsei* (literally, " junior ").
7. *Sessha* (literally, " awkward person ").
8. *Ware* (literally, " self "). These three are taken from the written language.

(*b.*)—Second Person (You)

1. *Anata* (literally, " that side "), the most common word.
2. *Kimi* (literally, " prince "), the counterpart of *boku*.
3. *O mae* or *o mae san* (literally " hon. front ") towards inferiors, members of the household, etc.
   These are the most usual but there are also—
4. *Sensei* (literally, " elder ") towards teachers, learned

men, physicians, etc.

5. *Danna* or *danna san* (literally " master ") towards employers and persons of superior station.
6. *Sono hō* (literally " that side ") used in law courts.
7. *Sonata* or *sochira* (literally, " thither ") towards inferiors.
8. *Kisama* (literally, " august Mr."). In the written language an honorific term, but now extremely disrespectful. Used jocularly among students and working men.

(*c.*)—Third Person (He, She, It)

1. *Ano hito,* " that person."
2. *Ano o kata,* " that gentleman."
3. *Ano otoko,* " that man."
4. *Ano onna,* " that woman," etc.; in fact, *ano* before any appropriate noun.
5. *Aitsu,* " that fellow." Impolite.
6. *Are* (literally, " that thing ").
7. *Kare,* the written form of *are,* and sometimes heard in the colloquial.
8. *Mukō de* (literally, " over there ").

We have further the following rather peculiar idioms:—

1. *Temae* (literally, " in front of hand ") may mean either " I " (modest, to superiors) or " you " (to inferiors).
2. *Danna san* and *sensei* may be used with reference to the third person as well as the second.
3. *Heika, denka,* and *kakka,* in like manner may mean respectively either " Your," or " His Majesty," " Your," or " His Highness," " Your " or " His Excellency."
4. *Yo* and *chin* are for " I." The latter is used only by the Emperor. *On mi* is occasionally heard for " you."

These pronouns like other nouns may have postpositions attached to them to indicate tense relationships (*watakushi no,* " my " ; *watakushi ni,* " to me," etc.) and furthermore usually employ the plural suffixes to indicate a change of number. *Watakushidomo,* " we," however, does not mean " you and I," but " I and my friend " as opposed to " you."

Various Pronominal Expressions

The genitive plus *no* also indicates the independent possessive pronoun. *Sore wa watakushi no desu,* " That is mine." *Are wa anata no desu,* " That is yours." The word *waga* for " our " in certain connections is fairly common. *Waga kuni,* " our country " ; *wagahai,* " we."

Reflexive pronouns are chiefly formed by the use of *jibun* (more rarely *jishin*) and is commonly followed by *de. Watakushi jibun,* " I myself " ; *anata jibun* or *go jibun* " you yourself." " By one self " is expressed by either *jibun* or *hitori de.* " By itself " or " spontaneously " is *shizen de. Tagai ni* means " each other," or " one another."

There are, it will be remembered, no relative pronouns in Japanese, their place being taken by verbal paraphrases. *Wareta chawan,* " the tea cup which was broken."

Demonstrative Pronouns

The following table of important demonstrative pronouns should be carefully memorized :—

kore	this (noun)	*sore*	that (near), (noun)	*are*	that (far), (noun)	*dore ?*	which ? (noun)
kono	this (adj.)	*sono*	that (near), (adj.)	*ano*	that (far), (adj.)	*dono ?*	which ? (adj.)
konna *kō iu*	this kind of such as this	*sonna* *sō iu*	that kind of, such as that	*anna* *ā iu*	that kind of, such as that	*donna ?* *dō iu ?*	what kind of ? what—like ?
kō	thus, like this	*sō*	like that	*ā*	like that	*dō ?*	how ?
koko *kochi(ra)*	here	*soko* *sochi(ra)*	there (near)	*asoko* *achi(ra)*	there (far)	*doko ?* *dochi(ra) ?*	where ?
koko-ira	hereabouts	*soko-ira*	thereabouts (near)	*asoko-ira*	thereabouts (far)	*doko-ira ?*	whereabouts ?
				anata	you	*donata ?*	who ? (polite)

Thus, *kō suru,* "to do like this," *sō shitara ii deshō,* "if (you) do it like that, it will be all right probably." *Kō iu hon, kōnna hon,* and *kō iu yō na hon* all mean "such a book," or "a book like this." *Dōshite sonna machigai wo nasaimashita ka?* "How did you make such a mistake?" *Baka no hoka ni sō iu koto wo iwanai,* "No body but a fool would say such a thing." *Ko suru, kō iu yō ni suru, konna ni suru, kono yō ni suru* all mean "to do or to act like this." *Sonna ni hayaku ittewa narimasen,* "You must not go as fast as all that."

There are a certain number of adverbs formed from combinations of these adjectives :—

Achikochi, here and there.
Yoshiashi, good and bad.
Kono uchi ni, herein.
sono uchi ni, therein.
Kono aida (or *konaida*) recently.
Sono aida, in the meantime.
Sono toki, at that time.

Kore kara, henceforth, from now.
Sore kara, after this, then.
Kore made, till now, up to here.
sore made, till then, up to there.
Kore de, with this.
Sore de, with that.
Sore nara, if that is so, well then.
Sore de wa, that being so, then.

Interrogative and Indefinite Pronouns

Japanese has a very peculiar system of interrogative pronouns, and a way by means of which interrogative pronouns may be turned into indefinite pronouns :—

dare ?	who ?	*dare ka*	somebody or other	*dare mo*	(with neg.) nobody	*dare de mo*	anybody, everybody
donata ?	who ? (polite)	*donata ka*	somebody or other (polite)	*donata mo*	(with neg.) nobody (polite)	*donata de mo*	anybody, everybody (polite)
dore ?	which ?	*dore ka*	one or other, some one thing	*dore mo*	every one, (with neg.) none	*dore de mo*	either one, any one
dochi(ra) ?	where ? which ?	*dochi ka*	one or the other	*dochi mo*	both, (with neg.) neither	*dochi de mo*	anywhere, any one
do ?	how ?	*do ka*	somehow or other	*do mo*	somehow	*do de mo*	anyhow
doko ?	where ?	*doko ka*	somewhere or other	*doko mo*	(with neg.) nowhere	*doko de mo*	anywhere, everywhere
doko ni ?	where ?	*doko ni ka*	somewhere or other	*doko ni mo*	(with neg.) nowhere	*doko ni de mo*	anywhere, everywhere
itsu ?	when ?	*itsu ka*	some time or other	*itsu mo*	any time, always	*itsu de mo*	any time whatever, always
ikura ?	how much ?	*ikura ka*	a certain amount	*ikura mo*	any amount	*ikura de mo*	any amount whatever
ikutsu ?	how many ?			*ikutsu mo*	any number	*ikutsu de mo*	any number whatever
iku a.n.? / *nan* a.n.?	how many ?			*iku* a.n. *mo* / *nan* a.n.*mo*	any number	*iku* a.n. *de mo* / *nan* a.n.*de mo*	any number whatever
nani ?	what ?	*nani ka*	something or other	*nani mo*	(with neg.) nothing	*nan de mo*	anything, everything

In this connection, one or two points deserve attention. *Mo* is chiefly used in the negative sense, *demo* in the affirmative. Interrogative pronouns may be used as quasi-adjectives by adding *no*. *Are wa doko no hito desu ka?* " Where does that man come from ? " (literally, " that as for of where man is it ? "). *Ano hon wa dare no desu ka?* " Whose book is that ? " Interrogative pronouns take all the postpositions after them except *wa* which is never expressed. The *ka* forms usually drop the nominative and accusative sign in addition. The *mo* and *demo* forms do the same, while the *no, ni,* etc., are placed in between the pronoun and the *mo* or *demo*. *Asuko ni dare ka no bōshi ga arimasu ka?* "Is someone's hat over there ? " *Iiye dare no bōshi mo mimasen,* "No I don't see any one's hat."

It should be remembered that these pronouns are very idiomatic, and that the literal translations used show only very imperfectly how they are used. A careful examination should be made of all examples given, before considering them mastered.

CHAPTER 11

Analysis: Numerals

Japanese Numerals

In Japanese there are two sets of numerals. One is purely indigenous, while the other is derived from China. With certain rare exceptions, the Japanese numerals extend at present only up to ten. Above ten the Chinese numerals must be used, but under that number the Japanese are more common, save when Chinese numeral classifiers are employed. The Japanese numerals have three forms, first, substantive form; second, adjective form, and third, enumerative form, and are as follows :—

	Substantive Form	Adjective Form	Enumerative Form
One -	*hitotsu*	*hito*	*hii*
Two -	*futatsu*	*futa*	*fū*
Three -	*mitsu*	*mi*	*mii*
Four -	*yotsu*	*yo*	*yō*
Five -	*itsutsu*	*itsu*	*itsu*
Six -	*mutsu*	*mu*	*mū*
Seven -	*nanatsu*	*nana*	*nana*
Eight -	*yatsu*	*ya*	*yā*
Nine -	*kokonotsu*	*kokono*	*ko(ko)no*
Ten -	*tō*	*to*	*tō*

The third form is the least used, and is employed only when counting, as for example, when going over the washing list, "one, two, three," etc. The second form is used when the numeral is compounded with some other noun, chiefly Japanese numeral classifiers. The first form is used when the numeral is employed separately.

Thus the first or substantive form is used either without a noun, or when it follows a noun or its postpositions, or when it precedes a noun with *no* between. *Botchan, o toshi wa ikutsu desu,* " I say, youngster, *how old are you ?* " (literally, " hon. years as for how many is it ? ") *Nanatsu desu,* " Seven." *Tamago futatsu,* or *futatsu no tamago,* " two eggs." *Kinō wa tamago wo futatsu tabeta ga kyō wa hitotsu dake tabemashita.* " Yesterday I ate two eggs, but today I ate only one." Note that *wo* comes between the noun and the numeral, but we may also say *futatsu no tamago wo,* etc.

Japanese Numeral Classifiers

The adjective form of the numeral is used when it is compounded with other words. Such words are, for the most part, numeral classifiers of Japanese origin. The most important are as follows :—

(*a.*)—*Kumi* (literally, " a company ") equivalent to the English " set," such as a set of toys, tea sets, pair of gloves, parties of travellers, etc. Thus :—*hito-kumi, futa-kumi, mi-kumi, yo-kumi, itsu-kumi, mu-kumi, nana-kumi, yo-kumi, kokono-kumi, to-kumi. Sakazuki hito-kumi,* " one set of *sake* cups," *tabibito mi-kumi,* " three parties of tourists."

(*b.*)—*Suji* (literally, " a line ") used in enumerating ribbon or rope-like things. *Obi,* " a belt " ; *yo-suji no obi,* " four belts.

(*c.*)—*Hashira* (literally, " post ") used in counting Shinto deities. *kami futa-hashira,* " two Gods."

(*d.*)—*Soroe* (literally, " a match ") used for sets of things of like nature, such as suits of clothes.

(*e.*)—*Hako* (literally, " box ") for " boxful." *Hito-hako,* " one boxful," etc.

(*f.*)—*Ma* (literally, " interval ") for counting rooms. *Zashiki mi-ma,* " Three reception rooms."

(*g.*)—*Tsuki* (literally, " moon ") for counting months. *Futa-tsuki,* " two months," etc.

Other such Japanese numeral classifiers are *ban* " night," *fukuro* " bagful," *kire* " slice," *yama* " heap," *sara* " plateful," *saji* " spoonful," *hari* " stitch," *bin* " bottleful," *tabi* " time," *tokoro* " place," *tsutsumi* " packet," *shina* " article," etc. There are also a few isolated expressions. *Hito-kuchi* " a mouthful," *hito-me ni* " at one glance," *futago* " twins," etc. Note the distinction between *hitotsu no hako* " one box," and *hito-hako* " one boxful " ; *hari futatsu* " two needles," and *futa-hari,* " two stitches " ; *mitsu no sara* " three plates," and *mi-sara* " three platefuls," etc. Since the Japanese numerals only go up to ten, above that number Chinese numerals are employed even when dealing with Japanese numeral classifiers.

Chinese Numerals

Chinese numerals are extremely simple and easy to remember :—

One	*ichi*	Six	*roku*
Two	*ni*	Seven	*shichi*
Three	*san*	Eight	*hachi*
Four	*shi*	Nine	*ku*
Five	*go*	Ten	*jū*

The higher numerals are nothing more than regular combinations of these :—

Eleven	*jū ichi*	Twenty-one	*ni jū ichi*
Twelve	*jū ni*	Twenty-two	*ni jū ni*
Thirteen	*jū san*	Thirty	*san jū*
Fourteen	*jū shi*	Thirty-one	*san jū ichi*
Fifteen	*jū go*	Forty	*shi jū*
Sixteen	*jū roku*	Forty-one	*shi jū ichi*
Seventeen	*jū shichi*	Fifty	*go jū*
Eighteen	*jū hachi*	Sixty	*roku jū*
Nineteen	*jū ku*	Seventy	*shichi jū*
Twenty	*ni jū*	Eighty	*hachi jū*

Ninety	*ku jū*
Ninety-five	*ku jū go*
Hundred	*hyaku*
Hundred and twenty-four	*hyaku ni jū shi*
Two hundred	*ni hyaku*
Five hundred and fifty	*go hyaku go jū*
Thousand	*sen*
Three thousand	*san sen*
Ten thousand	*man*
Twenty thousand	*ni man*
Thirty thousand	*san man*
Hundred thousand	*jū man*
Million	*hyaku man*
Two millions	*ni hyaku man*

In many cases, even with Chinese numerals *yo* or *yon* takes the place of *shi* ("four"), *nana* the place of *shichi* ("seven") (these two from the Japanese numerals), and *kyu* the place of *ku*. Thus *yon jū roku*, "forty-six"; *nana jū go*, "seventy-five"; *kyu jū hachi* "ninety-eight," etc.

Below ten Japanese words take the Japanese numerals, Chinese words the Chinese numerals. Above ten Japanese as well as Chinese words take the Chinese numerals.

Chinese Numeral Classifiers

Up to ten the Chinese numerals are used only with numeral classifiers, or with Chinese words of measure, weight, time, etc. Thus *ni sun,* " two inches " ; *san shaku,* " three feet " ; *go ken,* " five ken " (a *ken* is six feet) ; *ku chō,* " nine chō " (a *chō* is sixty *ken*) ; *ichi ji,* " one hour " ; *ichi nen,* " one year." etc. Above ten, in addition to these Chinese words are used in front of many Japanese nouns.

There are numerous Chinese numeral classifiers, and it is important that their exact use be learned, as a mistake sounds as ridiculous to Japanese ears as a wrong gender to French or German auditors. The following are those which are most commonly employed :—

1.—*Chō* for things with handles, such as utensils, guns, cannons, knives, tools, candles, slabs of ink. *Teppō ni chō,* " two guns " ; *rōsoku san chō,* " three candles."

2.—*Dai* or *Ryō,* used for all kinds of vehicles.

3.—*Fuku,* used for things like " cups " of tea, " smokes " of tobacco, "doses" of medicine. *Kusuri go fuku,* "Five doses of medicine" ; *tabako ni fuku,* " two whiffs of tobacco."

4.—*Hai,* for so many " cups," " glasses," " pails " of things. *Mizu ni hai motte kite kudasai,* " Please bring two cups of water."

5.—*Hiki,* for most living beings, excepting human beings and birds. Also for certain sums of money, and quantities of cloth. *Inu shichi hiki,* " seven dogs."

6.—*Hon* (literally " stem ") used for cylindrical objects, such as masts, trees, ropes, umbrellas, tubes, bottles, pencils, pens, newspapers rolled up to be posted, also for letters. *Empitsu shi hon,* " Four pencils."

7.—*Jō* for mats, or Japanese " tatami." The size of rooms is counted by the number of mats of fixed size which it contains. *Are wa hachi jō no heya desu,* " That is an eight mat room."

8.—*Ka* or *Ko*, used for various things which have no special numeral classifier, and especially for times and places. *Ni ka getsu,* " Two months " ; *san ka nen,* " three years."

9.—*Ken,* for all kinds of buildings and for law cases. *Ie ga ni ken yakemashita,* " Two houses were burnt."

10.—*Kyaku,* for all things with legs, such as chairs, tables, benches, etc. *Isu shi kyaku,* " four chairs."

11.—*Mai,* for all kinds of flat objects, such as sheets of paper, stamps, plates, coats, shirts, rugs, boards, etc. *Yūbin-kitte wo ni mai kudasai,* " Please give me two postage stamps."

12.—*Mei,* used for human beings, slightly more pedantic than *nin*. *Gakusei ga ni jū mei hodo shinda,* " About twenty pupils died."

13.—*Men,* for mirrors, and framed pictures. *Kagami hachi men,* " Eight mirrors."

14.—*Nin,* for human beings. *Onna roku nin,* " six women." In addition to *ichi nin, ni nin,* and *yo nin* (for *shi-nin*) there are respectively *hitori, futari,* and *yottari*. *Futari no Eikokujin ga kimashita,* " Two Englishmen have come."

15.—*Satsu,* for books. *Jibiki go satsu,* " five dictionaries." One literary work, without regard to the number of volumes is called *bu*. *Hyakkwazensho ichi bu,* " One set of an encyclopedia."

16.—*Shu,* for poems. *Hyaku nin Is-shu* (*ichi shu*) (literally, " one hundred men, one poem ") a famous poetical anthology of a hundred poems, in which each poem is by a separate author.

17.—*Sō* for boats of all kinds. *Jōkisen ni sō,* " Two steamships."

18.—*Soku* used in the sense of pair, for all foot coverings such as shoes, stockings, etc. *Kutsu roku soku,* "six pairs of boots."

19.—*Tō,* for a few kinds of the larger quadrupeds, such as cattle and horses. *Ushi san tō,* "three cows."

20.—*Tsū,* for letters and official documents. *Tegami ni tsū,* "two letters."

21.—*Tsui,* for pairs of all kinds. *Hanaike ni tsui,* "two pairs of vases."

22.—*Wa* for birds and for rabbits, etc. *Suzume shichi wa,* "Seven sparrows."

Phonetic Changes

When nouns are compounded in Japanese it is common for a certain number of phonetic changes to take place. A final *chi, tsu* or *fu,* the first part of a compound, tends to become silent, and to double the succeeding consonant. This is especially true before *ch, k, s, t, sh, f,* and *h.* The last two are changed to *p,* before doubling. Thus *Nippon* comes from *nichi hon; betto,* "jockey" or "groom," from *betsu to; ikko* from *ichi ko.* Double *ch* is usually written *tch,* and double *sh, ssh.* Thus *ketchaku* is from *ketsu chaku; zasshi* from *zatsu shi.*

K has a similar tendency, but only before *k, f,* and *h.* Thus *akkō* is from *aku kō; roppon* from *roku hon; roppun* from *roku fun.* *N* before *h* or *f* almost invariably changes to *m,* while *h* changes to *b,* and *f* to *b* or *p.* *Nm* becomes *mm.* *K* after *n* usually changes to *g.* Thus *sampo* comes from *san ho; samben* from *san hen; amma* from *an ma; sampun* from *san fun; sangen* from *san ken.* *S* after *n* is *z.* *San zen = sansen.*

All these rules have especial though somewhat irregular reference to assimilation between the Chinese numerals and the Chinese numeral classifiers. In combination *jū* is really *jifu,* so that the numbers affected are *ichi, san, roku, hachi, jū* (*jifu*), *hyaku, sen,* and *man.*

Ichi (one) has therefore the following combinations :—*itchō* from *ichi chō ; ippun* from *ichi fun ; ippon* from *ichi hon ; ikken* from *ichi ken ; issoku,* from *ichi soku ; isshaku,* from *ichi shaku ; ittō* from *ichi tō.*

San combines in the following way :—*sampun* from *san fun,* but *sambuku* from *san fuku ; sambon* from *san hon ; sangin* from *san kin ; sammai* from *san mai ; sanzo* from *san so.*

Roku (six) combines in the following way :—*roppuku* from *roku fuku ; roppon* from *roku hon ; rokken* from *roku ken.*

Hachi (eight) is slightly irregular since it has only four changes instead of seven. It is unaffected before *h,* and *f,* and usually before *k.* But *hatchō* from *hachi chō ; hassoku* from *hachi soku ; hasshaku* from *hachi shaku ; hatteki* from *hachi teki.*

Jū (ten) is *jifu.* Thus *jitcho* from *jifu cho ; jippuku* from *jifu fuku ; jippen* from *jifu hen ; jippa* from *jifu wa ; jikken* from *jifu ken ; jissoku* from *jifu soku ; jisshaku* from *jifu shaku ; jitteki* from *jifu teki.*

Hyaku (hundred) resembles *roku,* and *sen* (thousand) *san. Shichi* is entirely irregular since after it no phonetic change takes place.

Questions of Number and Quantity

When questions are asked as to the number of things, we have various modes of expression in Japanese. One is by asking *ikutsu* for any kind of object. *Tamago ga aru ka ?* " Are there any eggs ? " *Hai gozaimasu,* " Yes, there are." *Ikutsu aru ka ?* " How many are there ? " *Sō desu ne kokonotsu bakari desu,* " Let me see. There are about nine." *O toshi wa ikutsu de gozaimasu ka ?* " How old are you ? " Where numeral classifiers may be employed, however, or with words relating to measure, weight, or time, it is more usual to use simply *iku* or *nan* plus the numeral classifier, or the quantative nouns. Thus, *iku-nin,* or *nan-nin ; iku-satsu* or *nan-satsu ; iku-mai* or *nan-mai. Ima Tōkyō ni Seiyōjin ga nan-nin orimasu ka ?* " How many Occidentals are there in Tokyo now ? " *Ima wa nan ji desu ka ?* " What time is it now ? "

" How much ? " is usually rendered by *ikura,* but sometimes by *ika hodo, dore hodo,* or *dono gurai,* all meaning literally " about how much ? " Note the peculiar use of *suru* in the sense of " cost," and *kakaru* in the sense of " take." *Kono hon wa ikura shimasu ka ?* " How much does this book cost ? " *Ichi yen go jissen shimasu,* " It costs me one yen and fifty sen." *Kono tamago wa hitotsu ikura ?* " How much is one of these eggs ? " *Go sen desu,* " It (costs) five sen." *Tōkyō ye yuku no wa nan jikan kakarimasu ka ?* " How many hours does it take to go to Tokyo ? " *Nihongo wa dono gurai kenkyū shimashita ka ?* " About how much Japanese have you studied ? " *Mada sukoshi mo naraimasen,* " I have not studied any as yet."

Ordinal Numbers

There are four ways of forming ordinal numbers in Japanese. One is by placing *Dai* in front of the Chinese numerals. The second is by adding *Bamme* or *ban* to them, *e.g., ni ban,* or *ni bamme,* " the second " ; *san ban,* or *san bamme,* " the third." The third is by placing *Dai* in front and *ban* or *bamme* after the Chinese numerals. The fourth is by adding *me* after the Japanese numerals, or after any numeral classifier. *Nido me,* " the second time," etc. *Sanchō me,* " the third ward," etc. It should be remembered that the ordinal numbers are comparatively little used in Japan, the cardinal numbers being frequently used in their place.

Dates and Other Time Expressions

Dates have reference to years, months, weeks, days and hours.

YEARS are expressed by the numerals plus *nen*. Thus 1919 is *sen ku hyaku jū ku nen.*

MONTHS are expressed by the Chinese numerals plus *gwatsu* or *gatsu. Ichi* is generally replaced by *Shō.* Thus :—

January	*Shōgatsu*
February	*Nigatsu*
March	*Sangatsu*
April	*Shigatsu*
May	*Gogatsu*
June	*Rokugatsu*
July	*Shichigatsu*
August	*Hachigatsu*
September	*Kugatsu*
October	*Jūgatsu*
November	*Jūichigatsu*
December	*Jūnigatsu*

DAYS OF THE WEEK are expressed in the following manner :—

Sunday	*Nichiyō(bi)*	(literally, " sun day ")
Monday	*Getsuyō(bi)*	(literally, " moon day ")
Tuesday	*Kwayō(bi)*	(literally, " fire day ")
Wednesday	*Suiyō(bi)*	(literally, " water day ")
Thursday	*Mokuyō(bi)*	(literally, " wood day ")
Friday	*Kinyō(bi)*	(literally, " metal day ")
Saturday	*Doyō(bi)*	(literally, " earth day ")

Days of the Month are expressed as follows :—

The First of the Month		*Tsuitachi* or *ichinichi*	
2nd	*futsuka*	17th	*jū-shichi-nichi*
3rd	*mikka*	18th	*jū-hachi-nichi*
4th	*yokka*	19th	*jū-ku-nichi*
5th	*itsuka*	20th	*hatsuka*
6th	*muika*	21st	*ni-jū-ichi-nichi*
7th	*nanuka*	22nd	*ni-jū-ni-nichi*
8th	*yōka*	23rd	*ni-jū-san-nichi*
9th	*kokonoka*	24th	*ni-jū-yokka*
10th	*tōka*	25th	*ni-jū-go-nichi*
11th	*jūchi-nichi*	26th	*ni-jū-roku-nichi*
12th	*jū-ni-nichi*	27th	*ni-jū-shichi-nichi*
13th	*jū-san-nichi*	28th	*ni-jū-yokka*
14th	*jū-yokka*	29th	*ni-jū-ku-nichi*
15th	*jū-go-nichi*	30th	*san-jū-nichi*
16th	*jū-roku-nichi*	31st	*san-jū-ichi-nichi*

Misoka is " the last day of the month whether the 30th or 31st ; *ō misoka,* the " last day of the year."

In enumerating dates, the year comes first, followed by the month, and the day. " The thirtieth of September," *kugatsu no san-ju-nichi.*

Hours are indicated by the Chinese numerals plus *ji.* " One o'clock," *ichi-ji ;* " two o'clock," *ni-ji,* etc. *Gozen* is " A.M." and *Gogo* " P.M." Minute is *fun ; ippun, ni-fun, sampun, shi-fun, go-fun, roppun, shichi-fun, hachi-fun, ku-fun, jippun,* are one to ten minutes. *Sugi* means " after " or " past." *Mae,* " before," " to," *Hachi-ji jū-gofun sugi,* " fifteen minutes past eight," or " 8.15." *Roku-ji go-fun mae,* " five minutes to six," or 5.55."

Shinto temple

Kiyomizu Temple, Kyoto

TIME is indicated by the use of the numeral classifier *ka,* or a temporal number plus *kan.* Thus *ikka nen* or *ichi-nen kan,* " one year " ; *ni ka nen* or *ni-nen kan,* " two years," etc. *Ikka getsu* or *ichi getsu kan,* " one month " ; *ni ka getsu* or *ni getsu kan,* " two months," etc. *Shū,* week," *nichi,* " day," *ji,* " hour," take only the *kan* form. *Nichi* may be used alone with *kan.* Thus *jū-go-nichi,* " fifteen days," so with the irregular " day " forms except *tsuitachi, misoka, ō misoka.* *Yokka,* " four days " ; *nanuka,* " seven days " ; *isshūkan,* " one week " ; *ni shukan,* " two weeks " ; *ichi-ji-kan,* " one hour " ; *ni-ji-kan,* " two hours." *Han* means " a half," and is used as follows :—*ichi-ji-kan han,* " an hour and a half " ; or *ichi nen han,* " a year and a half " ; *rokuji han,* "half past six."

Arithmetical Expressions

The following methods are employed in arithmetical calculation, in the first four mathematical processes (*ka-gen-jo-jo.* *Ka* =*kuwaeru* or *yoseru,* " to add " ; *gen* = *hiku,* " to substract " ; *jo* =*kakeru,* " to multiply " ; *jo* = *waru,* " to divide."

2+3=5. *Ni to san to kuwaereba* (or *yosereba*) *go* (*ni naru*), or *ni to san to de go ni naru,* or *ni ni san wo tasu* (or *atsumeru*) *to go ni naru.*

9 - 6=3. *Ku kara roku wo hikeba san ni naru.*

5×4=20. *Go ni shi wo kakereba ni-jū ni naru.*

40÷5=8. *Shi-jū wo go de wareba hachi ni naru,* or *go de shi jū wo wareba hachi ni naru.*

Idiomatic numeral expressions are very common, so that it is impossible to present a complete list. The following points, however, deserve especial consideration :—

(*a.*) Fractions are expressed thus :—Two-thirds, *sam bun no ni ;* one-third, *sam bun no ichi ;* three-quarters, *shi bun no san ;* one-quarter, *shi bun no ichi ;* a/b equals *bii bun no ei.*

(*b.*) Percentage is slightly complicated. "Tenths" are indicated by *wari.* "Ten per cent.," *ichi wari ;* "twenty per cent.," *ni wari ;* "fifty per cent.," *go wari.*" "Hundredths" by *bu.* "One per cent.," *ichi bu ;* "two per cent.," *ni bu ;* "five per cent.," *go bu.* Compounded they are—"fifteen per cent.," *ichi wari go bu ;* "Twenty-three per cent.," *ni wari sam bu ;* "ninety-nine per cent.," *ku wari ku bu,* etc.

(*c.*) "Fold," or "times as much," is *bai* or *sōbai.* "Double," or "twice as much," or "two-fold" is *bai* or *sōbai ;* "treble," or "three-fold," etc., *sambai, san-sōbai,* etc.

(*d.*) "Time" (once, twice, etc.) is expressed by the Chinese numerals plus *do, hen,* or *kwai. Ichi-do, ni-do, san-do,* etc. ; or *ippen, ni hen, samben,* etc. ; or *ikkwai, ni kwai, san kwai.*

(*e.*) "Each," or "at a time" is expressed by *zutsu,* generally with the Japanese numeral or with the Chinese numeral, numeral classifier, etc. *Hitotsu zutsu,* "one each," or "one at a time" ; *sammai zutsu,* "three (plates) each," or "at a time."

(*f.*) "About" before a numeral is usually translated *kurai, hodo,* or *bakari* when it means approximate quantity ; by *goro,* when it means approximate moment or date. *Ni-jū yen gurai,* "About twenty yen," but *san-ji goro,* "about three o'clock."

(*g.*) "House floors." The Japanese count their stories or floors in the American, not in the English way. *Ikkai,* "first floor" = "ground floor" ; *ni-kai,* "second floor," *i.e.*, " the first floor (English) " ; *san-gai* (for *kai*), " third floor," *i.e.*, the English " second floor," etc.

(*h*.) " Portion " is expressed by *mae*, *e.g.*, *hitori mae* or *ichi nin mae*, " a portion for one," etc.

(*i*.) " Every other " is expressed by *oki*. *Hitotsu oki*, " every other one " ; *futatsu oki*, " every third " ; *ichi nichi oki*, " every other day " ; *futsuka oki*, " every third day " ; *ikken oki*, " every other house " ; *ni-ken oki*, " every third house," etc. " Every other day " may also be expressed *kaku jitsu*. " One of two " is *kata* or *katappo*. *Kata-te* " one hand " ; *kata-me*, " one eye," etc.

(*j*.) Vagueness is indicated by coordinating two numerals. *Shi go nichi mae*, " four or five days ago," or " a few days ago " ; *hon go roku satsu*, " five or six books."

(*k*.) Ages, and other dates are counted in rather a peculiar way. On January 1st everyone, irrespective of birthday adds one year to his age, and the day he is born he is considered one year old. Thus a child born on December 31st is one year old that day, and two years old the next. Most dates are inclusive.

CHAPTER 12

Analysis: Postpositions

Case Particles

The Japanese postpositions correspond to the English prepositions, conjunctions, and interjections. The most important are *wa, ga, no, ni, ye, wo, de, to,* and *kara.*

1.—*Wa* is the absolute particle and is used to disjoint a word or phrase from the remainder of the sentence. It has usually the significance of " as for," or " with regard to." The words which precede it are considered slightly parenthetical, so that a slight pause is generally made after *wa.* In most cases it is used as a sort of weak nominative, emphasizing the predicate rather than the subject. This should not lead the student astray for often its real meaning comes to the surface. Consider the example that follows : —*Anata wa keiba desu ka?* Literally, " You as for horse race is it ? " If *wa* were a real nominative the sentence would mean " Are you a horse race ? " but instead it implies " As for you, is it the races (to which you are going) ? " or more freely, " So you are off to the races, eh ? " Sometimes it takes the place of an accusative, especially in comparing one thing with another. *Nihon no satsu wo motte imasu ga Igirisu no satsu wa motte imasen,* " I have some Japanese paper money but as regards English paper money, I haven't paper money but as regards English paper money, I haven't any." *Wa* has also often an elliptical sense of "how about . . ." if used alone. Thus in answer to *Rainen watakushi ga Yōroppa ye yukimasu,* "Next year I am going to Europe," *Okusan wa* means "What about your wife (is she going too)?"

Except when it is used more or less as a nominative *wa* serves to emphasize the words which it qualifies, comparing it with others. *Kore wa furui, are wa atarashii* "This is old (but) that is new." *Kyō wa ii tenki desu,* "(The other day was unpleasant but) today the weather is fine." Even so, however, if the two subjects are to be emphasized at the expense of the predicates, *ga* may be substituted. Thus, *kore wa furui are wa atarashii* means more strictly, "this is *old;* that is *new.*" *Kore ga furui are ga atarashii,* "*This* is old; *this* is new." *Pari to Rondon to wa dochira ga ōkii,* "Which is the bigger, Paris or London?" *Rondon ga ōkii,* "*London* is bigger," but *Rondon wa ōkii ga Pari wa nigiyaka,* "London is *bigger,* but Paris is *more bustling.*" Note how the emphasis on the absolute word sometimes changes the whole meaning of the sentence. *Wakarimasu ka?* "Do you understand?" *Mina wakarimsen,* "I don't understand at all," but *Mina wa wakarimasen,* "I don't understand *all* (but most of it I understand)."

Sometimes *wa* has a peculiarly emphatic significance. If one should be shewn a rare curio, one should say, "*A kore ga ii wa,* "O, I say, this *is* good." Accordingly in some instances it indicates something like the *nai koto wa nai* form which we have already considered. *O kwashi ga aru ka?* "Are there some cakes?" *Aru ni wa arimasu ga amari arimasen,* "There *are* some, but not very many."

In most cases, however, the student may content himself with learning that the absolute particle may be used as a sort of weak nominative, to be employed when the predicate and not the subject needs emphasis. Thus, if you are expecting your Japanese teacher, you might be informed of his arrival by the following saying: *Sensei wa miemashita,* "The teacher has *come*" (literally "appeared"). But should the same person arrive in the middle of the night or at some other unusual hour, he would be announced by the saying, *Sensei ga miemashita,* "the *teacher* has come." So too of an unexpected death one would say, *Hayashi san ga shinimashita,* "Mr. *Hayashi* is dead," but if he had long been known to be past recovery the phrase would be *Hayashisan wa shinimaita,* "Mr. Hayashi is *dead.*"

Wa may be attached to a number of other postpositions especially *ni* and *de* to indicate indirect absolute forms, more or less corresponding to the above. *No wa* added to a verb often makes it into a noun, or an English (as opposed to Japanese) gerund. *Tōkyō ye yuku no wa nanjikan kakarimasu ka?* literally, "The affair of going to Tōkyō as for, how many hours, does it take ? " or " How long does it take to go to Tōkyō ? "

2.—*Ga* has three different meanings. Originally, and in the present written language it is the sign of the genitive, corresponding to *no*. For the most part this meaning has died out of the colloquial, but it is still retained in certain place names, and in certain idioms. Thus *onigashima,* " the island (*shima*) of (*ga*) devils (*oni*)," or " Devil's Island," the bogey land of fairy tales. *Takama-ga-hara,* " The high plain of heaven," the primæval abode of the gods ; *pan ga suki,* " to like bread," more literally " to be fond of bread," *pan ga kirai,* " to dislike bread," literally, " not-fond of bread " ; *pan ga hoshii,* " to want bread," literally, " desirous of bread." There are several other verbs which take *ga* in place of *wo*. These should be carefully remembered.

The second and more usual use of *ga* in the modern colloquial is to indicate the nominative, or rather the nominative in which the subject as opposed to the predicate is emphasized. *Otō san ga yonde orimasu,* " Father is calling." Nouns are not the only possible subjects. *Ga* may be added to verbs as well as to substantives, and in fact whole phrases may serve either as subjects or objects of sentences. . . . . *ga aru* often means " there is." *Nihon ni wa hebi to iu mono ga arimasu ka?* " In Japan are there any snakes ? " literally, " Are there things called snakes ? " Sometimes the clause corresponds to the English word " have." *Watakushi wa tokei ga arimasu,* " I have a watch," or more literally, " As for me, there is a watch."

The third use of *ga* is as a conjunctive, when it has the meaning of " but " or " whereas," occasionally " so " or " and." *Ikitaku arimasen ga ikanakereba narimasen,* " I don't want to go, but I must go."

3.—*No* has also a number of different meanings, the most important being to denote the possessive, subjective, objective, attributive, and explicative genitive. *Watakushi no hon* (possessive) " my book " ; *watakushi no kaita tegami* (subjective) " The letter which I wrote " (note this peculiar construction) ; *oya no mo* (objective), " Mourning for parents " ; *kinu no kimono* (attributive), " Silk clothes "; *kamakura no machi* (expressive), " The town of Kamakura."

The use of *no* to indicate the subject of a relative sentence is peculiar, and requires special attention. It owes its existence to the fact that in relative clauses the relationship between two nouns can only be expressed by *no* with or without other postpositions. *Watakushi ga tegami wo kaku* but *watakushi no kaita tegami wa dō narimashi ta ?* " What has become of the letter which I wrote ? " *Gakkō ni omoshiroi hon ga arimasu,* " There is an interesting book at school," but *gakko no omoshiroi hon wa nan to iu hon desu ka?* "What is the name of the interesting book at school?" *Tōkyō kara Yokohama made no tetsudō,* "the rail road from Yokohama to Tōkyō"; *gakkō no michi,* "the road to (or from) school"; *Beikoku kara dempō ga kita,* "A telegram has come from America," but *Amerika kara no dempō,* "The telegram from America." This of course means that in translating from Japanese *no* has a wide variety of renderings. *Atami no onsen,* "The hot-springs *at* Atami"; *Fuji no yuki,* "the snow *on* Mount Fuji"; *Chibus no yobō,* "precautions *against* typhus," etc.

No is often used as a contraction of *mono,* "thing," or "one." *Akai no wa doko desu ka?* "Where is the red one?" *Are wa akai no deshō,* "That is the red one is it not?" *Kore wa ii no desu,* "This is a good one." *Namben mo mita no desu,* "It is a thing which I have seen several times." This *no* is often contracted in conversation to *n'*. It is this form with which we are familiar in connection with adjectives and verbs. *Kyō wa samui n' desu,* etc. *Kyō wa konai n' deshō,* "It probably is that he is not coming," or more freely, "I suppose that he is not coming." Compare *Nani wo shimasu ka?* "What are you doing?" with *Nani wo suru n' desu ka?* "What is it that you are doing?" *Massugu ni ikimasu ka?* "Am (I) going straight on?" with *Massugu ni yuku n' desu ka?* "Is it that I am to go straight on?" or "Am I to go straight on?" The use of *no* or *no wa* to make a noun of a verb has already been mentioned. In this as in many other cases, *no* is equivalent to *koto.*

Dano is like the English *etc.* *Tabako dano, sake dano,* "tobacco, etc., wine, etc." *No* is also used with the numeral.

4.—*Ni* is one of the most common postpositions, and its uses are legion. It is used for the indirect object, *kodomo ni yaru,* "to give *to* the boy," for the locative with verbs of existence (as opposed to verbs of action), *tsukue no ue ni pen ga aru,* "There is a pen *on* the top of the table," or *Kikuchi san wa Rondon ni sunde orimasu,* "Mr. Kikuchi lives *in* London,"; for time relationship, *jū-ichi-ji-ni kimasu* "(He) will come *at* eleven." *Nichi-yōbi ni ikō,* "Let us go *on* Sunday." Occasionally to express direction. *Tōkyō ni kita,* "Came *to* Tōkyō"; *ano hito wa gakkō ni haitta,* "That man has gone into the school." Like Latin Japanese has also a Possessive Dative. "To me there is a cow." = "I have a cow." This *to* may be expressed by *ni* or *ni wa* (in addition to the simple *wa* form mentioned previously). *Watakushi ni tsuno ga nai,* "I have no horns," etc. *Dōbutsu ni wa ashi ga aru,* "Animals have feet," etc.

In addition a number of verbs govern the dative in place of, or together with the accusative. The most important of such verbs are:—

(*a.*)—*Naru,* "to become." *Baka ni naru,* "To become a fool"; *byōki ni naru,* "to become ill."

(*b.*)—*Au,* "to meet." *Kinoshita san ni aimashita,* "(I) met Mr. Kinoshita."

(*c.*)—*Someru* and *somaru* "to dye," the first transitive and the second intransitive. *Murasaki iro ni someru,* "to dye purple."

(*d.*)—*Ataru,* "to hit against." *Mato ni atarimashita,* "(It) hit the target." *Ataru* sometimes means "to be equal to." *Ni mairu han wa ichi ri ni ataru,* "Two miles and a half equal one *ri.*"

(*e.*)—Shitagau, "to follow," "to obey." *Fujita san no chūkoku ni shitagaimashita,* "I followed Mr. Fujita's advice."

(*f*.)—*Tsuku,* " to adhere," " to arrive." *Kino otōto ga Kobe ni tsuita,* " My younger brother arrived at Kobe yesterday." *Kutsu ni doro ga tsuku,* " Mud is sticking to the shoes." *Ki ni tsuku* (literally, " to arrive at the spirit "), *i.e.,* " to perceive," " to be aware of."

(*g*.)—*Tou,* " to ask," and other verbs relating to asking, requesting, imploring, etc., such as *kiku, tazuneru, ukagau, inoru, negau, tanomu. Ano hito ni kiite kudasai,* " Please ask that man."

There are numerous other examples. Some such verbs imply the sense of " on." *Uma ni noru,* " To ride on a horse " ; *tatami ni suwaru,* " to sit on the *tatami,*" etc. Some imply " as." *Yome ni iku,* " To go as a bride," *i.e.,* " to marry " (for a woman). Where English would have a double accusative Japanese puts the second object in the dative. " The German soldiers made the English officer a prisoner." *Doitsu no heitai ga Eikoku no shikwan wo toriko ni shimashita.*

When used after the second base of a verb, and preceding a verb indicating motion, *ni* expresses purpose. *Kaki ni yuku,* " Go in order to write."

When used with a passive or potential verb *ni* means " by." *Tarō wa Jirō ni makemashita,* " Taro was defeated by Jiro." *Ka ni sasaremashita,* " (I) was bitten by mosquitoes " (from *sasu,* " to sting "). *Segare wa anata no inu ni kamaremashita,* " My son was bitten by your dog."

When used with a causative verb *ni* denotes the person who is caused to perform the action. *Tarō ni tegami wo kakasete kudasai,* " Please make Taro write the letter."

The adverbial form of quasi-adjectives is formed by adding *ni* to the noun. In fact *ni* may be called an adverbial ending. *Jōzu na,* " Skillful " ; *jōzu ni,* " skillfully."

Finally, when several things are to be enumerated *ni* is employed to express " and " or " as well as " or "besides the foregoing." *Iroiro na hito ga orimashita. Nihonjin ni, Eikokujin ni, Shinajin ni, Indojin ga orimashita,* "There were all sorts of people. Japanese, Englishmen, Chinese, and Indians were (there)."

5.—*Ye,* the other form of the dative is much more restricted in its use. Its chief use is to indicate direction to or towards. *Tōkyō ye yuku,* "to go to Tōkyō."

6.—*Wo* chiefly serves to denote the direct object. *Yome wo morau,* "to receive a bride," *i.e.,* for a man to marry. Occasionally *wo* is used after verbs where English would have some other particle. Particularly is this so with certain verbs of motion and emotion. In the former case *wo* indicates the place from which the motion starts, or where it takes place, and never direction (which would be *ye* or *ni*). With verbs of emotion the cause is put into the accusative. Such verbs are numerous, but the most important are (of motion) : —

(*a.*)—*Tatsu,* "to depart." *Rondon wo tatsu,* "to depart from London," or as we should say, "to leave London."

(*b.*)—*Deru,* "to go out." *Ie wo deru,* "to go out of a house." *Dekakeru* has almost the same meaning and is used in the same way.

(*c.*)—*Magaru,* "to turn around." *Kado wo magaru,* "to turn a corner"; *mawaru,* "to go around" or "wander." *Yōroppa wo mawarimashita,* "I wandered all over Europe." *Chikyū ga taiyō wo mawaru,* "The earth turns round the sun."

(*d.*)—*Yuku,* "go." *Hashi no ue wo yuku,* "to go on a bridge." *Aruku* is used in the same way. *Machi wo aruku,* "to walk about a town."

(*e.*)—*Oriru,* "descend." *Yama wo oriru,* "to go down a mountain."

The most important of the second class or emotional

verbs, are as follows :—

(*a.*)—*Tanoshimu,* "to take pleasure in." *Hana wo tanoshimu,* "to take pleasure in flowers" or "to like flowers."

(*b.*)—*Shimpai suru,* "to be anxious." *Wazawai wo shimpai suru,* "to be anxious about disaster."

(*c.*)—*Hajiru,* "to be ashamed." *Mugaku wo hajiru,* "to be ashamed of one's ignorance."

Originally *wo* was nothing more than an interjection emphasizing or calling attention to some particular word, and occasionally we find traces of its origin. As a result the accusative sign is not infrequently omitted. This is especially so before *suru,* and in fact *suru* is now considered to be more an auxiliary making the noun into a verb than a verb governing an object.

7.—*De* is like *ni* in that it has a wide variety of meanings. Most commonly it denotes means or instrument. Connected with this is the conception of material and of price. *Kisha de yuku,* "to go by train"; *kinu de dekite arimasu,* "it is made of silk"; *ichi yen de kaimashita,* "I bought it for one yen"; *chizu de miru,* "to see from (-by) a map." *Nihongo de iu,* "to say in Japanese." Note also the numeral expression, *futatsu de ii,* "two will be enough," or more literally, "with two (it) is-good." *Kore de takusan,* "This is enough" (literally, "With this it is many"). *Mina de ikura,* "How much is it altogether?" or "With all, how much?"

The other most common use of *de* is to denote the predicate. *Kore wa pen de arimasu,* "This is a pen." This special particle for the predicate case is peculiar to Japanese and should be carefully memorized.

De has also a locative sense, and means "in" or "at" when most verbs of action are employed. *Koko de go zen wo tabete imasu,* "I am eating my dinner here," compare with *koko ni orimasu,* " I am here." *Pen wa doko de urimasu ka?* " Where do they sell pens?" (where = at what place ?) *Muko no chiisai mise de urimasu,* " They sell them at that small shop."

Finally *de* is used to denote the predicate form of quasi-adjectives, and in this sense often takes the place of a gerund. *Ano hana wa kirei de nioi ga ii,* " That flower is beautiful and it smells nice," literally, " That flower being beautiful smell is good."

8.—*To* now means chiefly " with " (in the sense of accompaniment) or " and." *Watakushi wa Takeuchi kun to keiyaku shimashita,* " I made a contract with Mr. Takeuchi." *Ano hito to ikimashita,* " I went with him." *Tarō to Jirō wa kyō kuru hazu da ga,* " Tarō and Jirō ought to come today but . . ."

With certain verbs *to* is used concurrently with *ni,* but somewhat less in the colloquial than in the written language. Such, for example, are :—*au,* " to meet " ; *chigau,* " to differ from " ; *naru,* " to become," etc.

To added to the indicative tenses of the verb gives a quasi-conditional form, equivalent to " if " or " when."

It is also frequently used to express quotation, where it means " that " or " thus," or better still, is equivalent to quotation marks. In such a connection *to* is almost always found before verbs meaning " to say " or " to think." *Uso da to iimasu,* " He says that it is a lie " literally, " (It) is a lie, thus (he) says "). *Hontō da to omoimasu,* " I think that it is true."

9.—*Kara* usually means " from," " out of," or " since." *Tōkyō kara Kyōto ye itta,* " He went from Tōkyō to Kyōto." *Heian Chū Gakkō wa koko kara toi n' desu ka?* " Is the Heian Middle School far from here ? " *Ima kara,* " from now," " henceforward " ; *sakunen kara,* " since last year " ; *kore kara,* " from this " or " from now onwards," etc.

When after the gerund of verbs *kara* signifies " after " or " since." *Asuko ni itte kara uchi ye kaerimashita,* " After going there I went home," or " After I went there," etc. *Tanaka san to hanashite kara kakimashō,* " After I have talked with Mr. Tanaka I shall write you a letter."

Incidentally the Japanese often use *kara,* " from," where English people would be more apt to say " at " or " by." Thus *Enzetsu wa ni ji kara hajimarimasu,* " The lecture begins *at* (literally, ' from ') two o'clock."

Kara following an indicative verb, whether past or present, has an entirely different meaning, and implies reason, or causality, " therefore," " because," " so," etc. *Kinō wa warukatta kara ikananda,* " Yesterday was bad so I did not go." *Baka da kara ate ni narimasen,* " He is a fool. Therefore he cannot be trusted."

10.—Miscellaneous Postpositions. Among the other postpositions which are frequently met with are *ka, mo, made, shi, ya,* and *yori.*

Ka serves to change a sentence into an interrogative. Note that in a compound interrogative sentence the *ka* is repeated. *Iku ka ikan ka?* " Will you go or not ? " (literally, " Will you go ? Will you not go ? ") *Shiremasen* " (I) cannot know," is often added to this form to express doubt. *Ii ka warui ka shiremasen,* " I don't know whether it is good or bad." *Ka* when added to the interrogative pronouns also serves to change them into indefinite pronouns.

Mo (not to be confounded with the adverb *mō* already) means " also," or " too." *Watakushi mo mairimasu,* " I am coming also." Attached to the gerund it indicates the concessive. *Itte mo,* " even though you go." *Mo* . . . mo, means " both . . . and," with a positive verb, and " neither . . . nor," with a negative verb. *Otōsan mo okkasan mo orimasu,* " Both father and mother are here." *Watakushi ga Furansugo mo Doitsugo mo wakarimasen,* "I understand neither French nor German." Both *mo* and *demo* are used with interrogative pronouns to form indefinite pronouns.

Made means "up to," "until," "as far as," etc., and corresponds in a general way to *ye. Ima made,* "until now"; *rainen made matanakereba narimasen,* "you must wait until next year"; *gakkō made itta ga are kara doko ye itta ka shiranu,* "he went as far as the school, but after that I don't know where he went"; *made ni,* "by"; *ni ji made ni,* "by two o'clock."

Shi cannot be exactly rendered into English, but corresponds in a general way to "and," or the conjunctive use of the Japanese gerund. *Isogashii toki mo aru shi yōji no nai toki mo aru,* "There are both times when I am busy, and times when I have no business."

Ya in the written language is both an interrogative and an exclamatory particle. In the colloquial it seldom has this significance, but is to be rendered by "and," "etc." "Such things as . . . or." *Watakushi wa tabako ya, biiru ya, budōshu wo nomimasen,* "I take (drink) neither tobacco, beer, nor wine."

Yori corresponds to *kara* and means "from" or "since," but cannot be used in the sense of "because." It is also used to compare adjectives, and then means "more than."

II.—Quasi-Postpositions. There are a large number of words which though in reality other parts of speech yet are used as postpositions. Generally speaking they are of two kinds, verbs and nouns.

Verbal postpositions consist of *ni* plus the gerund. Thus *ni tsuite,* "with regard to," or "concerning"; *ni yotte,* "in accordance with"; *ni shitagatte,* "following from," etc. Occasionally we have other forms. *Wo motte* as in *empitsu wo motte kakimasu,* " I write with a pencil " (literally, " having a pencil I write.").

Nominal postpositions consist of *no* plus a noun plus *ni.* The most common are as follows :—

(*a.*)—*No ue ni* (at top of) on, above.
(*b.*)—*No shita na* (at bottom of) under.
(*c.*)—*No naka ni* (at middle of) inside.
(*d.*)—*No soto ni* (at out of) outside.
(*e.*)—*No uchi ni* (at interior of) inside, in.
(*f.*)—*No tame ni* (for sake of) for, in order to.
(*g.*)—*No mae ni* (at front of) before.
(*h.*)—*No ushiro ni* (at back of) behind.
(*i.*)—*No kawari ni* (for change of) instead of.
(*j.*)—*No hoka ni* (at exterior of) besides, etc.

For example :—*Biiru no hoka ni nani ka nomu mono ga aru ka?* " Is there anything to drink except beer ? " *Suzuki san ga byōki da kara Sasaki san ga kawari ni yatte imasu,* " As Mr. Suzuki is ill Mr. Sasaki is doing it instead." *Teiburu no shita ni kami ga arimasu,* "There is some paper under the table."

In relative sentences the *ni* must of course change to *no.* *Teiburu no shita no kami,* " The paper which is under the table," etc.

CHAPTER 13

Analysis: Verbs

The Structure of the Verb

In Japanese the verb is a part of the *Hataraki-Kotoba* which also include the English adjective and adverb. In this connection one important point deserves attention. In the treatment of the *Na*, or uninflected words (including therein the Noun, Pronoun, and Numeral) as well as the *Teniwoha*, the spoken language does not materially differ from the written language. The verb and adjective, however, undergo a widely different inflection in the two styles.

Apart from the Chinese verbs formed by adding *suru* to the uninflected form the Colloquial has but two conjugations, a vowel and a consonant. The literary language has four, a consonant conjugation, two *uru* conjugations (corresponding to the *eru* and *iru* forms of the Colloquial), and an *iru* conjugation. The Colloquial has but one past tense, the written has five, as well as a perfect tense. The oblique forms are also much more numerous in the latter than in the former. Finally, while there is only one form for each tense in the spoken language, in the written style there is an attributive, and a conclusive form for each indicative tense, corresponding to the Attributive, and Predicate forms of the Adjective.

In spite of these differences, however, the essential structure of the verb is the same in both styles. In both the verb is unaffected by the number and gender of the subject. In both, conjugation is effected by means of suffixes, bases, stems, and roots. Suffixes, such as *nai*, *masu*, *ta*, *ba*, etc., are added to the five bases to indicate some particular tense or mood. The bases consist of certain fixed verbal forms which serve as the starting point of conjugation. In the consonant conjugation they are formed by adding the five vowels to the stem. Thus the five bases of " write " are, *kaka*, *kaki*, *kaku*, *kake*, *kakō*. With vowel verbs the first, second, and fifth bases are formed by dropping the *ru* of the third base (which is the familiar present), while the fourth base is formed by changing the *ru* to *re*.

The stem of a consonant verb is found by dropping the last vowel of the base. Thus the stem of " write " is *kak*. With vowel verbs the stem and the second base is the same. The stem is never used alone. For practical purposes the stem is all that a student need know, but philologists have discovered that several different verbs have, in many cases, a common origin. Thus *sameru* (" to cool "—intransitive, stem *same*) *samasu* (" to cool "—transitive, stem, *samas*) as well as the adjectives *samui*, "cold," and *sabishii*, "lonesome," are all derived from a common root *sab* or *sam*.

For the most part, however, all such etymological questions may be neglected, and the complete conjugation of any verb may be found by learning first its five bases, and second a complete list of the suffixes which are most frequently attached to them.

The five bases (as well as the assimilated second base) of the two classes of vowel verbs, and the six classes of consonant verbs have already been explained (pages 29 and 31), so that we may now concern ourselves immediately with the important suffixes, and their general meanings and use.

VERBAL CHART OF BASES AND SUFFIXES

1ST BASE	2ND BASE	3RD BASE	4TH BASE	5TH BASE
Tabe, etc. *Kaka*, etc.	*Tabe*, etc. *Kaki*, etc.	*Taberu*, etc. *Kaku*, etc.	*Tabere*, etc. *Kake*, etc.	*Tabe*, etc. *Kakō*, etc.
1. *nai** 2. *n[u]** (*mai*) *zu* 3. *(*ra*) *reru* 4. *(*sa*) *seru*	1. *masu** 2. *tai** 3. *sō na** 4. *ni* 5. *na* 6. (*ro*) ASSIMILATED 2ND BASE 1. *te* 2. *ta* 3. *tarō* 4. *tara* 5. *taredo* 6. *tari*	1. *deshō* 2. *mai* 3. *to* 4. *na* 5. *koto* 6. *mono* 7. *toki* 8. *aida* 9. *hazu* 10. *tsumori* 11. *tokoro*	1. *ba* 2. *do* 3. [*ru*]	1. (*yō*)

Those forms marked with an * may themselves be conjugated through all the tenses. Those in () marks refer only to vowel verbs. The second and third bases of vowel verbs, and the second, third, fourth and fifth bases of consonant verbs may be used alone. [] indicate optional forms.

Analysis of Suffixes

Suffixes Added to the First Base

(*a.*)—*Nai* (the negative form of *aru*) denotes the familiar negative, and has itself the following full conjugation :—

Present -	- *nai*
Past - -	- *nakatta*
First Future -	- *nakarō* or *nai deshō*
Second Future -	- *nakattarō* or *nakatta deshō*
First Conditional	- *nakereba*
Second Conditional	- *nakattara*
Gerund -	- *nakute*, or *nai de*
First Concessive	- *nakeredo*
(Second Concessive	- *nakattaredo*)
Frequentative -	- *nakattari*

The meaning of the first seven tenses has already been explained (page 23); the two concessive forms as well as the frequentative will be considered hereafter. The second concessive of the negative is very seldom used. Examples :—*kakanakatta*, " did not write " ; *butanakeredo*, " if (one) does not beat " ; *tabenai deshō*, " probably does not eat," etc.

(*b*.)—*N*(*u*) is an alternative form of *nai*. There is no difference in meaning between the two forms, and *n* (*u*) like *nai* may be conjugated through all the tenses as follows :—

Present -	- *n*(*u*)
Past - -	- *nanda*
First Future -	- (*mai*) *n*(*u*) *deshō*
Second Future -	- *nandarō*
First Conditional	- *neba*
Second Conditional	- *nandara*
Gerund -	- *n*(*u*) *de* or *zu* (*ni*)
First Concessive	- *nedo*
(Second Concessive	- *nandaredo*)
Frequentative -	- *nandari*

These forms are for the most part somewhat less used than the *nai* form, except for the irregular future and

Statue of Buddha

Rock garden

gerund. *Mai* is added to the first base of vowel verbs, and to the third base of consonant verbs. The *u* in *nu* is generally omitted.

(*c.*)—(*Ra*)*reru* stands for the passive, a voice which is comparatively little used in Japanese. *Rareru* is added to the first base of vowel verbs, and *reru* to that of consonant verbs. In reality such words are transformed into independent vowel verbs, and are conjugated accordingly. Examples :—*mirareru,* "to be seen"; *butareru,* "to be beaten"; *mirareta* or *miraremashita; butareta* or *butaremashita,* etc.

(*d.*)—(*Sa*)*seru* stands for the causative, a voice which is peculiar to Japanese, Hindi, and a few other languages. As with the passive, *saseru* is added to vowel, and *seru* to consonant verbs. In this manner both become independent vowel verbs and are conjugated accordingly. Examples :—*kakaseru,* "to cause to write," as in "I made him write a letter," or "I had him write a letter"; *tabesaseru,* "to cause to eat"; *kakaseta,* or *kakasemashita; tabesaseta,* or *tabesasemashita,* etc.

Both passives and causative present several difficulties, and will be considered more fully hereafter.

Suffixes Added to the Second Base

(*a.*)—The Second Base Alone. In the written language the second base is frequently employed by itself, as an indefinite tense corresponding very closely to the colloquial use of the gerund. Although in conversation it is very seldom heard, one constantly comes across it in lectures, and stories, so that the student should be able to recognize it. *Sekai ni baka mo ari, rikō mo ari, bimbō mo ari, kanemochi mo arimasu,* "In the world there are fools, there are wise men, there are paupers, and there are rich men."

(*b.*)—*Masu* when added to the second base gives the polite conjugation, and has itself different forms for each tense. These are, it will be remembered :—

Present -	- *masu*
Past - -	- *mashita*
First Future -	- *mashō* or *masu deshō*
Second Future -	- *mashitarō* or *mashita deshō*
First Conditional	- *masureba*
Second Conditional	- *mashitara*
Gerund -	- *mashite*

First Concessive	- *masuredo*
(Second Concessive	- *mashitaredo*)
Frequentative -	- *mashitari*

Theoretically *masu* like any other verb may be conjugated in the negative in both forms through all the tenses. Actually, however, they are very seldom used, the periphrastic conjugation by means of *desu*, after *masen* being adopted. Thus *masen deshita*, *masen deshō*, etc. Occasionally the past *masenanda*, and the gerund, *masezu*, may be heard.

(*c.*)—*Tai.* The desiderative adjective *tai* (derived from *itai*, "painful") is added to the second base to denote desire or wish. It may be conjugated like any other adjective either in the polite form (*tō gozaimasu*, etc.) or the impolite form. The latter is as follows :—

Present -	- *tai*
Past - -	- *takatta*
First Future -	- *takarō* or *tai deshō*
Second Future -	- *takattarō* or *takatta deshō*
First Conditional	- *takereba*
Second Conditional	- *takattara*
Gerund -	- *takai de* or *takute*

First Concessive	- *takeredo*
(Second Concessive	- *takattaredo*)
Frequentative -	- *takattari*

The polite negative is formed by conjugation *gozaimasu* in the negative, and the impolite or familiar form, by changing *tai* to *taku nai*, and conjugating the *nai*.

(*d.*)—*Sō na* is a quasi-adjective, and added to the second base of the verb expresses likelihood, or probability with especial reference to the future. *Ame ga furi-sō desu*, " Rain seems likely to fall " (not " Rain is probably falling now "). Like other quasi-adjectives, *na* follows if attributive, *ni* if adverbial, and *de* if predicative. By adding the various forms of " to be " to the last we may conjugate in all tenses. *Ame ga furi-sō deshita*, " It looked as if rain were going to fall."

(*e.*)—*Ni* added to the second base and followed by a verb denoting motion indicates purpose. *Kinō shibai wo mi ni itta*, "Yesterday (I) went (in order) to see (the) theater." In most cases the purpose is so weak that the sentence had best be translated merely by the English infinitive.

(*f.*)—*Na* added to the second base of either vowel or consonant verbs denotes a familiar or impolite imperative. It is not very frequently used. Examples :—*tabe na*, " Eat ! " ; *kase na*, " lend ! " etc.

(*g.*)—(*Ro*) added to the second base is the more usual way of denoting the familiar imperative of vowel verbs. *Miro*, " look " ; *tabero*, " eat."

The Assimilated Second Base and its Suffixes

The gerund and all the tenses derived from the gerund are attached to the contracted or elliptical form of the second base which is usually known as the Assimilated Second Base. In the vowel verbs the assimilated second base and the second base are the same while the rules for forming the assimilated second base for the consonant verbs has already been given (page 31). The usual suffixes are :—

(*a.*)—*Te* for the Gerund. (*b.*)—*Ta* for the Past.
(*c.*)—*Tarō* for the 2nd Future. (*d.*)—*Tara* for the 2nd Cond.
(*e.*)—*Taredo* for the 2nd Concessive.
(*f.*)—*Tari* for the Frequentative.

The absolute gerund (*te wa* or *cha*) is equivalent to the conditional, while *te mo* denotes the concessive. The last two suffixes (concessive and frequentative) though not frequently met with are yet sufficiently important to make memorization necessary. The exact meaning of these and of other tenses will be discussed hereafter.

Suffixes Added to the Third Base

(*a.*)—THE THIRD BASE ALONE indicates the familiar present, which like all other familiar or impolite forms is used when addressing servants, inferiors, intimate friends, members of the family, and so on, as well as in practically all relative and subordinate sentences.

(*b.*)—*Deshō* OR *Darō* added to the present indicates the first future, or the probable present or future.

(*c.*)—*Mai,* as we have seen, when added to the third base of consonant verbs or to the first base of vowel verbs denotes the negative first future.

(*d.*)—*To* added to the third base is equivalent to either the first or the second conditional. *Iku to,* "If I go," "when I go," "if I went," "when I went," etc.

(*e.*)—*Na* attached to either vowel or consonant verbs denotes an impolite negative imperative. *Kaku na,* "don't write."

(*f.*)—*Koto* AND *mono* are often attached to verbs and renders them into sort of nouns, with *koto* abstractness, and with *mono* concreteness. *Koto* means the "act" or "thing"; *iku koto,* "the going" or "the act of going." This form is chiefly used with such idioms as *koto ga dekiru, itta koto ga aru, nai koto ga nai,* etc. (*cf.* page 69). *Mono* is a material "thing." Compare *yomu koto,* "reading," with *yomu mono,* "a thing to read."

(*g.*)—AUXILIARY NOUNS. The following nouns are often added to the third base of verbs to denote some peculiar idiomatic expression. 1.—*Toki* (literally "time") indicates the definite period of an event, and is an emphatic demonstrative or relative "when." *Nihon ni otta toki ni Nihongo wo naraimasen deshita,* "When I was in Japan, I did not study Japanese." 2.—*Aida* (literally, "interval") is equivalent to the English "while," or "during." *Aruku aida ni hon wo yonda,* "While walking I read a book." 3.—*Hazu* (literally, "necessity") corresponds to "ought" or "should." *Iku hazu desu ga ikitaku nai,* "I should go but I don't want to." 4.—*Tsumori* (literally, "intention") is equivalent to "intend to . . ." *Indo ye yuku tsumori desu,* "I intend to go to India."

One of the most common auxiliary nouns is *tokoro,* the meaning of which is often impossible to convey in English. Literally *tokoro* signifies "place," and after either the present or the past tense it may often be rendered in this way. More usually, however, it has a more metaphorical rendering, such as "stage" (of time, or of progress) while in other places it is equivalent to *koto,* or abstraction. Examples :—*Chōdo tsuku tokoro ye Tarō ga mukai ni kita,* "Just as I arrived, Tarō came to meet me" (more literally, "exact arrive stage at," etc. ; *hau tokoro ja nai yoku aruke masu,* "It is not a matter of creeping. (He) can walk well," (more literally, "creeping stage it is not," etc.) ; *tattoi tokoro wo tattonde,* "reverencing all matters reverential."

Suffixes Added to the Fourth Base

(*a*)—THE FOURTH BASE ALONE (for consonant verbs only) denotes the impolite imperative.

(*b.*)—*Ba* denotes the present conditional, as for example, *Are ga sumeba hayaku o ide nasai,* "When that is finished please come quickly."

(*c.*)—*Do* is the sign of the present concessive. More correctly it is *domo,* but the *mo* is usually omitted. In any case the concessive is not often employed.

(*d.*)—[*Ru*]. A number of verbs have a potential form formed by adding *ru* to the fourth base, and thus creating a new independent vowel verb. Examples:—*Aruku,* "To walk"; *arukeru,* "to be able to walk"; *arukemasu ka?* "are you able to walk?" etc.

Suffixes Added to the Fifth Base

(*a.*)—THE FIFTH BASE OF CONSONANT VERBS if used alone denotes the ordinary first future. Strictly speaking this is not an independent base at all, but rather a radical transformation of the first base. In the earlier written language *mu* was added to the first base to indicate the future (*e.g., kakamu,* "probably will walk"). This *mu* became *n,* a form which is still employed by the modern written language, but which the colloquial has further changed into *u.* This is still the correct form, and when written with the *kana, kakō* is seen to be *kaka-u. Au,* however, is pronounced *o,* and the *a* of the first base having thus entirely disappeared, it is best to consider it as a separate base.

(*b.*)—*Yō.* Vowel verbs form their future by adding *yō* to the first base, but since a special future base has been constructed for consonant verbs, it is better to class the vowel verbs in the same way. In any case the first, and fifth bases of vowel verbs are the same.

Periphrastic Forms of the Verb

There are certain periphrastic forms of the verb which are extremely common, and must, in fact, be considered as inherent parts of the conjugation. Two or three of these are especially worthy of note.

The First Periphrastic Form

One of the most frequently employed is the gerund plus *iru, oru,* or *irassharu,* all more or less identical in meaning, the last being the most polite. Needless to say all three may be used with the *masu* or polite form, and for *irassharu* this is the only suitable one. They may be put into any tense, but more especially the present, the past, the first future, and the second future. Thus the conjugation of the first periphrastic form is :—

1. PRESENT—
   (Positive) *kaite iru* (*imasu*) ; *oru* (*orimasu*) ; *irasshaimasu.*
   (Negative) *kaite inai* (*imasen*) ; *oranai* (*orimasen*) *irasshaimasen.*

2. PAST—
   (Positive) *kaite ita* (*imashita*) ; *otta* (*orimashita*) ; *irasshaimashita.*
   (Negative) *kaite inakatta* (*imasen deshita*) ; *oranakatta* (*orimasen deshita*) ; *irasshaimasen deshita.*

3. FIRST FUTURE—
   (Positive) *kaite iyō* or *iru deshō* (*imashō* or *imasu deshō*) ; *orō* or *oru deshō* (*orimashō* or *orimasu deshō*) ; *irasshaimashō* or *irasshaimasu deshō.*
   (Negative) *kaite imai* (*imasumai*) ; *orumai* (*orimasumai*) ; *irasshaimasumai.*

4. SECOND FUTURE —
   (Positive) *kaite itarō* (*imashitarō*) ; *ottarō* (*orimashitarō*) ; *irasshaimashitarō.*
   (Negative) *kaite inakattarō* (*imasen deshitarō*) ; *oranakattarō* (*orimasen deshitarō*) ; *irasshaimasendeshitarō.*

In addition to the above there is another way of forming the negative of each of the tenses. Instead of keeping the gerund in the positive and adding the negative forms of *iru, oru,* etc., we may put the gerund into the negative, and add the positive conjugation of *iru, oru,* etc., *e.g., kakanai de iru,* or *kakazu ni iru,* etc.

The meaning of these forms is not difficult to understand since they do not differ radically from the English participial expressions—("I am writing," "I was writing," I shall be writing," etc.). They are sufficiently important, however, to make more detailed explanation necessary :—

(*a.*)—Simple Present. In Japanese, as we have seen, the simple present (*e.g., kaku*) expresses (1) frequent or (2) habitual action; (3) action irrespective of time, and (4) present action without reference to past or present. Idiomatically it is also used to denote (5) the definite future, and occasionally, like the English historical present (6) the definite past.

(*b.*)—Periphrastic Present. The first periphrastic present (*e.g., kaite iru*) on the other hand denotes (1) an incomplete action, (2) an action which began in the past and is still continuing, and (3) a present state as the result of a former action. This last is almost equivalent to the English present perfect.

As examples of the differences we have :—*Ningen ga go-zen wo tabemasu,* "Men eat food" (literally, "rice"). *Tarō wa go-zen wo tabete imasu,* "Taro is eating (his) food." *Watakushi wa tabi-tabi shibai ye ikimasu,* "I often go to the theater." *Watakushi ga tabako wo kau toki ni itsudemo Kameya de kaimasu,* "When I buy tobacco, I always buy it at Kameya's." *Segare wa ichi nen mae kara heitai ni natte imasu,* "My son has been (become) a soldier since one year ago." *Go shisoku wa mada nagaku gakkō ye yukimasu ka?* "Will your son go to school much longer?" (future). *Go shisoku wa mō nagaku gakkō ye itte imasu ka?* "Has your son been at school long?"

(*c.*)—THE SIMPLE PAST (*e.g., kaita*) denotes (1) an action which took place at some definite past time, as well as (2) habitual past action, and (3) past action simultaneous with some other past action. The idea of completion is generally implied.

(*d.*)—THE PERIPHRASTIC PAST (*e.g., kaite ita*) is in some ways very idiomatic for in addition to the usual sense of (1) a past action continuing for some time, it has (2) a pluperfect sense denoting an action which was complete when another action began, and also (3) the past state as the result of a prior action.

As examples of these tenses we have:—*Kinō ame ga furimashita,* "Rain fell yesterday." *Kinō asa kara ban made ame ga futte orimashita,* "Rain was falling yesterday from morning until night." *Eikoku ni oru aida ni mainichi gakkō ye yukimashita,* "When I was in England, I went to school every day."

(*e.*)—THE SIMPLE FIRST FUTURE (*kakō* or *kaku deshō*) denotes (1) a probable future, (2) a probable present, (3) a phrase like the English "isn't it?" or the French "*n' est ce pas,*" and also such idiomatic expressions as (4) "let us," (5) "am I to . . ." or "shall I . . ." and (6) "I will."

(*f.*)—THE PERIPHRASTIC FIRST FUTURE (*e.g., kaite iru deshō*) has but one meaning—the probable present. It can never refer to future action.

Examples of this tense are very common :—*Biiru wo motte kimashō ka?* "Shall I bring (some) beer?" *Sa, kore kara isshōkemmei benkyō shimashō,* "I say, from now on, let us study with all our might and main." *Tarō wa doko?* "Where is Taro?" *Nikai de benkyō shite iru deshō,* "He is probably upstairs studying."

(*g.*)—THE SIMPLE SECOND FUTURE (*e.g., kaitarō*) refers to a probable past action.

(*h.*)—THE PERIPHRASTIC SECOND FUTURE (*e.g., kaite itarō,* etc.) refers to a probable past state, or to a continued action which was probably going on in the past, a sort of probable pluperfect.

Thus, for example :—*Ano hito wa demashita deshō,* "He probably went out." *Ano hito wa mō dete imashitarō,* "He has probably gone out." *Asa kara ban made ame ga futte imashtarō,* "Rain was probably falling from morning until night."

The above mentioned perfect use of the periphrastic forms deserves especial attention. Thus, *kite orimasu* means "he has come," and not "he is coming"; *shinde imasu,* "he has died" or "he is dead," and not "he is dying." *Shinda* would mean "he died."

The *te* of the gerund and *iru* often contract into *tteru.* This is often found in such a colloquial phrase as *shitteru wa* (from *shite iru wa*), "I know it indeed," or "Of course I know it."

Occasionally in place of *iru, oru,* etc., we find *aru* employed. This, however, has a somewhat different significance. Such a form denotes a sort of passive, or more correctly a state which is the result of an action described by the verb. Thus from *tsutsumu,* "to wrap," we have *kami ni tsutsunde arimasu,* "(it) is wrapped up in paper," or "it has been wrapped up in paper." From *oku,* "to put," we have *asuko ni oite aru mono wa nan desu ka?* "What is that thing which has been put over there?"

The Second Periphrastic Form

Desu (or *da*) with or without *no* or *n'* before it, is often added to a verb in the first four tenses. This gives us an additional periphrastic conjugation of the Present, Past, First Future, and Second Future, as follows :—

1. PRESENT—
   (Positive) (*taberu desu*) or *taberu no desu.*
   (Negative) (*tabenai desu*) or *tabenai no desu.*
2. PAST—
   (Positive) (*tabeta desu*) or *tabeta no desu.*
   (Negative) (*tabenakatta desu*) or *tabenakatta no desu.*
3. FIRST FUTURE—
   (Positive) *taberu deshō* or *taberu no deshō.*
   (Negative) *tabenai deshō* or *tabenai no deshō.*
4. SECOND FUTURE—
   (Positive) *tabeta deshō* or *tabeta no deshō.*
   (Negative) *tabenakatta deshō* or *tabenakatta no deshō.*

In this connection several points deserve attention. One is that in all cases *da* may be substituted for *desu*, and *darō* for *deshō*, and *n'* for *no*. The second is that the first and second periphrastic forms may be combined, *e.g.*, *kaite iru desu, kaite inakatta n' desu*, etc., and in fact in the future this combined form is the one most in use so that we have given it in our list of the first periphrastic forms. So in the simple forms also, *kaku deshō* is more common than *kakimashō*. The latter refers more to the first person, and the former to the actions of the second or third person. In the second and past, the second periphrastic form without the *no* or *n'* is not very common, so that these forms have been put in () marks.

Furthermore, in addition to the negative forms which are given above, there are several others which are sometimes met with. Thus in place of keeping the main verb in the negative and *desu* in the positive, we may put the main verb in the positive, and *desu* in the negative. There is no direct negative of *desu,* so that this must be done in a round about manner, such as *taberu de wa nai,* or *taberu de wa nai n' desu,* and so on with the other forms. Again in place of inflecting the main verb in the past and the second future, leaving the *desu,* or *deshō* unchanged (*e.g.*, *kakanakatta desu, kakanakatta deshō*) we can reverse the inflectional processes and say *kakanai deshita* and *kakanai deshitaro.* In fact, there are numerous other modes of expressions, but those given above are the most common.

This second periphrastic form is very common, and in ordinary conversation is even more common than the simple forms. The difference in meaning between the simple tenses and these is very slight, and may be understood by the following example :—*Nani wo shimasu ka?* " What are you doing ? " *Nani wo suru no desu ka?* " What is it that you are doing ? " In almost all cases this *desu,* etc., corresponds to a weak " it is that . . ." or " the fact is that . . ." This the Japanese consider to be more expressive in all cases, and especially when denoting anger, astonishment, repulsion, etc.

Minor Periphrastic Forms

The first and second periphrastic forms have especial reference to the first four tenses. In addition there are several periphrastic modes of expressing the conditional concessive and other oblique tenses. Chief among these are :—

(*a.*)—*Naru,* " to be " (to be carefully distinguished from *naru,* " to become ") is a very common auxiliary in the written language, but in the colloquial is found only in the forms *nara* (occasionally *naraba* or *nareba*) and *naredo.* The latter denotes the concessive, and the former the conditional. Thus for *ikeba* we may say *iku nara,* and for *ittara, itta nara.* *Nara* may also be used with adjectives either real or quasi in the same way. *Utsukushii nara,* or *kirei nara,* " if beautiful."

(*b.*)—*Keru,* an old perfect form of *kuru,* " to come," is now found in the words *keredo* (or *keredomo*), " but," attached to the indicative past or present to form the concessive past or present. *Kereba* is the conditional form of the same word.

(*c.*)—*Iu* (literally, " to say ") is also used with the indicative to denote the periphrastic conditional or concessive, *e.g.*, *Aru to iu to,* " if there be " (literally, " is thus say if ") or " if you say that there is." *Aru to iedo,* " Even though there be " (literally, " is, thus even-though-say ") or " even though one say that there is." For the most part this *iu* is entirely redundant.

(*d.*)—Finally, the honorific mode of expression should not be forgotten. This applies for all tenses, and is formed by *o* plus the second base plus either *de gozaimasu,* or *ni narimasu.* These auxiliary words may of course be fully conjugated themselves, *e.g.*, *o kaeri de gozaimasu,* or *o kaeri ni narimasu,* etc. The polite imperative forms mentioned on page 66 should be borne in mind.

The Complete Conjugation of the Verb

The complete structure of the verb, with its roots, stems, bases, and suffixes, as well as most of the important periphrastic modes of expression having been mastered, we are now in a position to frame a complete conjugation of the verb, more or less in accordance with European verbal systems.

Certain forms in each one of the two classes of vowel verbs, and of the six classes of consonant verbs, differ, of course, from one another, but since these changes are in accordance with a rule already mastered (cf. page 31) the conjugated of any one, as for example, *kaku,* will serve as a model for all others.

KAKU

(FIVE BASES :—*kaka, kaki, kaku, kake, kakō*)

(ASSIMILATED SECOND BASE :—*kai*)

TENSE	POSITIVE	NEGATIVE
1. PRESENT—		
(*a.*)—Familiar	*kaku*	*kakan* or *kakanai*
(*b.*)—Polite	*kakimasu*	*kakimasen.*
(*c.*)—First Periphrastic	*kaite iru,* (etc.)	*kaite inai* (etc.)
(*d.*)—Second Periphrastic	*kaku no desu* (etc.)	*kakanai no desu* (etc.)
2. PAST—		
(*a.*)—Familiar	*kaita*	*kakananda* or *kakanakatta*
(*b.*)—Polite	*kakimashita*	*kakimasen deshita.*
(*c.*)—First Periphrastic	*kaite ita* (etc.)	*kaite inakatta* (etc.)
(*d.*)—Second Periphrastic	*kaita no desu* (etc.)	*kakanakatta no desu* (etc.)
3. FIRST FUTURE—		
(*a.*)—Familiar	*kakō*	*kakumai* or *kakanakarō*
(*b.*)—Polite	*kakimashọ*	*kakimasen deshō.*
(*c.*)—First Periphrastic	*kaite iyō* (etc.)	*kaite inakarō* (etc.)
(*d.*)—Second Periphrastic	*kaku deshō* or *kaku no deshō* (etc.)	*kakanai deshō* or *kakanai no deshō* (etc.)

4. SECOND FUTURE—		
(*a.*)—Familiar	*kaitarō*	*kakanandarō* or *kakanakattarō*
(*b.*)—Polite	*kakimashitarō*	*kakimasen deshitarō*
(*c.*)—First Periphrastic	*kaite itarō* (etc.)	*kaite inakattarō* (etc.)
(*d.*)—Second Periphrastic	*kaita deshō* or *kaita no deshō* (etc.)	*kakanakatta deshō* or *kakanakatta no deshō* (etc.)
5. FIRST CONDITIONAL—		
(*a.*)—Familiar	*kakeba*	*kakaneba* or *kakanakereba*
(*b.*)—Polite	*kakimasureba*	*kakimasenakereba*
(*c.*)—Additional	*kaku nara*	*kakan nara* (etc.)
	kaku to	*kakan to* (etc.)
	kaku to iu to	*kakan to iu to* (etc.)
	kaite wa	*kakanakute wa* (etc.)
6. SECOND CONDITIONAL—		
(*a.*)—Familiar	*kaitara*	*kakanandara* or *kakanakattara*
(*b.*)—Polite	*kakimashitara*	*kakimasen deshitara*
(*c.*)—Additional	*kaita nara*	*kakananda nara* (etc.)
	kaku to	*kakan to* (etc.)
	kaite wa	*kakanakute wa* (etc.)
7. GERUND—		
(*a.*)—Familiar	*kaite*	*kakazu*, or *kakanai de* (etc.)
(*b.*)—Polite	*kakimashite*	*kakimasezu* or *kakimasen de* (etc.)

These seven are the tenses which are the most commonly employed, and in addition there are several others which are sufficiently important to require that they at least be recognized.

TENSE	POSITIVE	NEGATIVE
8. FIRST CONCESSIVE—		
(*a.*)—Familiar	*kakedo*	*kakanedo* or *kakanakeredo*
(*b.*)—Polite	*kakimasuredo*	*kakimasenakeredo*
(*c.*)—Additional	*kaku keredo*	*kakanu keredo* (etc.)
	kaku to iedo	*kakanu to iedo* (etc.)
	kaku naredo	*kakanu naredo* (etc.)
	kaite mo	*kakanakute mo* (etc.)
9. SECOND CONCESSIVE—		
(*a.*)—Familiar	*kaitaredo*	*kakanandaredo* or *kakanakattaredo*
(*b.*)—Polite	*kakimashitaredo*	*kakimasen deshitaredo*
(*c.*)—Additional	*kaita keredo*	*kakananda keredo*
	kaita naredo	*kakananda naredo*
	kaite mo	*kakanakute mo* (etc.)
10. ALTERNATIVE—		
(*a.*)—Familiar	*kaitari*	*kakanandari* and *kakanakattari*
(*b.*)—Polite	*kakimashitari*	

There are in addition the following derivative forms:—

TENSE	POSITIVE	NEGATIVE
IMPERATIVE—		
(*a.*)—Familiar	*kake* or *kaki na*	*kaku na, kakinasanna*
(*b.*)—Polite	*o kaki nasai* or *kaite kudasai*	*o kaki nasaruna* or *kaite kudasaruna*

(*a.*)—CAUSATIVE VERB—
kakaseru

(*b.*)—PASSIVE VERB—
kakareru

(*c.*)—POTENTIAL VERB—
kakeru

(*d.*)—NOMINAL FORMS—
kaku koto, mono, toki, aida, hazu, tokoro, tsumori, etc.

(*e.*)—ADJECTIVAL FORMS—
kakitai, kaki sō na

The Meanings and Uses of the Tenses

The First Four Tenses

The present, past, first future, and second future have already been considered at length and need no longer take our attention. In a word they may be said to represent the certain present or future, the certain past, the probable present or future, and the probable past respectively.

Both forms of the future have also a semi-interrogative meaning. Both may indicate "I suppose that," or "I think that." The first future may mean "let us," or "shall we." The first three ordinary forms, *yobō, yobimashō, yonde iyō*, etc., when used alone generally refer to the first person. In the "let us" sense, however, they may be used for all persons.

The second periphrastic form, *yobu deshō*, etc., generally refers to the second or third person. When, however, it is used in the quasi-interrogative sense it may be used for any person. The combination of the first and second periphrastic forms, *yonde iru deshō*, is used for all persons when the state and not the action is intended.

The following idioms deserve attention. The future plus *to omou* means "thinking of doing . . ." or "intend to . . ." *e.g.*, *ikō to omou*, "I am thinking of going." The future plus *to shite*, "at the point of . . . ing." *Ikō to shite*, "at the point of leaving."

In a few cases the use of the past and the present in Japan differs from the English custom. Thus the Japanese present sometimes has a past meaning, *e.g.*, *shimbun wa mada mimasen*, "I have not seen the newspaper yet." *Beikoku ni oru aida ni*, "While I was in America." On the other hand the English present is sometimes translated by the Japanese past. *Wakarimashita* may mean "I understand" or "I understood." *Arimashita* (literally, "was") for "here it is," said when a searched-for article has been found. These and other occasional differences, however, will cause the student no serious difficulty.

The *ta* or past tense form of the colloquial is the perfect tense sign of the literary language. In the colloquial, however, it more frequently indicates the imperfect than the perfect. Occasionally, it will be remembered, the first periphrastic form of the present has a perfect significance. *Kite orimasu,* "He has come." The first periphrastic form of the past also serves to indicate the pluperfect, but for the most part no account is taken of such difficulties.

The Conditional Forms

The present form of the conditional is due to a curious contraction of two earlier forms, the hypothetical and the conditional proper. In the written language the present conditional of *kaku* is *kakeba,* the past *kakitareba,* the hypothetical present *kakaba,* and the past *kakitaraba.* The interesting point is that the colloquial has adopted the conditional present and the hypothetical past.

The additional forms are frequently employed and should be remembered. There is a slight difference between all other forms of the conditional and the absolute gerund. The former denotes a general condition, or even one which is contrary to fact, while the latter is limited to a particular case. All forms of the conditional may be used to indicate "when," as well as "if."

In practice there is very little distinction made between the present and the past conditional. Both may be used indifferently when relating to some general or actual fact but the past is especially met with when describing conditions contrary to fact.

Other meanings of the conditional are also very common. "as soon as," "in as much as," "after," "while." Two conditionals coming together, the second often means " provided that " or " so long as." If *moshi* is prefixed to the conditional it becomes distinctly hypothetical and with *moshi mo* even concessive.

A conditional clause followed by some form of *ii* (*yoi*, etc.) has a somewhat idiomatic significance expressing a mild " hope " or " fear," " desire " or " regret." In many such cases *ga* (but), *ni* or *no ni* (where as) are added and the sentence left unfinished, the words " unfortunately it was (*or* was not) so," be understood. Thus, for example, *kureba ii n' desu ga . . .* " I wish he would come."

In certain cases the Japanese employ the conditional where we should expect the gerund, and is to be translated " but," " and," " whereas."

The Remaining Tenses

For the most part the remaining tenses do not require especial consideration. The gerund has already (page 58) been fully analyzed. The concessive is almost equivalent to the concessive gerund (*itte mo* = *Ikedo*) but in the colloquial is seldom used.

The alternative or frequentative form is chiefly used in pairs and corresponds to the English " sometimes . . . and sometimes . . ." " now (eating) now (drinking)," " (reading) as well as (talking)," etc. It is always followed by *suru*. Take the following example given by Plaut :—

Hokori ga tattari suna ga mattari suru toki ni kaze ga tatsu to iimasu. " When the dust rises and the sand whirls people say that the wind springs up."

4.—*Passive Potential and Causative Forms.*

Further consideration of the various adjectival and substantive forms may be omitted, but the exact meaning

Local restaurant

Buddha

and use of the passive potential, and causative forms should be carefully mastered.

The Japanese passive is somewhat complicated, and it cannot be adequately described in English. *Areru* which is added to the first base of consonant verbs is derived from *ar*(*u*) " to be," and *eru* " to get." The idea of " getting " is retained throughout. Thus, *Kuruma ga nusumaremashita* means not so much "My car was stolen" as "My car got stolen."

With the passive, agent is expressed by *ni. Ashi wo inu ni kuitsukaremashita,* "I have had my leg bitten by a dog."

For this reason also the passive may be used with intransitive verbs, *e.g.*, *kyaku ni korareru,* " to get a coming by guests," *i.e.*, to be visited by guests. *Ame ni furareru,* " to get a falling by rain," *i.e.*, to be rained upon.

For the most part Japanese abhors the passive and employs many circumlocutions to retain the active voice. In general the passive may only be used with a conscious agent.

In addition to the passive sense the same form is employed to denote two other ideas. One is potentiality " can," " may," etc., *e.g.*, *taberaremas,* " am able to eat " ; *koraremasu,* " am able to come." The other is still more peculiar. The passive forms are used as polite active verbs to denote the actions of the second and third persons. They are then treated as ordinary active verbs governing the same case as the plain verbs from which they are derived.

The so-called potential form of the verb is really an intransitive verb which frequently has a potential meaning. In many cases it is used interchangeably with the passive form (in its potential sense) but the passive denotes more *may* or moral ability, the potential *can* or general ability. *Ikemasu,* "One can go" (because the way is easy or because one is a good walker). *Ikaremasu,* "One can go" (because there is no prohibition against so doing).

The various periphrastic methods of expressing potentiality (*e.g.*, by the use of *dekiru, ka mo shiremasen*) must not be forgotten.

The causative serves to express the following meanings :—"to cause to do," "to cause a person to do something," "to allow a person to do something," "to let a person do some thing." In addition to the ordinary forms (*seru* to the first base of consonant verbs, *saseru* to the first base of vowel verbs) there is a frequently used alternative form *sasu* added to the first base of vowel verbs, and *su* to the first base of consonant verbs, *e.g.*, *tabesasu,* "to cause to eat"; *kakasu,* "cause to write."

In all causative constructions the agent is expressed by *ni*, the object of the action performed by *wo, e.g., isha wo yobaseta,* "he had a doctor called"; *ototo ni isha wo yobaseta,* "he made his younger brother call a doctor."

Miscellaneous Verb Idioms

It is impossible, of course, in the short space allotted to us to attempt to cover the whole field of the Japanese verb. Enough has been said to outline its main features.

Two final points, however, require consideration. One is the great distinction made between transitive and intransitive verbs, the other is the frequent use made of compound verbs.

Regarding the first point, note the interesting explanation below:

In English the same word commonly does duty both as a transitive and as an intransitive verb, the context alone determining in which of these acceptations it is to be understood. . . . In Japanese the transitive and intransitive meanings are almost always expressed by different verbs derived from the same root, thus :—

INTRANSITIVE	TRANSITIVE
aku, " to be open."	*akeru*, " to open."
hajimaru, " to begin."	*hajimeru*, " to begin."
kaeru, " to return."	*kaesu*, " to return."
naoru, " to get well."	*naosu*, " to cure."

Regarding the second point, we find that Japanese is much addicted to the use of compound verbs. In most cases both parts consist of verbs themselves, the first half, of course, being kept in the second base. Examples are :—

tobi-agaru, " to jump up."
tobi-komu, " to jump in."
tobi-kosu, " to jump across."
wake-ataeru, " to give in shares."
deki-agaru, " to be completed."
omoi-dasu, " to call to mind."

Analysis: Adjectives

In the Japanese language the adjective is a form of the verb, and though it is not affected by number, person or gender, it is conjugated through all the tenses.

In all there are four distinct types of adjective; (1) real adjectives such as *samui*, "cold"; *takai*, "high," etc., the present tense of which always ends in an *i*. (2) quasi-adjectives formed from nouns usually by adding *no* or *na* *e.g.*, *Amerika no*, "American"; *jōzu na*, "skillful." (3) verbal adjectives or verbs used attributively to qualify a noun which they precede. (4) a certain number of idiomatic and uninflected words used as adjectives such as *mina*, "all"; *zutsu*, "each," etc.

Real Adjectives

We have already dealt with most questions regarding the conjugation of adjectives. (*cf*. pages 44 to 48). We have seen that adjectives have three forms:—the *i* form, used either predicatively or attributively; the *ku* form, used adverbially or in front of a verb, and the *sa* form, which changes the adjective into a noun.

Furthermore we have examined the five modes of conjugation and have seen that they consist of (1) the adjective alone; (2) of the adjective plus *desu* or *da*; (3)

of the adjective plus *n' desu,* etc. ; (4) of the adverbial or *ku* form of the adjective plus *arimasu* (though this form is seldom used in the positive), and (5) of the contracted adverbial form of the adjective (formed by the dropping *k* of *ku*) plus *gozaimasu.* Nor need it be repeated that though theoretically all modes may be conjugate of the five forms only the first and fifth of the positive, and the first, fourth and fifth of the negative are used in other tenses than the present.

The tenses of the fourth and fifth forms are gained by conjugating the auxiliary verb (*arimasu* and *gozaimasu*) while the first form is conjugated in the positive by dropping the *u* of the adverbial form and adding the familiar tenses of *aru,* and in the negative by adding the tenses of *nai* to the full adverbial form.

There are also several classes of real adjectives. The three most important categories we may call the simple adjective, the compound adjective, and the complex adjective.

The first class or simple adjectives consist of those words which like *samui, takai,* etc., are used by themselves.

The second class or compound adjectives consist of two or more words which are run together to form a new or compound meaning. The last part of the compound is, of course, always an adjective, but the first part may be either a noun, a verb, or another adjective. If a verb it is the second base, if an adjective the stem. Thus from the noun *kokoro,* " heart," and the adjective *yasui,* " easy," we have the word *kokoro-yasui,* " familiar " ; from *na,* " name " and *takai,* " high," we have *nadakai,* " famous." From the verb *miru,* " see " and *kurushii,* " distressing," we have *mi-gurushii,* " ugly " (literally, " painful to look at "). From *wakaru,* " understand " and *yasui,* we have *wakari-yasui,* " easy to understand." From the two adjectives *hosoi*, " narrow " and *nagai*, " long," we have *hoso-nagai*, " slender." From *usui*, " light-colored " and *akai*, " red," *usu-akai*, " pink."

Complex adjectives consist of nouns (occasionally of verbs in their second bases) followed by *no* and an adjective, *e.g.*, *yama no ōi*, " mountainous," as in *yama no ōi kuni*, " a mountainous country " ; *un no yoi*, " fortunate," " lucky " ; *sei no takai*, " tall," etc. The words *yoi*, *warui*, *ōi*, *fukai*, *nai*, etc., are the most common adjectives used in these forms but several others occur.

These complex adjectives are very numerous, but among the most common are :—

benri no yoi, " convenient."
hyōban no yoi, " reputable."
kimari no yoi, " systematic."
kokoro-mochi no yoi, " agreeable."
genki no yoi, " lively."
hito no ōi, " populous."
ame no ōi, " rainy."
ishi no ōi, " stony."
ki no mijikai, " impatient."
ki no hayai, " impulsive."
naka no fukai, " intimate."
yoku no fukai, " covetous."
ki no ōkii, " generous."
aji no nai, " flavorless."
kagiri no nai, " boundless."

Most of these forms have also their opposites such as *benri no warui*, *hito no sukenai*, etc.

This *no* form is used only when the complex adjective is used attributively. When used predicatively the *no* invariably changes to *ga*, *e.g.*, *Ano hito wa un ga yoi. Nihon wa yama ga ōi.*

There are in addition a few such complex adjectives ending in *de nai* or *mo nai*, *e.g.* :—

shōjiki de nai, " dishonest."
arisō mo nai, " unlikely."
zōsa mo nai, " easy."

Quasi-Adjectives

Practically all nouns may be made into adjectives by one of three ways :—(1) by compounding with another noun ; (2) by adding *no* to nouns dealing with time, place, country, or material, and (3) by adding *na* to abstract nouns.

The *na* form is used only attributively. When the quasi-adjectives are in the predicate, the *na* changes to *de* when followed by some verb implying existence (*aru*) etc. or *ni*, when followed by any other verb. The *de* form may also be used as a sort of gerund. With the negative the *de* changes to *dewa.*

Among the quasi-adjectives most commonly employed are *sō na, yō na,* and *sō na.* The first *sō na* when added to the stems of adjectives or the second base of verbs indicates probability, with more especial reference to the future. The forms *yosasō na* and *nasasō na* from *yoi* and *nai* are irregular. This form is also attached to quasi-adjectives directly.

Yō na is suffixed to the full forms of adjectives and verbs, and *no yō na* to nouns to indicate present probability. *Sō na* when added to the full forms of adjectives and verbs means " they say that . . ." or " I hear that . . ."

Important examples of quasi-adjectives are :—

eikyu no, " eternal."
ue no, " upper."
kin no, " golden."
gwaikoku no, " foreign."

rambō na, " disorderly."
rippa na, " splendid."
chūgi na, " loyal."
jōzu na, " skillful."
muri na, " unreasonable."
zannen na, " unfortunate."

Verbal Adjectives

Since there are no relative pronouns in Japanese many such relative clauses are expressed by the attributive use of verbs. In many cases such verbs correspond to and take the place of adjectives. In the modern colloquial only two tenses are used in this manner, the present and the past, but each of these in turn has a simple form, and a complex form.

The following are important instances of each form :—

SIMPLE PRESENT

mieru, visible
kikoeru, audible
dekiru, possible
yomeru, legible
dekinai, impossible
shireru, knowable
hiiki suru, partial
shinjirareru, credible
yomenai, illegible
motte ikeru, portable

(Note the large number of potentials, etc.)

COMPLEX PRESENT

doku ni naru, poisonous
kusuri ni naru, wholesome
ki ni iru, agreeable
ki ni iranai, disagreeable
yaku ni tatsu, useful
yaku ni tatanai, worthless
tame ni naru, beneficial
shimpai ni naru, harassing
kagiri no aru, finite
katachi no aru, material
tsumi no aru, guilty
mottai no aru, dignified
hone no oreru, arduous
shochi no dekinai, inadmissable

SIMPLE PAST

aita, empty
chanto shita, steady, still
chigatta, dissimilar
futotta, stout, fat
hakkiri shita, explicit
iri-kunda, complicated
nareta, experienced
kusatta, rotten
sappari shita, frank
shinda, dead

COMPLEX PAST

do ni sugita, ultra
hō ni kanatta, legal
kōbai ni natta, sloping
ki no kiita, attentive
sei no nuketa, crestfallen
choito shita, slight

All the above are attributive forms. Most of them can also be used predicatively but in all cases where the past is used, it must be replaced by the gerund plus *iru*, etc., *e.g.*, *futotta hito* but *ano hito wa futotte imasu*. Furthermore in those complex forms which employ *no*, the *no* must be changed to *ga*.

Miscellaneous Notes on Adjectives

In the written language there is a different form even for real adjectives according to whether they are attributive or predicative. The common *i* of the colloquial is *ki* for the former, and *shi* for the latter. Though these forms have been dropped from the colloquial one occasionally meets instances where they are used so that the student should be able to recognize them.

Many adjectives are used in two senses (1) to refer to the objective quality of a thing, and (2) with reference to the subjective feeling of a person, *e.g.*, *omoshiroi koto*, "an interesting thing," but *omoshirokatta*, "(I) was amused," etc.

An adjective may often have the force of a noun when *no* is added to it, *e.g.*, *chiisai*, "small," and *chiisai no*, "a small one"; *kirei*, "pretty," *kirei na no*, "a pretty one." Quasi-adjectives ending in *no* do not add another *no* added to them.

A few derivative forms deserve attention :—

(*a.*)—The desiderative and negative forms of the verb (*tai* and *nai*) are true adjectives and may be conjugated accordingly. It will be remembered that *tai* is added to the second base and *nai* to the first base.

(*b.*)—The apparitional form of the verb (*sō na* added to the second base) is a quasi-adjective, and may be inflected like all other quasi-adjectives.

(*c.*)—An adjective may be formed from certain nouns by adding *rashii*. This usually means "having the appearance of," but frequently it denotes a real quality, like the English suffixes "ish," "ly," etc., *e.g.*, *bakarashii*, "foolish"; *otokorashii*, "manly"; *yakusharashii*, "actor-like"; *sōrashii*, "seemingly so." Occasionally *rashii* is added to verbs and adjectives. These forms are all conjugated like true adjectives.

(*d.*)—Much more infrequently we find *gamashii*, which also denotes a resemblance or a quality described by the word to which it is attached, *e.g.*, *tanin-gamashii*, " behaving like a stranger, distant in manner " ; *katte-gamashii*, " seemingly inconsiderate " ; *shitte iru gamashii*, " pretending to know."

(*e.*)—*Beki* is the old written form of an adjective and is still occasionally employed to denote " ought " or " should," and is often equivalent to our adjectives in ". . . able." It is only used attributively (*i.e.*, in front of nouns) and is attached only to verbs—to the second base of vowel verbs, and the third base of consonant verbs. *Kubeki* from *kuru ;* *subeki* from *suru ;* and *mibeki* or *mirubeki* from *miru* are peculiar, *e.g.*, *subeki koto*, " a thing to be done " ; *shinzubeki koto*, " a credible thing." *Kono kinjō ni mirubeki tokoro ga gozaimasu ka ?* " Is there any thing worth seeing in this vicinity ? "

(*f.*)—*Ppoi* added to a few specified nouns, adjectives, and verbs (in the latter two cases to the stem) forms an adjective, and generally denotes excess, *e.g.*, *mizuppoi*, " watery " ; *okorippoi*, " quick-tempered."

(*g.*)—Finally, it should be noted that a number of adjectives are transformed into verbs by adding *garu* to the stem. Thus *kowagaru* from *kowai.* It may also be added to the desiderative base, *e.g.*, *ikitagaru* from *ikitai.* *Garu* implies " to think . . ." or " to feel . . ." These verbs are, of course, conjugated in all the moods and tenses like all other verbs.

CHAPTER 15

Analysis: Adverbs

Japanese has but few real adverbs. Practically all the words corresponding to the English adverb are peculiar forms of other parts of speech. Thus nouns, adjectives and verbs have all adverbial uses.

(1.)—NOUNS. Many words relating to time, place, degree, etc., which in English would be expressed by adverbs belong to the *Na* (nouns, pronouns, etc.) class in Japanese. Such, for example, are *koko,* "here"; *soko,* "there"; *konnichi,* "today"; *sakujitsu,* "yesterday"; *tashō,* "more or less"; *daitai,* "generally, for the most part." Like ordinary nouns all such words may have postpositions attached to them, *e.g., koko ni, ashita no,* etc. In fact, there are a number of such nouns which are now found only when followed by some particular postposition, *e.g., jiki ni,* "immediately"; *sude ni,* "already"; *maru de,* "entirely." Occasionally adverbs are formed by the duplication of substantives, *e.g.* :—

tabitabi, frequently	*hōbō,* everywhere
tokidoki, occasionally	*nakanaka,* very, just so
oriori, rarely	*dandan,* gradually

(2.)—ADJECTIVES. Adverbs formed from adjectives are of two kinds, first those derived from real adjectives (ending in *i*) and second, those derived from quasi-adjectives (ending in *na*, and occasionally in *no*). Real adjectives, it will be remembered, have a special adverbial form by changing the final *i* to *ku*. This, of course, applies to the negative (by adding *naku*) as well as to the positive. Quasi-adjectives have an adverbial sense when the *na* is changed to *ni*. Important examples are :—

ōki ni, greatly
tashika ni, certainly
katte ni, inconsiderately
tsune ni, always
sen ni, formerly
saiwai ni, fortunately
muri ni, unreasonably
kari ni, provisionally
betsu ni, especially
chokusetsu ni, directly

In many cases there is no corresponding adjective, *e.g.* :—

koto ni, specially
tama ni, occasionally
metta ni, seldom (with negative)
jiki ni, immediately

All of these forms are frequently used when English would not require an adverb.

(3.)—VERBS. A number of verbs are used with an adverbial sense. The gerund, either positive or negative, is the form most frequently employed. Important examples are :—

aratamete, again, anew
hatashite, after all
kaette, on the contrary
sadamete, doubtless
subete, in general, all
kesshite, never
hajimete, for the first time
itatte, very
kanete, previously
semete, at least
tatte, urgently
shiite, compulsorily

hakarazu, unexpectedly
oboezu, unconsciously
ai-kawarazu, as always
nokorazu, all
kanarazu, without fail
shirazu-shirazu, unawares

In addition to the preceding derivative adverbs there are a number of uninflected words of several kinds which may be called real adverbs. For present purposes they may be divided into three catagories :—(1) simple adverbs ; (2) *to* adverbs, and (3) onomatopœic adverbs.

(1.)—The most important of the simple adverbs are :—

goku, extremely ; *taihen*, very ; *taisō*, very ; *yohodo*, very ; *hanahada* very ; *mada*, yet ; *naze*, why ; *yahari*, also ; *sappari*, wholly ; *ikaga*, how ; *mazu*, well then, in the first place ; *mō* or *mohaya*, already ; *narutake*, " as . . . as possible " ; *sate*, well ! ; *zehi*, without fail ; *zuibun*, rather ; *sukoshi*, a little, etc.

(2.)—There are a number of adverbs ending in *ri* to which, properly speaking, *to* should always be added, but which is frequently omitted. The most important are :—

bikkuri, an expression of surprise
bonyari, dimly, perplexedly, dully
dossari, abundantly, luxuriantly
hakkiri, distinctly, explicitly
kitchiri, precisely, tightly
sukkari, entirely
shikkari, firmly, faithfully
yukkuri, slowly, leisurely

These may also be made into verbs by adding *suru*. There are also a number of adverbs with which *to* is invariably used, in many cases being assimilated into the word itself. Among these are :—

motto, more
kitto, surely
sotto, softly
hyotto, suddenly
tonto, totally, at all
zutto, all the way, very much
chitto, a little
chanto, precisely

(3.)—Many of the adverbs in the preceding class are onomatopœic in origin, but this has now been forgotten, and they are looked upon as true adverbs. In addition, however, there are a number which retain their onomatopœic association. For the most part they are duplicated words. In many cases they can not be translated into English. Among them are :—

barabara, of the falling of rain, etc
gishigishi, of creaking timbers
buruburu, trembling or shuddering
chibichibi, of driblets
gasagasa, of rustling sounds
gatagata, of rattling, slamming sounds
guruguru, round and round
pikapika, of shining, glittering objects

Finally, with regard to responsives, it may seem strange that the foregoing list (of adverbs) should contain no equivalent for our adverbs of affirmation and negation, *yes* and *no*. The reason is that there are no words corresponding exactly to our *yes* and *no* in the Japanese language. There is, it is true, a word *iie* which means *no*. But it is little used except when the denial is an indignant one. The word *he*, *hei*, or *hai* which may sometimes be translated by *yes* is properly an interjection used to show that one has heard and understood what has been said to one. It does not generally imply assent to a statement. Thus when a tea-house girl is called, she will immediately call out, *hei*, to show that she is coming immediately. Instead of *yes* the Japanese say 'that is so,' *sō da* ; more politely, *sō desu* ; still more politely, *sayō de gozaimasu*. Similarly for *no* they say *sō ja nai* ; politely, *sayō de gozaimasen*. Or else they repeat the verb of the question.

It should further be noted that in response to a negative question the use of *yes* and *no* is exactly opposite to that of English. *Kimasen ka?* "Won't he come?" *Hai kimasen*, "*Yes*, he won't come," where, of course, we would say, "*No*, he won't come."

CHAPTER 16

Analysis: Miscellaneous

Syntax

The chief rules of syntax have already been given (page 17) but in addition a few idiomatic constructions require attention.

(*a.*)—QUOTATION. Strictly speaking there is no indirect quotation, the words quoted being given in their original form followed by *to* and some form of the word " to say," " to think," etc. In certain cases *to* is replaced by *yō ni*.

(*b.*)—NEGATIVES. There is a complete negative conjugation contrary to English grammar, but, as in English, two negatives destroy one another; *nai koto wa nai*, " there *is*." The most difficult feature of Japanese negatives is that there are no negative pronouns, viz., no-one, never, etc., and in their place we have positive pronouns followed by a negative verb. *Watakushi wa kesshite ikimasen*, " I never go " (literally, " I always do not go "). *Daremo orimasen*, " There is no one " (literally, " Everyone is not ").

(*c.*)—ELLIPSES. Japanese are very fond of leaving their sentences incomplete. The most common form of ellipsis is by the omission of the final verb in certain stereotyped phrases, *e.g.*, *Tanaka san ni yoroshiku* (*negaimasu*). " Best wishes to Mr. Tanaka." Another common form is by ending the sentence with *ga*, "but," etc., leaving the remainder to be understood by the context.

(*d.*)—COORDINATION. When the verbs of several clauses are intended to express the same tense or mood, it is only the last of these verbs that takes the suffix by which such tense or mood is indicated. The previous verbs all assume the gerundial (or in the higher style the indefinite form, *i.e.*, the second base). Adjectives assume either the gerundial or indefinite (*i.e.*, ordinary) form. . . . In the case of nouns it is only the last of a set of nouns that takes the postpositions common to all. *Mo* (with any post-position which may precede it) is, however, suffixed to every noun of a set.

(*e.*)—ABSENCE OF SUBJECT AND OF PERSONIFICATION. Japanese if compared with English is extraordinarily impersonal. Personal pronouns are usually omitted, and in many cases sentences have no expressed subjects. Finally, the personification of natural objects is almost unknown. Thus we find nothing corresponding to "the hand of Time," "the fates decided," etc. In place of "lightning killed him" we must say "He was killed by lightning." Various honorific paraphrases have already been discussed (page 64).

Interjections

Japanese makes frequent use of interjections. The most frequent are :—

a, shows attention, assent, admiration, grief, or weariness.

aita, a cry of pain, like the English "ouch."

ara denotes joy, fear, or surprise.

dokkoisho is a signal of encouragement when lifting a heavy weight, like the English "up she goes," or "altogether." It is also a sigh of relief when the weight is lifted into place.

dōmo shows the speaker to be puzzled, not knowing just what to do, or as telling how difficult was the situation which he is describing. It also expresses astonishment, and sometimes corresponds to our " really," " indeed," *e.g.*, *dōmo arigatō gozaimasu*, " Thanks very much indeed."

e denotes wonderment, sympathy, and occasionally dislike.

hai or *hei* denotes assent, attention, or in answering a call.

ma denotes surprise and wonder, like the English " oh ! " but more frequently entreaty, corresponding to " do, please do," etc.

moshimoshi, " hello." In calling out to catch attention *ano ne* is preferred.

naruhodo, " indeed," " really," " is that so ? " " you don't say so ? "

nē when attached to a verb is like the French "*n'est ce pas*," but is chiefly used to soften an affirmative. *Kyō wa samui nē*, " It is cold today, isn't it ? " After a noun it is rather more like the English " y' know."

oi, a call summoning a servant or an intimate friend.

oya denotes astonishment.

sa is an exclamation to arouse one to action.

ya denotes pleasurable excitement.

yo after verbs or at the end of sentences denotes emphasis or often warning.

zo, in like manner expresses strong emphasis.

Needless to say much of the exact meaning of interjections and other words depends upon the intonation of the voice.

Auxiliary Verbs

There are a small number of very important auxiliary verbs, whose meaning is frequently ambiguous. In fact in many cases they cannot be rendered into English at all. They are all used after the gerund of the main verbs. The most important of such verbs are *miru*, *kuru*, *oku*, *shimau*, and the various words meaning " give."

(*a.*)—*Miru* (literally, " to see ") denotes " try," " attempt," " to take a shot at," etc. *Itte mimashō ka?* " Shall I try to go? " *Nete mite mo neraremasen deshita,* " Though I tried to sleep I could not sleep." For the second and third persons the polite form *goran nasaru* is usually substituted. *Cf.* the English, " I'll *see* what I can do."

(*b.*)—*Kuru* (literally, " to come ") is often used where the English idiom would require " go and . . ." *Kippu wo katte kimasu,* " I shall go and buy the ticket." *Yonde kimashō ka?* " Shall I go and call him? " Occasionally *kuru* is placed after the word which it logically precedes, *e.g., omoshiroi koto wo itte kita.* Again, in addition to motion, it denotes the coming into existence. *Ame ga futte kimashita,* " It has begun to rain."

(*c.*)—*Oku* (literally, "to put") is used after the gerund to express the full and complete settling of the matter for the time being with a view to its future use. Generally it is employed only with transitive verbs, *e.g., kippu wo katte okimashita* " I've already bought my ticket "; *kangaete oite kudasai,* " please think it well over."

(*d.*)—*Shimau* (literally, " to finish ") following a gerund indicates the completion of an action, though sometimes it is merely emphatic. *Nete shimaimashita,* " At last he fell asleep " (after several restless hours). *Itte shimaimashita,* " He has gone away (and won't come back)." *Shimbun wo yonde shimatta ka?* " Have you finished reading the newspaper? "

(*e.*)—The verbs *yaru, kureru, ageru, kudasaru,* all mean " to give." The distinction between these words has already been examined.

These verbs are all very commonly employed, and the student should familiarize himself with their use. Two points especially deserve attention. One is that sometimes we find two such auxiliary verbs used together, the one affecting the other. The other is that such verbs are frequently employed in their original and literal sense, even when following the gerund at the end of a sentence.

Idiomatic Verbal Constructions

Although not very frequently used the following peculiar verbal paraphrases deserve attention.

(*a.*)—An emphatic form is obtained by means of the second base of any verb followed by *wa* and the positive or negative past, present or future of *suru.* In such instances *wa* is usually pronounced *ya.* This form expresses either partial concession or contradiction, and is equivalent to the English "I admit . . . but," "I *do* . . . but," etc. *e.g., Wakari wa shimasu ga yoku wakarimasen,* "I do understand but not very well." *Iki wa shimasen,* "I certainly shall not go."

(*b.*)—A paraphrase having a very similar meaning is the absolute gerund (page 60) followed by another verb, usually the verb "to be," *e.g., Nete wa orimasen ga utouto shite imasu,* "I am not sleeping, I am only dozing." *Iiye watakushi wa netcha inakatta.* "No, I was *not* sleeping."

(*c.*)—Still another way of expressing the same thing is by the use of *koto.* The negative form (*nai koto wa nai*) has already been explained, but the affirmative form should also be learned. This consists of two positives instead of two negatives, but does not differ in meaning, *e.g., aru koto wa aru* = *nai koto wa nai* = "there *are* some but . . ." The other two important uses of *koto,* the perfect (*e.g., itta koto ga aru ka?* = "have you ever gone?") and the potential (*yomu koto ga dekimasu ka?* = "can you read?") should not be forgotten. An equivalent of the second is found in *wake ni wa ikemasen, e.g., sō iu muri na koto wo shinjiru wake ni wa ikanai,* "I cannot believe such an unreasonable thing."

(*d.*)—A very complicated paraphrase consisting of the past plus *no* plus the negative present (of the same verb) plus *no de wa nai* is occasionally employed. It corresponds to our "not a little," "extremely," etc., *e.g., nodo ga kawaita no kawakanai no de wa nai,* "I am extremely thirsty" (more literally, "It was not a question of whether I was thirsty or not—I was without a doubt").

Various Idiomatic Phrases

Even after a very complete vocabulary has been acquired and the complicated rules of grammar mastered, the student of Japanese will constantly find himself in difficulty owing to the large number of idiomatic phrases which are so frequently employed, which cannot be parsed, analyzed, or in many cases even translated. It would be impossible in a work such as this to attempt to give a complete list, but the following are among the most important :—

o hayō gozaimasu	good morning.
konnichi wa	good day.
komban wa	good evening.
sayonara	good bye.
gomen kudasai	excuse me.
arigatō gozaimasu	thank you.
dō itashimashite	don't mention it.
chitto haiken . . .	please let me see it.
o yasumi nasai	good night.
kore de takusan	this is enough.
osaki ni	please go ahead of me, *or* excuse my going ahead of you.
makoto ni shibaraku . . .	it is a long time since we met.
memboku ga nai	I feel ashamed.

Japanese block print

Incense burning ritual

EXERCISES AND TRANSLATIONS

Exercises on Nouns

A.

1—*Kotoshi no atsusa wa nakanaka hidoi desu.* 2—*Hitogoroshi wa hidoi mon' desu.* 3—*Kono yu no atsusa wa nan do gurai desu ka?* 4—*San ju go do gurai desu.* 5—*Fuji san no takasa wa dono gurai desu ka?* 6—*Tashika ni zonjimasen ga tonikaku ichi man shaku ijō desu.* 7—*Tōkyō no Kandaku ni furu-honya ga ōi.* 8—*Eibun no hon mo aru shi muron Nihon bun no hon mo aru.* 9—*Kinjo ni shitateya ga gozaimasu ka?* 10—*Arimasu keredomo amari ii no wa arimasen.* 11—*Tanabe san no okusan wa kodomo ga dekimashita.* 12—*Otoko no ko desu ka onna no ko desu ka?* 13—*Otoko no ko desu.* 14—*Ouma wa memma (meuma) yori tsuyoi ga, memma no hō ga hayai.* 15—*Sono kuromegane wa nan no tame ni tsukaimasu ka?* 16—*Hōbō sagashite mo mitsukaremasen deshita.* 17—*Ano o kata no semmon wa bankoku kōhō desu.* 18—*Nambei no kuniguni ni wa jinkō ga sukenai.* 19—*Uekiya ga hasami de ki no eda wo kitte orimasu.* 20—*Itami wa doko desu.* 21—*Kono fujingata wa mada Nikkō ye irasshaimasen deshitarō.* 22—*Omaera wa sonna ni yakamashiku shite wa ikemasen.* 23—*Hanahada shitsurei desu ga, anata no shashin wo kudasaimasen ka?* 24—*Ima kita hito wa dare desu?* 25—*Nihon no tenugui wa hontō ni chiisō gozaimasu.* 26—*Nihonjin wa tebukuro wo tsukaimasu ka ?* 27—*Nihon no tabemono wa goku kantan desu.* 28—*Mono-oki ni wa nani ga haitte arimasu ka ?* 29—*Ironna furudogu ga arimasu.*

Translation

1—This year's heat is very dreadful. 2—Murder is a terrible thing. 3—What is the heat of this water ? 4—About thirty-five degrees (C.). 5—What is the height of Mount Fuji? 6—I don't know exactly, but in any case it is over ten thousand feet. 7—In the Kanda Ward of Tōkyō there are many secondhand book shops. 8—There are English books, and of course, there are Japanese books. 9—Is there a tailor in the neighborhood ? 10—There is, but not a very good one. 11—Mrs. Tanabe has given birth to a child. 12—Is it a boy or a girl ? 13—It is a boy. 14—A horse is stronger than a mare, but a mare is faster. 15—For what reason does one use black goggles ? 16—Although I looked everywhere I could not find it. 17—That man's speciality is International law. 18—In the countries of South America the population is small. 19—The gardener is cutting the branches of the tree with some scissors. 20—Where is the pain ? 21—I suppose that these ladies have not yet been to Nikko. 22—You all must not make such a racket. 23—It is extremely rude (of me to ask you) but won't you give me your photograph ? 24—Who is the man who came now ? 25—Japanese towels are really small. 26—Do Japanese people use gloves ? 27—Japanese food is extremely simple. 28—What is there in the store-house ? 29—There are various kinds of old utensils.

B.

1—*Teishaba ye yuku michi wa dochira desu ka?* 2—*Sakuragichō ni komeya ga arimasu.* 3—*Are wa Akasaka byōin desu ka?* 4—*Konaida Tōkyō ye itte shashinki wo kaimashita.* 5—*Ano kakemono wa zuibun kirei desu nē.* 6—*Nihon ni wa kwasan to jishin ga ōi.* 7—*Ō-bei ni wa jishin ga arimasu ka?* 8—*Anata no tonari wa dare desu ka?* 9—*Konogoro Kyōto kara kita hito desu.* 10—*Ano o kata no shokugyō wa nan desu?* 11—*Akindo de gozaimasu.* 12—*Are wa?* 13—*Bengoshi de gozaimasu.* 14—*Ano shitateya wa yasui keredomo heta desu.* 15—*Kippu wo katte kite kudasai.* 16—*Ōfuku desu ka, katamichi desu ka?* 17—*Ni tō no katamichi wo sammai kudasai.* 18—*Ano tegami wo mō kaita ka?* 19—*Iiye, fude mo jōbukuro mo nakatta.* 20—*Kinō Yamada san ga saishi wo tsurete katsudōsashin ye ikimashita.* 21—*Tanabe kwaisha wa kabushiki kwaisha desu ka, gōmei kwaisha desu ka?* 22—*Kabushiki kwaisha deshō.* 23—*Ano wakai otoko wa nakanaka gakusha ni naru mikomi desu. Dai Ichi Kōtōgakkō to Tōkyō no Teikoku Daigakkō wo sotsugyō shimashite kara Yōroppa ye itte kenkyū shimashita. Kaette kite kara Teidai no fuku-kyōju ni natte shimaimashita.* 24—*Doko de jōbukuro wo urimasu ka?* 25—"*Yokohama Specie Bank*" *wa Nihongo de nan to iimasu ka?* 26—*Yokohama Shōkin Ginkō to iimasu.* 27—*Anata wa Nihon ryōri ga suki desu ka?* 28—*Kirai demo nai ga betsu ni suki demo nai.* 29—*Shikwangata ga oide ni narimashita.* 30—*Yoku irasshaimashita.*

Translation

1—Which is the road which leads to the station? 2—In Sakuragicho there is a rice dealer. 3—Is that the Akasaka Hospital? 4—The other day I went to Tōkyō and bought a camera. 5—That *kakemono* is very beautiful isn't it? 6—In Japan there are many volcanoes and earthquakes. 7—Are there any earthquakes in Europe and America? 8—Who is your next door (neighbor)? 9—A man who has recently come from Kyōtō. 10—What is that gentleman's profession? 11—He is a merchant. 12—And that man . . . ? 13—A lawyer. 14—That tailor is cheap but unskillful. 15—Please go and buy a ticket. 16—A return ticket or a single ticket? 17—Three second class single tickets, please. 18—Have you written that letter yet? 19—No, I had neither writing brush nor envelopes. 20—Yesterday Mr. Yamada took his family to the cinematograph. 21—Is the Tanabe Company a Joint Stock Company or a Limited Liability Partnership? 22—It is probably a Joint Stock Company. 23—That young man has the prospect of becoming a great scholar. After he had graduated from the First Higher School and the Tōkyō Imperial University he went to Europe and studied. After his return he ended by becoming an Assistant Professor in the Imperial University. 24—Where do they sell envelopes? 25—In Japanese what do they say for "The Yokohama Specie Bank"? 26—They say "Yokohama Shōkin Ginkō." 27—Are you fond of Japanese food? 28—I don't dislike it but I am not particularly fond of it. 29—The officers have come. 30—Welcome.

Exercises on Pronouns

A.

1—*Kore wa watakushi ga chūmon shita no to chigaimasu.* 2—*Kimi wa doko ye yuku no?* 3—*Ueno kōen ye ikō to omotte orimasu.* 4—*Sore ja boku mo ikō.* 5—*Watakushi-domo no uchi ni tetsugaku wo kenkyū shitai mono mo gozai-*

masu. 6—*Omae wa nani wo shite orimasu ka?* 7—*Ya, washi no fuku ga kita.* 8—*Temae wa nani shite wa yō gozaimasu ka?* 9—*Are wa nan to iu o kata desu ka?* 10—*Boku mo chūgakusei desu.* 11—*Watakushi ga yonde shimattara sugu ni o kashi mōshimashō.* 12—*Ano hito wa jibun no uchi ye kaette shimatta.* 13—*Hitori de yukimashita ka?* 14—*Hitori de ugokimasu ka?* 15—*O taku wa doko desu ka?* 16—*O hima de gozaimasu ka?* 17—*O katte ni shi nasai.* 18—*Wagakuni ni sonna koto ga arimasen.* 19—*Kyō wa sensei ga gakkō ye irasshaimasen deshita.* 20—*Sore wa anata no jidōsha de gozaimasu ka?* 21—*Ima dare ka watakushi no tokoro ye tsutsumi wo motte kita ja nai ka?* 22—*Omae san no bōshi wa koko ni aru.* 23—*Kore wa Oishi sama de wa gozaimasumai ka?* 24—*O medetō gozaimasu.* 25—*Go zonji no tōri Nagaoka kun ga ototoi naku narimashita.* 26—*Hanahada o ki no doku san de gozaimasu.* 27—*Jiyū bōeki to hogozei no koto wa dō iu go setsu desu ka?* 28—*Gijido ye yuku no wa dono michi wo ittara yokarō.* 29—*Soko ni aru kutsu wa donata no de gozaimasu?*

Translation

1—This is not the one which I ordered. 2—Where is it that you are going? 3—I am thinking of going to Ueno Park. 4—Well then, I think that I'll go also. 5—There are some of us who would like to study philosophy. 6—What are you doing? 7—O, I say, my clothes have come. 8—What shall I do? 9—Who is that gentleman? 10—I am also a Middle School student. 11—When I have finished reading it I shall lend it to you immediately. 12—He has gone back to his own house. 13—Did you go alone? 14—Does it move by itself? 15—Where is your house? *or* Where do you live? 16—Are you free? = Are you busy? 17—Do as you please. 18—In our country there is no such thing. 19—Today our teacher did not come to school. 20—Is this your motor car? 21—Has not some one brought a parcel to my place? 22—Your hat is here. 23—Isn't this Mr. Oishi? 24—Congratulations. 25—As you know Mr. Nagaoka died the year before last. 26—I sympathize with you very greatly (literally, August spirit poison Mr.). 27—What do you think of Free Trade and Protection? 28—What is the best way to get to the Houses of the Diet? 29—Whose are the shoes which are over there?

B.

1—*Kimi no uchi no meshi-tsukai wa jōzu desu nē.* 2—*Iiye are wa inaka no mon' desu kara mada yaku ni tatanai.* 3—*Ano hitodachi wa doko ye ikimasu ka?* 4—*Kisama wa nan no yō da?* 5—*Kimi, kore kara doko ye yuku ka?* 6—*Kotoshi no fuyu no samusa wa nakanaka hidō gozaimasu.* 7—*Anata no dempō wa anata to chōdo onaji toki ni kimashita.* 8—*Kono koto wa dō iu wake desu ka?* 9—*Watanabe sensei to Hiroe sensei no oshiekata wa daibu chigaimasu.* 10—*Kō iu yō na hon wa Eikoku ni arimasen.* 11—*Dō iu shinamono wo go ran ni iremashō ka?* 12—*Kyō wa nan no o matsuri de gozaimasu?* 13—*Ano o kata wa doko no gakkō de oshiemasu ka?* 14—*Dare ka no kōmori kasa wo karite ikimashō.* 15—*Rusu chū donata ka mairimashita ka?* 16—*Iiye dare mo konakatta.* 17—*Shujin wa itsumo asa no rokuji ni okimasu.* 18—*Dochira no te ga itō gozaimasu?* 19—*Ryōhō tomo itai.* 20—*Nanji ni kitara yō gozaimasu ka?* 21—*Itsudemo ii n' desu.* 22—*Kono zasshi ni nanimo omoshiroi koto ga kaite arimasen.* 23—*Dare ka yonde kudasai.* 24—*Donata wo yobimashō?* 25—*Masao demo ii deshō.* 26—*Doko wo sagashite mo mitsukenakatta.* 27—*Mō sukoshi o sake wo sashi-agemashō.* 28—*Iiye, mo kekkō desu.* 29—*Kanji no uchi ni oboeyasui no mo arimasu shi, oboenikui no mo arimasu.* 30—*Dōmo mōshi-wake ga gozaimasen.*

Translation

1—Your servant is skillful, isn't he? 2—No, as he is a man from the country as yet he is worth nothing. 3—Where are those people going? 4—What is it that you want? 5—O, I say (literally, You!), where are you going? 6—This winter's cold (literally, The cold of the winter of this year) is exceptionally severe. 7—Your telegram came at the same time as yourself. 8—What is the meaning of this? 9—The manner of teaching of Mr. Watanabe and Mr. Hiroe is quite different. 10—In England there are no such books as this. 11—What sort of articles (goods) shall I show you? 12—What is the festival today? 13—In what school is that gentleman teaching? (literally, In the school of where?). 14—I'll borrow some one's umbrella and go. 15—While I was away did anyone come? 16—No, no one has come. 17—My husband always gets up at six o'clock. 18—Which hand hurts? 19—Both hurt. 20—What time had I better come? 21—Anytime will do. 22—In this magazine there is nothing interesting written. 23—Please call some one. 24—Whom shall I call? 25—Masao will do. 26—No matter where I looked I could not find it. 27—Can't I give you a little more *saké?* 28—No, I have had enough (literally, Already it is excellent). 29—Among the Chinese idiographs some are easy to remember, and some are difficult to remember. 30—Indeed I have no excuse (to offer).

Exercises on Numerals

A.

1—*Kono jūbako wa ikura desu ka?* 2—*Sore wa jū go yen de gozaimasu.* 3—*Sore nara mukō no chiisai no wa ikura?* 4—*Jū ichi yen desu.* 5—*Kyō wa nani yōbi desu?* 6—*Suiyōbi desu.* 7—*Nan nichi desu ka?* 8—*Kinō wa tōka datta kara kyō wa jū ichi nichi desu.* 9—*Matsumoto san no uchi wa doko ni arimasu ka? Azabu no ichibeichō ni arimasu.* 10—*Namban desu ka?* 11—*Jū ni banchi deshō.* 12—*Yūbinkyoku ye itte hagaki wo katte o kure.* 13—*Nammai kaimashō ka?* 14—*Go mai de ii deshō.* 15—*Tamago wa ikutsu arimasu ka?* 16—*Itsutsu arimasu.* 17—*Kore wa dono gurai shimasu ka?* 18—*Ichi yen ni jissen shimasu.* 19—*Mō sukoshi yasuku shite o kure.* 20—*Sore ja go sen makemasu.* 21—*Rondon ni wa jū ni kai no tatemono wa hotondo arimasen.* 22—*Anata wa namben Amerika ye itta ka?* 23—*Kondo wa sandome desu.* 24—*Ototo wa nikai ni imasu ka?* 25—*Iiye shita ni orimasu.* 26—*Nihon ni nan nen kan orimashita?* 27—*Go nen kan deshita.* 28—*A sō desu ka. Nihongo wa o jōzu de gozaimasu ne.* 29—*Iiye sukoshi mo.*

Translation

1—How much is this lacquer box? 2—That is fifteen yen. 3—Well then, how much is that small one over there? 4—Eleven yen. 5—What day of the week is today? 6—Wednesday. 7—What day of the month is it? 8—As yesterday was the tenth, today is the eleventh. 9—Where is Mr. Matsumoto's residence? It is in Azabu

(Ward). 10—What number? 11—It is No. 12 I think. 12—Go to the post office and buy some post cards. 13—How many shall I buy? 14—Five will probably be enough. 15—How many eggs are there? 16—There are five. 17—About how much does this cost? 18—One yen and twenty sen. 19—Won't you make it a little cheaper? 20—Well, I shall come down five sen (literally, defeat five sen). 21—In London there are almost no twelve story buildings. 22—How many times have you been to America? 23—This will be the third time. 24—Is my (or your) younger brother upstairs? 25—No, he is downstairs. 26—How many years were you in Japan? 27—I was there about five years. 28—O, indeed! Your Japanese is very fluent (skillful), isn't it? 29—Oh, not at all!

B.

1—*Empitsu ni hon to kami wo motte koi.* 2—*Kono daikon wa ikura?* 3—*Hitotsu jissen shimasu.* 4—*Watashi wa neko wo ippiki to inu wo ni hiki katte imasu.* 5—*Kumamoto kun wa kodomo ga arimasu ka?* 6—*Hai onna no ko ga futari, otoko no ko ga san nin arimasu.* 7—*Ano gakkō no seito wa nan nin hodo arimasu ka? Hyaku go jū mei arimasu.* 8—*Watakushi wa mainichi makitabako wo ni jippon nomimasu.* 9—*San sen no yūbin kitte ga go mai arimasu ka?* 10—*Tōyō Gakuin ni Nihongo wo keiko suru gakusei ga go jū nin orimasu.* 11—*Konogoro no bōfū de fune ga hyaku sō ijō nansen ni aimashita.* 12—*Senshū Nihon kara tegami ga san tsū kimashita.* 13—*Kono mura ni yadoya wa nangen aru ka? Ni ken bakari arimasu.* 14—*Tōbun no aida hima desu kara shōsetsu wo jissatsu katte yonde orimasu.* 15—*Ni mai zutsu yaru to tarimasen.* 16—*Waraji wa issoku ikura desu ka?* 17—*O cha wa mō ippai ikaga de gozaimasu?* 18—*Sakujitsu budōshu wo go hai nonda ga sukoshi mo yowanakatta.* 19—*Tabako wo ippuku meshi agarimasen ka?* 20—*Kore kara inaka ye ikō to omotte imasu kara nagagutsu wo sanzoku kaimashita.* 21—*Konaida no kwaji de ie ga ni san hyakken yakemashita.* 22—*Buritania hyakkwazensho wa ichi bu wa nanzatsu desu?* 23—*Jū ichi han de wa ni jū ku satsu desu.* 24—*Dai Ni Kōtōgakkō wa doko ni arimasu ka?* 25—*Takeo wa Makino san no sambamme no ko desu.* 26—*Kiyomizu shi no ushi wa nan tō arimasu ka?* 27—*Ni jittō arimasu.* 28—*Ashita no asa ichiban no kisha de Kyōto ye yuku no desu kara kanarazu hayaku okoshite kure.* 29—*Dōbutsuen ni shishi wa roppiki arimasu.*

Translation

1—Please bring two pencils and some paper. 2—How much is this radish? 3—One costs ten sen (more freely, they cost ten sen each). 4—I keep one cat and two dogs. 5—Has Mr. Kumamoto any children? 6—Yes, he has two girls and three boys. 7—How many pupils are there in that school? There are one hundred and fifty. 8—I smoke twenty cigarettes a day. 9—Have you five three sen stamps? 10—At the School of Oriental Studies there are fifty students who are studying Japanese. 11—In the recent typhoon over one hundred ships were shipwrecked (literally, Met to shipwreck). 12—Last week three letters came from Japan. 13—How many hotels are there in this village? 14—For the time being I am at leisure so I bought ten novels and am reading them. 15—There are not enough to give them two each. 16—How much is one pair of straw sandals? 17—What about one more cup of tea? 18—Yesterday I drank five glasses of wine but I did not get at all intoxicated. 19—Won't you smoke some tobacco? (literally, One whiff of tobacco?) 20—Soon (literally,

From now) I am thinking of going to the country so I bought three pairs of boots. 21—In the fire of the other day two or three hundred houses were burnt. 22—In one set of the *Encyclopædia Britannica* how many volumes are there? 23—In the eleventh edition there are twenty-nine volumes. 24—Where is the Third High School? 25—Takeo is Mr. Makino's third child. 26—How many cows has Mr. Kiyomizu? 27—He has twenty. 28—As I am going to Kyōtō by the first train tomorrow please be sure and call me early. 29—There are six lions in the Zoological Gardens.

Exercises on Postpositions

A.

1—*Ano hito wa yoku fune ni yoimasu.* 2—*Wareware wa asuko no mise de yasaimono wo kaimasu.* 3—*Kesa yo ji han ni okimashita.* 4—*Kore de tarimasu deshō ka?* 5—*Taiwan ni amari ka ga inakereba ii n' desu ga.* 6—*Nihon ni kiken na kwazan ga daibu arimasu.* 7—*Kono pan ni shio ga haitte iru ka?* 8—*Anata wa Ōshū de umaremashitarō.* 9—*Sekai de nan to iu shima ga ichiban ōkii darō?* 10—*Kono hako no naka ni ni jū yen satsu ga irete arimasu.* 11—*Kono shatsu ni botan ga hitotsu mo tsuite arimasen.* 12—*Hombako no ue ni nani ga oite aru ka?* 13—*Hanabi wo mi ni Sumida gawa ye ikō ja nai ka?* 14—*Kudanzaka no hō ye sampo shiyō ka?* 15—*Otōto wa go ji made hataraite imasu.* 16—*Koko kara Tsukiji made nan ri hodo arimasu ka?* 17—*Kore wa daiku ni koshiraesasemashita.* 18—*Tōkyō ni tsuitara denshin de shirasete kudasai.* 19—*Kono fude wo ippon kudasai.* 20—*Ore no uchi wa hakubutsukwan no soba ni oite arimasu.* 21—*Komban made ni jumbi ga dekimasu deshō?* 22—*Zōkin de o fuki nasai.* 23—*Yūbe tonari no musuko wo tsurete shibai ye ikimashita.* 24—*Kono tegami wa kitte nashi ni kimashita.* 25—*Kono hako wa kagi ga nakereba akeru koto ga dekimasen.* 26—*Hiru meshi wo tabezu ni Ōsaka ye itta.* 27—*Kono tsutsumi ni tegami ga tsuite konakatta ka?* 28—*Kono kwashi wa nan de dekimashita ka?* 29—*Kona to tamago to mizu de dekita mon' de gozaimasu.*

Translation

1—He always becomes sea-sick. 2—We buy our vegetables at that shop. 3—I got up at half past four this morning. 4—Will this be enough do you think? 5—I hope there are not too many mosquitoes in Formosa. 6—There are many dangerous volcanoes in Japan. 7—Is there any salt in this bread? 8—You were born in Europe, weren't you? 9—Which is the biggest island in the world, do you think? 10—There is a twenty yen note placed inside this box. 11—There is not even one button on this shirt. 12—What is that (placed) on top of the book case? 13—Let's go to the Sumida river to see the fire-works. 14—Suppose we take a walk towards Kudanzaka. 15—My younger brother works until five o'clock. 16—How many *ri* is it from here to Tsukiji? 17—I had the carpenter make this. 18—When you arrive in Tōkyō please inform me by telegraph. 19—Please give me one of these writing brushes. 20—My house is (placed) near the museum. 21—I suppose that we can make all preparations by tonight. 22—Please dust this with a rag. 23—Last night I went to the theater with my neighbor's son. 24—This letter came without a stamp. 25—You can't open this box without a key. 26—I went to Osaka without eating lunch. 27—

Didn't a letter come with this parcel? 28—With what was this cake made? 29—It is a thing made from flour eggs and water.

B.

1—*Ano seito wa Daigakkō ni hairu tame ni isshōkemmei hatarakimashita.* 2—*Nihonjin ni shite wa Eigo ga taihen jōzu ni dekimasu.* 3—*Kono hombako no kagi ga nai ka?* 4—*Kawa no mukō ni tatte iru hito wa dare desu ka?* 5—*Yaoya no mae ni yūbinbako ga arimasu.* 6—*Uma ni notte oru hito wa watakushi no ani da.* 7—*Jibun no uchi to gakkō no aida ni kwashiya ga gozaimasu.* 8—*Kyūka chū dochira ye irasshaimasu ka?* 9—*Nihon no seito wa Eigo no hoka ni gwaikokugo wo manabimasen ka?* 10—*Kore shika arimasen ka?* 11—*Kore kiri desu.* 12—*Keimburiji ye ikazu ni Okusuhorudo ye yukimashita.* 13—*O Yuki san no ningyō wa todana no ue ni arimasumai ka?* 14—*Norinaga san no katta ie wa doko ni arimasu ka?* 15—*Danna! Nihongo no sensei ga miemashita.* 16—*Sore wa Nihon no fūzoku ni kanaimasu ka?* 17—*Yasumi to iu ji wa nimben ni ki to iu ji wo kakimasu.* 18—*Indojin wa te de tabemasu.* 19—*Komban kyaku ni ikimasu kara embi fuku wo dashite kure.* 20—*Nihonjin wa tatami ni suwarimasu.* 21—*Yūbe wa samukatta kara kaze wo hiita.* 22—*Hito ni oshieru no wa jibun no keiko ni narimasu.* 23—*Fujimura san ni aimashita ka?* 24—*Kore wa nani ni shimasu ka?* 25—*Konaida gakkō no tomodachi to futari de yukimashita.* 26—*Ano hito wa gakusha demo nai ga kyōshi ni wa taihen ii n' desu.* 27—*Kono bunshō wo Nihongo ni honyaku shite kudasai.* 28—*Takakusu san wa Kodama san no kodomo wo yōshi ni moraimashita.* 29—*Kore wa tame ni naru hanashi ja nai.* 30—*Kodomo no byōki ga ki ni natte hitoban jū nerarenakatta.*

Translation

1—That student worked with might and main in order to enter the University. 2—For a Japanese he speaks English very skillfully. 3—Isn't there a key for this box? 4—Who is that standing on the other side of the river? 5—In front of the grocer's there is a post-box. 6—The man who is riding on the horse is my brother. 7—Between my house and the school there is a confectioner's. 8—Where are you going during the vacation? 9—Don't Japanese students learn any foreign language except English? 10—Isn't there anything except this? 11—There is only this. 12—I went to Oxford without going to Cambridge. 13—Isn't Miss Yuki's doll on the shelf? 14—Where is the house which Mr. Norinaga bought? 15—Master! Your Japanese teacher has come (literally, Has appeared). 16—Is this in accordance with Japanese custom? 17—The ideograph for *yasumi* (vacation) is written with the man radical (or, the radical for man) and the ideograph for tree. (The Chinese ideograph for "rest" is the picture of a man under a tree.) 18—Indians eat with their hands (*i.e.*, fingers). 19—As I am going out tonight (literally, as a guest) please put out my evening dress (literally, swallow tail clothes). 20—Japanese people sit on the *tatami* (straw mats). 21—As last night was cold, I caught a cold. 22—To teach other people is good practice for oneself (literally, Teach people one's own practice becomes). 23—Have you met Mr. Fujimura? 24—What do you do with this? 25—The other day my school friend and I, the two of us, went (more freely, I went with my school friend the other day). 26—He is not a scholar but as a teacher he is very good. 27—Please translate this sentence into Japanese. 28—Mr. Takakusu has adopted Mr. Yamad's child. 29—This is not a worth while conversation.

30—My child's illness got on my nerves so that I was not able to sleep all one night.

Exercises on Verbs

A.

1—*Watakushi wa Nihon no mono wo atsumetō gozaimasu.* 2—*Watashi wa Nihon no Kempō no koto wo tori-shirabetō gozaimasu ga tekitō no hon ga arimasumai ka?* 3—*Komban wa sashitsukai ga arimasen nara dōzo o ide nas'tte kudasai.* 4—*Ato kara kangaete miru to boku wa jitsu ni baka wo shimashita.* 5—*Kō shiyō ja nai ka?* 6—*Sonna ni yoku nakutemo yō gozaimasu.* 7—*O iriyō naraba dōzo o mochi nasai.* 8—*Sore wa arisō na koto desu.* 9—*Neta to itte mo necha inakatta.* 10—*Komban wa konai no desu ka?* 11—*Kusuri wo nomedo naoranai deshō.* 12—*Areba ii to omotte tazunemashita keredomo gozaimasen.* 13—*Senjitsu yuku hazu deshita ga ikimasenanda.* 14—*Ima wa yuki ga futte inai kara sugu ni ikimashō.* 15—*Inu ni kono niku wo tabesasete kudasai.* 16—*Ano hito wa dare ni demo homerarete orimasu.* 17—*Sō shite wa otōsan ni shikararemasu yo.* 18—*Watakushi wa sashimi wo taberaremasen.* 19—*Ano kodomo wa hitori de arukemasu ka? Arukemasu tomo.* 20—*Kono surippa wo kutsuya ni naosasete o kure.* 21—*Oi! Henji ga arimasu kara ano tsukai wo matashite oke.* 22—*Sumisu san ni Manyōshu wo yomasemashita.* 23—*O mae wa haori wo dare ni kashita no desu ka?* 24—*Ima kite oru hito wa nan to iimasu?* 25—*Dōmo ha ga itakute tatte mo suwatte mo oraremasen.* 26—*Kodomo wa nanatsu ni naru to gakkō ni hairu no desu.* 27—*Nimotsu no shitaku ga dekitara sassoku tachimasu.* 28—*Mō iriyō ga gozaimasen kara kaeshimasu.* 29—*Washi no itoko wa tadaima Yōroppa wo ryokō shite imasu.* 30—*Ima wa benkyō shitai kara damare.*

Translation

1—I wish to collect Japanese things (*i.e.*, curios, etc.). 2—As I wish to study the Japanese Constitution do you know of any suitable books ? (literally, Whereas I wish-to-investigate Japan's Constitution suitable books probably-aren't-there ?) 3—If you have no business tonight, please come (to my place). 4—When I come to think about it afterwards I really acted the fool. 5—Isn't one supposed to do it this way. 6—It need not be such a good one. 7—If you need it, please take it. 8—It seems probable that such is the case. 9—Even though you say I was sleeping, I was *not* asleep. 10—(Is it that) you are not coming tonight ? 11—Even though he takes medicine he probably won't recover. 12—I thought it would be good to have some so I enquired but there isn't any (literally, If there be is-good (I) thought (so) enquired but not-is). 13—I ought to have gone the other day but I did not go. 14—It is not snowing now, so let us go immediately. 15—Please feed the dog this meat. 16—That man is praised by everyone. 17—If you do that you will be scolded by father. 18—I cannot eat raw fish. 19—Can that child walk by himself? Of course he can. 20—Please have the bootman mend these slippers. 21—Hey there ! There is an answer so make the messenger wait. 22—I made Mr. Smith read the Manyoshu. 23—To whom did you lend your *haori* (cloak) ? 24—Who is that man who has just come called ? 25—My tooth is so painful that I can't stand or sit down. 26—When children are seven they go to school. 27—I shall leave as soon as my baggage is ready. 28—I do not need it any more so I shall return it. 29—My cousin is now touring in Europe. 30—As I wish to study now, be silent.

B.

1—*Anata wa Nihon ni o ide nasaimashita toki ni Nihongo ga o wakari ni narimasen deshitarō.* 2—*Hai sukoshi shika wakarananda.* 3—*Watakushi ga kita toki ni Yokoda san ga mō dekaketa.* 4—*Sukoshi matte o kure. Oku san wa mō jiki kaette kuru deshō.* 5—*Kyō wa sukoshi zutsū shite yasumu n' desu. Ashita kara benkyō suru tsumori desu.* 6—*Kyonen Taiwan ni ōki na bōfu ga atta sō desu.* 7—*Mainen Tōyō kara satō wo ōku yunyū shimasu ka?* 8—*Chinda san ga kaettara Beikoku ye taishi ni yarareru sō desu.* 9—*Entotsu ni tsuru ga su wo tsukutte imasu.* 10—*Kaku to ittaredo kakanandarō.* 11—*Kono yu wo samenai tokoro ni oite kudasai.* 12—*Kinjo ni kwaji ga areba dō shite mo neraremasen.* 13—*Ōki na koe de iimashita ga kikoemasen deshita.* 14—*Tarō wa mada konandarō.* 15—*Sonna nimotsu wo hiku koto no dekiru uma wa goku sukenō gozaimasu.* 16—*Chokusetsu ni Seiyō kara chūmon shita hō ga ii ka mo shiremasen.* 17—*Kinō o tegami ga kitara kyō ikimashitarō ga.* 18—*Otō san kara hima wo moratte Asakusa no hō ye asobi ni ikō.* 19—*Ano hito wa shijū ki ni iranai koto wo itte imasu.* 20—*Kore wo naku shi nai yō ni ki wo tsukete.* 21—*Sonna ni asa-ne wo shite wa ikemasen.* 22—*Kore wa o iriyo desu ka. Iiye irimasen.* 23—*Nodo ga kawakimashite mizu ga hoshii.* 24—*Mō matanakute mo ii n' desu yo.* 25—*Iku to iedomo nan no yō ni narimasu ka?* 26—*Mukashi Kyōto no Kamo-gawa wo fune de watatta ga ni jū nen mae kara rippa na hashi ga dekite arimasu.* 27—*Wakatte mo wakaranai kao wo shite imasu.* 28—*Kinō wa jitsu ni omoshirokatta. Jidōsha ni nottari shibai wo mitari go chisō wo tabetari shite orimashita.*

Translation

1—When you came to Japan I suppose that you did not know Japanese? 2—Yes, I knew only a little. (Note the fact that the Japanese say "yes" where we would say "no," after negative questions.) 3—When I came Mr. Yokoda was already leaving. 4—Please wait a little. 5—As I have a slight headache today I am taking a vacation. I intend to study from tomorrow. 6—It seems that there was a great typhoon in Taiwan last year. 7—Every year do they import much sugar from the Orient? 8—They say that when Mr. Chinda comes back he will be sent as Ambassador to the United States. 9—The cranes are building a nest in the chimney. 10—Though he said he would write I should imagine that he did not write. 11—Please put the hot water in a place when it won't cool. 12—If there is a fire in the neighborhood I cannot possibly sleep. 13—He spoke in a loud voice but I could not hear him. 14—Tarō has not come yet, has he? 15—There are very few horses which can pull such luggage. 16—Perhaps it would be better to order direct from the Occident. 17—If I had received your letter yesterday I should probably have gone. 18—Let's get father to let us off (literally, Let's receive leisure from father) and go to amuse ourselves in the direction of Asakusa. 19—That man is always saying disagreeable things. 20—Be careful not to lose this. 21—You must not sleep so late in the morning. 22—Do you need this? No, I do not need it. 23—My throat has become very dry (*i.e.*, I am thirsty) and I want some water. 24—You need not wait any longer. 25—Even if you go of what use will it be? 26—Previously (literally, Anciently) one crossed the Kamo River in Kyōtō by boat, but about twenty years ago a splendid bridge was built. 27—Though he knows he pretends that he does not know (literally, He makes a do-not-know face). 28—Yesterday I really had a fine time, riding in motors, seeing plays, and eating feasts (I was doing).

Exercises on Adjectives

A.

1—*Kono hon wa wakari-nikukute mo omoshirō gozaimasu.* 2—*Sono ki wa hoso-nagakute kirei de gozaimasu.* 3—*Konna benri no yoi tsukue wa mezurashū gozaimasu.* 4—*Kono heya wa mado ga sukunakute hon ga yomi-nikui desu.* 5—*Matsumoto kun wa genki no ii hito desu kara taihen ki ni irimasu.* 6—*Sore wa zōsa mo nai mon' desu kara kanarazu dekimasu.* 7—*Are wa amari shōjiki de nai hito desu.* 8—*Hito wa aji no nai mono wo taberu no wa kirai desu.* 9—*Yūbe no sekkyō wa yokatta ka?* 10—*E. Taihen yō gozaimashita.* 11—*Konaida no ban wa samukattarō?* 12—*Samukattara naze futon wo tori ni konakatta ka?* 13—*Konogoro dekita Ei-wa jibiki ga nai no desu ka?* 14—*Wa-ei no jibiki ga takusan arimasu shikashi Ei-wa no ga tonto arimasen.* 15—*Ittemo yokarō.* 16—*Tōfu wa yosasō na mono desu ga mada tabeta koto ga arimasen.* 17—*Sonna bakarashii koto wo iu na.* 18—*Fukuzawa shi wa yohodo yūmei na gakusha datta.* 19—*Kesa tabeta mono wa karakatta kara nodo ga kawaite kimashita.* 20—*Sore wa dekiru koto dewa gozaimasen.* 21—*Yaseta hito ga hayaku arukemasu.* 22—*Kido to Ōkubo wa taihen jimbō no aru hito deshita.* 23—*Kyonen iroiro no o sewa ni narimashita. Kotoshi mo aikawarazu ni negaimasu.* 24—*Ano hito wa shirōto de nakute nakanaka nareta mono desu.* 25—*Sake wa doku ni naru mon' ka, kusuri ni naru mon' ka dochira deshō?* 26—*Omae no jiji wa taisō futotta hito desu nē.* 27—*Sō de gozaimasu. Moto wa sō dewa nakatta ga konogoro daibun futotte kimashita.* 28—*Nikai no heya ga aite imasu ka?* 29—*Tanaka san wa itsudemo yomenai ji wo kakimasu.* 30—*Sore wa totemo shinjirarenu koto desu.*

Translation

1—Even though this book is difficult to understand it is interesting. 2—That tree is so slender that it is beautiful. 3—Such convenient desks are rare. 4—As there are so few windows in this room, the books are difficult to read. 5—Mr. Matsumoto is a lively person, so I like him very much. 6—That is not at all a difficult thing, so I can certainly do it. 7—He is a not too honest person. 8—People do not like to eat tasteless things. 9—Was last night's sermon good? 10—Yes, it was very good. 11—You were very cold the other night, weren't you? 12—If you were cold why did you not come and get some comforters? 13—Are there not any recently published English-Japanese Dictionaries? 14—There are plenty of Japanese-English Dictionaries but almost no English-Japanese ones. 15—I think it will be alright for you to go. 16—*Tofu* (bean curd) is a tasty-looking thing, but I have never eaten any. 17—Don't say such foolish things. 18—Mr. Fukuzawa was a very famous scholar. 19—As the things which I ate this morning were acrid I have become thirsty. 20—That is impossible (literally, That is not a possible thing). 21—Thin people can walk fast. 22—Kido and Okubo were very popular people. 23—Last year I was much indebted to you (literally, Various assistance became). This year also I hope our relations may go on without change (literally, Without changing I beg). (This is the usual greeting amongst friends at New Year.) 24—That person, far from being an amateur, is a very

Wish tree-heian, Jingu shrine

Rice planting

experienced man. 25—Do you think that *saké* (in this case equivalent to any form of alchoholic beverages) is injurious or beneficial? 26—Your grandfather is a very fat man, isn't he? 27—Yes. It was not so originally but recently he has become very stout. 28—Is the room upstairs empty? 29—Mr. Tanaka always writes illegible letters. 30—That is a quite incredible thing.

B.

1—*Chiisai no ga nakereba ōkii no wo kaimashō.* 2—*Chōsen wa wariai ni yama no ōi kuni desu kara jinkō ga sukunai.* 3—*Kore wa atarimae no fuku desu ka?* 4—*Soko no hon wa hijō ni furui sō desu.* 5—*Kore wa umitate no tamago desu ka?* 6—*Hito ga kusuri wo nomu to iya na kao shimasu.* 7—*Are wa gakusha da to iimasu ga hontō wa monozuki na hito desu.* 8—*Kono shigoto wa nakanaka mendokusai desu.* 9—*Nihon wa ki no ōi kuni desu ga Nihon no ki wa mina chiisai n' desu.* 10—*Sono sakaya no kami san wa seji ga ii nē.* 11—*O ko san wa jitsu ni benkyō suru kodomo desu.* 12—*Iiye, segare wa namake mon' desu.* 13—*Sore wa subeki koto desu ga, dekiru ka dō ka shiran.* 14—*Hajimete shinsetsu ja nai to omotta ga yahari taisō shinsetsu na hito desu.* 15—*O isha san wa kono byōki ga sō omoku nai to iimashita.* 16—*Kono bin wa aite imasu ka?* 17—*Kono ahiru wa makoto ni yasete imasu.* 18—*Sono gasu wo motto ōkiku shite o kure.* 19—*Gasu wo chiisaku shite mo ii ga keshitara ikemasen.* 20—*Dōmo kyō wa isogashikute totemo koraremasen.* 21—*Kojiki to Nihongi wa Nihon no ichiban furui rekishi desu.* 22—*Fuji san wa Nihon no ichiban ōkii yama desu ga Taiwan no Niitaka yama hodo takaku nai.* 23—*Ginza wa Tōkyō no mottomo nigiyaka na michi desu.* 24—*Sore wa dekinai koto wa nai desu ga mutsukashii no desu.* 25—*Kono tabako wa amari kitsukute nomaremasen.* 26—*Nihon ni wa Kirisutokyō no shinja yori Bukkyō shinja no hō ga ōi.* 27—*Tanaka san no hidari ni suwatte iru hito wa dare da?* 28—*Aitsu wa okorippoi no de iya desu.* 29—*Narutake hayaku motte koi.* 30—*Konaida itta hon wo kashite kuremasu ka?*

Translation

1—If you have not got a small one I shall buy a large one. 2—As Korea is comparatively mountainous the population is small. 3—Are these the usual clothes? 4—They say that that book over there is very old. 5—Are these fresh eggs? 6—When they drink medicine people make a wry (literally, bad) face. 7—They call him a scholar, but he is really a dilletante. 8—This affair is really very troublesome. 9—Japan is a well treed country but the Japanese trees are all small. 10—The mistress of that wine-shop has ingratiating manners. 11—Your child is indeed a very diligent child. 12—Oh, no! he is a loafer. 13—That is a thing which ought to be done, but how can it be done, I wonder (literally, How can do I don't know). 14—At first I thought he was not kind, but after all he is a very kind man. 15—The doctor said that this illness is not very severe. 16—Is this bottle empty? 17—This duck is really thin. 18—Please turn the gas up (literally, Make big the gas). 19—You may turn the gas down, but don't turn it out. 20—Really I am so busy that I shall be unable to come. 21—The *Kojiki* and the *Nihongi* are Japan's oldest histories. 22—Mount Fuji is Japan's highest mountain but it is not so high as Mount Niitaka (Morrison) in Taiwan. 23—Ginza is Tōkyō's busiest street. 24—It is not an impossible thing, but it will be difficult. 25—This tobacco is so strong that I can't smoke it. 26—In Japan Buddhists are more numerous than Christians. 27—Who is the man who is sitting on Mr. Tanaka's left? 28—That fellow is so bad tempered I dislike him. 29—Bring it as soon as possible. 30—Will you kindly lend me the book you spoke of the other day?

Exercises on Adverbs

A.

1—*Kono honyaku wa umaku dekimashita.* 2—*Daigakkō ni haitte kara tabitabi jū ni ji made okite imasu ga yoku asa-ne shimasu.* 3—*Hajimete Nihongo wo naratta toki ni mutsukashikatta ga konogoro dandan yasuku natte kimashita.* 4—*Ōki ni arigatō gozaimasu.* 5—*Kore kara chokusetsu ni gakkō ye ikimasu ka?* 6—*Watakushi wa metta ni Ōsaka ye ikan.* 7—*Kore wa koto ni mutsukashii hon desu.* 8—*Jiki ni mairimasu.* 9—*Watakushi wa tama ni yose ye yukimasu keredomo amari suki dewa gozaimasen.* 10—*Ano koto wo kiite bikkuri shimashita.* 11—*Fuji san ni nobottara sazo tōku made miemashō.* 12—*Eikokujin wa subete jiyū ga suki desu.* 13—*Boku wa hisashiku mairimasen kara michi ga wakaranai ka mo shiremasen.* 14—*Konnichi wa dōshite konna ni nigiyaka deshō ka?* 15—*Kutabiremashita kara yukkuri mairimashō.* 16—*Ano hito wa ureshii n'de maru de kichigai no yō ni shite imashita.* 17—*Fujimura san wa goku teinei ni shite kuremashita.* 18—*Kore wa makoto ni rippa na tera desu ne.* 19—*Jochū wa amari rikō ja nai kara, hakkiri setsumei sen to wakarimasen.* 20—*Mizuguruma wa guruguru mawatte imasu.* 21—*Tarō wa omoshiroi hon wo yonde nikoniko shite orimasu.* 22—*Kaminari wa narazu ni inabikari dake pikapika shimasu.* 23—*Shōshō o machi nasai.* 24—*Ozei no hito ga achikochi yuku niwa gatagata itte imasu.* 25—*Koko wa Saigo san no jisatsu shita tokoro desu.* 26—*Kitanai tokoro desu ga dōzo kochira ye.* 27—*Ima wa chōdo shōgo desu.*

Translation

1—This translation was done very well. 2—Since I entered the University I am frequently up until twelve o'clock, but I often sleep in the morning. 3—When I first studied Japanese it was very difficult, but recently it has become gradually more easy. 4—Thank you very much. 5—From here (literally, From this) are you going directly to school? 6—I very seldom go to Osaka. 7—This is an especially difficult book. 8—I am coming immediately. 9—I occasionally go to a music hall but I am not very fond of it. 10—When I heard about that thing I was greatly surprised. 11—If one were to ascend Mount Fuji one could see for a very great distance. 12—Englishmen all like liberty. 13—As I have not been for a long time I am not sure but that I do not know the way. 14—Why do you suppose the streets are so bustling today? 15—As I am tired let us go slowly. 16—He was so happy that he behaved entirely like a maniac. 17—Mr. Fujimura kindly acted very politely. 18—This is really a splendid temple, isn't it? 19—As the maid is not very clever unless you explain very clearly she won't understand. 20—The water wheel revolves round and round. 21—Tarō is reading an interesting and amusing book and keeps grinning to himself. 22—The thunder does not strike (*i.e.*, there is no thunder) but the lightning comes flickering. 23—Please wait a little. 24—The going of many people to and fro makes much clattering. 25—This is the place where Saigo committed suicide. 26—This is a dirty place but please hitherwards . . . (said on inviting a guest into one's home). 27—Now it is exactly noon.

B.

1—*Kinō o kai nas'tta hon wa doko ni gozaimasu ka?* 2—*Kore wa zutto mae kara wakatte ita.* 3—*Asuko de koshiraete iru mono wa nan desu ka?* 4—*Koko wa fune ni noru tokoro desu ka?* 5—*Moto kara Eikokujin ga fune wo jōzu ni tsukurimashita.* 6—*Ano hito wa itsudemo hon wo yonde imasu.* 7—*Tarō wa shijū itazura wo shite komarimasu.* 8—*Taitei koko ni kuru hito wa Amerikajin desu.* 9—*Ima demo oriori kurabu ye yukimasu ka?* 10—*Anata wa metta ni kaze wo hikanai yō desu ne.* 11—*Ima made wasure te imashita ga hyotto omoi-dashimashita.* 12—*Watakushi wa kesshite ittō no kisha ni noranai.* 13—*Dōzo mō ichido oide kudasaimase.* 14—*Sore ja mata mairimasu.* 15—*Sore ga sundara nikai ni oide.* 16—*Kane ga naru to kisha ga demasu.* 17—*Hirumeshi wo taberu aida ni tokusho shimasu ka?* 18—*Aruki nagara hanashimashō.* 19—*Kinō honya ye itte mitara iroiro na Eibun no furuhon ga arimashita. Shikashi mō urete shimaimashita deshō.* 20—*Moto wa Nihon ni jidōsha to iu mono ga nakatta.* 21—*Kinjitsu ni Hokkaidō ye itte mitai desu.* 22—*Kono tsutsumi wo sassoku okutte agemasu.* 23—*Shibaraku Nihon ni o ide desu ka?* 24—*Yatto sukoshi zutsu wakaru yō ni natta.* 25—*Mō sukoshi de san ji ni narimasu.* 26—*Kore wa zehi shinakereba naran mon' desu.* 27—*Bonyari shitara ikemasen yō.* 28—*Ame ga barabara futte kimashita.*

Translation

1—Where is the book which you bought yesterday? 2—I have known this for a long time. 3—What is that thing which they are making over there? 4—Is this the place where one gets on the boat? 5—

From the beginning the English have constructed ships skillfully. 6—That man is always reading books. 7—Tarō is always getting into mischief (literally, Doing mischief) so that I am perplexed. 8—For the most part the people who come here are Americans. 9—Even now do you occasionally go to the club ? 10—It seems that you very seldom catch cold. 11—I forgot it until now and then suddenly recollected it. 12—I never ride in a first class carriage. 13—Please come again (literally, once more). 14—Well then, I shall come again. 15—When you have finished that please come up stairs. 16—When the bell strikes the train leaves. 17—Do you read while you are eating lunch ? 18—Let us talk as we walk. 19—Yesterday when I went to see the book-shops there were many old English books, but I suppose that they are already sold out. 20—Originally there were no motor cars in Japan. 21—In the near future I want to go and see Hokkaido. 22—I shall send this parcel (on to you) immediately. 23—Are you going to be in Japan for some time ? 24—At last I came to understand it little by little. 25—It is nearly three o'clock. 26—This is a thing which must be done without fail. 27—You must look lively, mind ! 28—The rain has come falling plop-plop.

Miscellaneous Exercises

A.

1—*Oya ! Boku no bōshi wa dō natta deshō nē.* 2—*Aita ! Kono tetsubin wa atsui desu.* 3—*Senjitsu Kuwahara san ni aimaishitara chikai uchi ni kuru to iimashita.* 4—

Dōzo nanibuno kokoro yasuku negaimasu. 5—*Tanabe san ga kuru to ii n' desu ga . . .* 6—*Shimbun ni yoreba Beikoku no Daitōryō wa taihen na byōki ni narimashita.* 7—*A sō desu ka? Nan no go byōki de gozaimashō?* 8—*O mae wa byōki deshitara o isha san ni mite morau hō ga ii ja nai ka?* 9—*Anata! Sumida san ga o ide ni narimashita.* 10—*Sore ja kochira ni o tōshi nasai.* 11—*Ya! Konnichi wa. Yoku irasshaimashita. Dōzo go enryo sezu ni o kake nasaimase.* 12—*Nani mo gozaimasen ga mā—dōzo o agari nasai.* 13—*Kyō wa o atsū gozaimasu.* 14—*Itsu kara o kaeri desu ka?* 15—*Kesa kaetta bakari de gozaimasu.* 16—*Naruhodo. Sore de wa zuibun o tsukare de gozaimashō.* 17—*Kyō wa go isshō ni Ueno kōen ye ikō to omoimashita ga . . . ikaga de gozaimasu?* 18—*Kyō wa totemo ike wa shimasen ga ashita o ide kudasattara o tomo wo itashimasu.* 19—*Shōchi itashimashita Sore ja asu no san ji goro mairimasu.* 20—*Mō sukoshi o machi kudasaimasen ka?* 21—*Arigatō gozaimasu. Ima wa sukoshi yō ga gozaimasu kara o itoma wo itashimashō.* 22—*A sō de gozaimasu ka? O mae! O kyaku wa o kaeri desu yo.* 23—*Ano hito no iu koto wa mina uso desu.* 24—*Hitori de bonyari shite orimashita kara nemuku narimashita.* 25—*Kitto kuru yō ni itte o kure.* 26—*Konna hombako wa doko de kaemasu ka?* 27—*Nannen hodo keiko shitara Nihon no hanashi ga dekiru yō ni narimasu ka?* 28—*Kondate wa omahen ka?* (*Omahen* is the Osaka dialect for *arimasen.*) 29—*Taihen ase ni natta kara kimono wo sukkari ki-kaemasho.* 30—*Ryokōken wo misete kudasai.*

Translation

1—Oh, I say! What do you think can have become of my hat? 2—Ouch! This teapot is hot. 3—The other day I met Mr. Kuwahara, and he said that he would come in the near future. 4—Please I beg a little familiarity (said on meeting a person for the first time). 5—I hope that

Mr. Tanabe will come. 6—According to the newspapers the American President has become very ill. 7—Oh, indeed! What sort of an illness is it, I wonder? 8—If you are ill wouldn't it be better to see a doctor? 9—You! (This is the polite way in which a wife calls to her husband.) Mr. Sumida has come (for a visit). 10—Well then, please escort him in (to the drawing room). 11—Well, well! You are welcome. Please sit down (and make yourself at home) without standing on ceremony. 12—(Offering cakes, the host says) Really there is nothing . . . but please eat (this). 13—Today is hot. 14—When did you return? 15—I came back only this morning. 16—Really? Then you must be very tired. 17—I thought that we might go to Ueno park together today. How about it? 18—Today I simply *can't* go, but if you kindly come tomorrow I shall accompany you. 19—Right O! Well then, I shall come about three o'clock tomorrow. 20—Won't you wait a little longer? 21—Thank you. As I have a little business, I am afraid I must be going. 22—Is that so? O you [calling to wife] the guest is returning. 23—Everything that man says is a lie. 24—I was fooling along doing nothing so I became sleepy. 25—Please tell him to be certain and come. 26—Where can one buy such a bookcase? 27—How many years will it take me to be able to speak Japanese? 28—Haven't you got the bill of fare? 29—I have perspired a great deal so I shall completely change my clothes. 30—Please show me your passport.

B.

1—*Are wa nan to itte iru ka?* 2—*Sore wo ano hito ni itcha ikemasen.* 3—*Dō shita no desu?* 4—*Sono imi wa nan de gozaimasu?* 5—*Omae wa motto toshi wo totte iru to omotta.* 6—*Ano o kata no okkasan wa chikagoro taihen toshi wo totta yō da.* 7—*Ame ga potsupotsu futte kimashita.* 8—*Ima wa hokori ga hidoku tatte kimashita.* 9—*Watakushi no kuru made o machi nasai.* 10—*Budōshu wo ippai ikaga de gozaimasu?* 11—*Iu koto ga aru kara kochira ni o ide.* 12—*Washi wa muika bakari mae ni ni ju ni sai ni natta.* 13—*Kyō wa tenki darō.* 14—*Mada san ji han ni nari-masumai.* 15—*Itsu kaeru ka? shitteru ka?* 16—*Anata no uchi ye yuku tokoro desu.* 17—*Uchi ye kaeru tokoro desu.* 18—*Watakushi ni nan no go yō desu ka?* 19—*Nan no wake de sō itta deshō ka nē.* 20—*Donata wo o tazune nasaru no desu ka?* 21—*O mae wa machigatte iru.* 22—*Sōridaijin ga shinda to kiita ga hontō deshō ka?* 23—*Sonna ni hayaku itte wa ikemasen.* 24—*Ano kata wa nani wo nasaru hito desu?* 25—*Are wa betsu ni shokugyō ga arimasen.* 26—*Nodo ga kawaite shiyō ga nai.* 27—*Isshō ni o ide nasaimasu ka?* 28—*Aru hito ga sō itta.* 29—*Tenki nara Utsuki san ga kuru yō ni yakusoku shita.* 30—*Yūshoku ni wa nani ga ii deshō ka?*

Translation

1—What is he saying? 2—You must not tell him that. 3—What has happened? 4—What is the meaning of this? 5—I thought you were older. 6—His mother seems to have aged recently. 7—It is begun to sprinkle (literally, Rain has come to fall *potsupotsu*). 8—It has become very dusty (literally, Dust has come to stand). 9—Please wait until I come (more literally, Please wait my arrival). 10—Won't you have a glass of wine? 11—As I have something to say, come here. 12—About six days ago I became twenty-two (years). 13—I think we are going to have a fine day. 14—It is not half-past three yet, is it? 15—Do you know when he will come back? 16—I was on my way to your house. 17—I am going home. 18—What is it that you want with me? 19—What made him say so,

I wonder? (literally, What reason was it . . .?) 20—Whom are you seeking? 21—You are mistaken (or making a mistake). 22—I heard that the Prime Minister is dead. Do you suppose that is true? 23—You must not go so fast. 24—What does this man do? 25—He has no especial occupation. 26—I am dreadfully thirsty. 27—Will you come with me? 28—Someone told me so. 29—Mr. Utsuki promised to come if the weather were fine. 30—What would you like for supper?

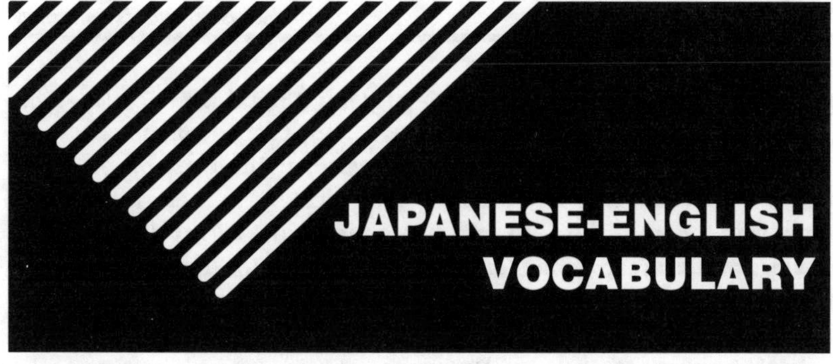

JAPANESE-ENGLISH VOCABULARY

A few words have been included which do not occur in the exercises, but which are sufficiently common and important to require memorization. Short *i* and *u* have been indicated thus:—*hĭto, desŭ.*

A

aa ! or **ā !** ah !

ā, like that, in that way : *ā iu,* that kind of, such as that.

abunai, dangerous.

abura, a general name for all oil, grease, and fat.

achi or **achira,** there.

agari, ascent, produce.

agaru, to rise ; to get clear (said of the weather) ; also to take, to eat or drink (honor).

ageru, to raise, hence to give to a superior.

ahiru, a tame duck.

ai, (properly *ayu*) a kind of trout.

aida, an interval, time, while.

ai-kawarazu, without change, the same as heretofore.

aikokŭshin, patriotism.

aisatsu, salutation, acknowledgment, response, answer; *aisatsu suru,* to salute, etc.

aisuru, to love.

aita ! or **aitata !** oh ! how painful.

aji, taste, flavor.

akagane, copper.

akai, red, brown.

akambō, a baby.

akami, a tinge of red.

akari, a light.

akarui, light (not dark).

akeru, to open (trans.) ; to begin (intrans.).

aki, autumn.

akinai, trade, commerce.

akinau, to trade.

akindo, a merchant, a dealer.

akiraka (na), clear, evident.

akkō, bad or scurrilous language, abuse.

aku, evil, vice.

aku, to open (intrans.), to become vacant : *aite iru,* to be open, to be unoccupied, not used.

ama, a (Buddhist) nun.

amai, sweet.

amami, a tinge of sweetness.

amari, too much, too ; (with a negative) not very.

amuru, to exceed.

ambai, way, manner, bodily feelings: *ambai ga Warui,* I feel unwell; *dō iu ambai?* how? *yoi ambai ni,* fortunately.

ame, rain: *ame ga furu,* to rain; *ame ni naru,* to come on to rain.

Amerika, America, the United States: *America-jin,* an American; *Amerika no,* American.

amma, a shampooer.

ana, a hole, a cave, a tunnel.

anata, you.

ane, an elder sister.

ani, an elder brother.

anjiru, to be anxious.

anna, that kind of, such as that.

annai, guidance, knowing one's way about, a guide: *annai suru,* to guide.

ano, that (adj.): *ano hĭto,* he, she.

anshin, mental ease: *anshin suru,* to feel at ease.

aoi, green, blue.

ara! An interjection.

arai, rough.

arare, hail.

arashi, a storm, a typhoon.

arasoi, a dispute.

arasou, to dispute.

aratamaru, to be renewed, overhauled, altered, rectified.

aratameru, to renew, overhaul, alter, rectify.

arau, to wash.

are, that (subst.); *are hodo,* as much as that; *are kara,* after that.

ari, an ant.

arigatai, thankful: *arigatō (gozaimasŭ),* thank you.

arimasŭ, polite form of *aru.*

aru, (irreg.) to be. Sometimes *aru* means a certain, some, as in *aru toki,* on a certain occasion, sometimes.

aruku, to walk.

asa, the morning: *asa-gao,* the morning glory, or convolvulus; *asa-han,* breakfast; *asa-ne,* morning sleep, late sleeping.

asatte, the day after tomorrow.

ase, perspiration: *ase ga deru,* to perspire; *ase ni naru,* to get into a perspiration.

ashi, the foot, the leg: *ashi no yubi,* the toes.

ashĭta, tomorrow; *ashĭta no asa,* tomorrow morning.

asobasu, an honorific equivalent of the verb *suru,* to do.

asobi, a game.

asobu, to play, to amuse oneself.

asŭko, there: *asŭko kara,* thence; *asŭko ye,* thither.

asŭkoera, thereabouts.

atama, the head.

atarashii, new.

atari, neighborhood, hence near, on or about.

atarimae, ordinary, generally: *atarimae no,* usual, natural, proper.

ataru, to hit the mark, also to be near, as *hi ni ataru,* to sit near the fire: *ni atatte,* just at; *dochira ni atatte?* where?

atatameru, to warm.

ate, reliance: *ate ni naru,* to be reliable; *ate ni suru,* to rely on.

ateru, to apply one thing to, or use it for, another; to hit.

ato, traces, effects, a sign, behind, afterwards, the rest: *ato de,* afterwards; *ato no,* the remaining, other; *ato-saki,* the context, circumstances.

atsui, hot.

atsui, thick.

atsusa, heat, the degree of heat.

atsusa, thickness, the degree of thickness.

atsumaru, to collect (intrans.).

atsumeru, to collect (trans.).

atsuraeru, to order (*e.g.*, things at a shop).

au, to meet, to agree, to suit: *ame ni au,* to get rained upon.

awa, millet.

ayamatsu, to make a mistake.

ayu, a species of trout.

azana, a nickname.

B

ba, a place:—used only in composition, as *furo-ba,* a bath-place.

babā, an old woman (rude).

bai, double; see page 102.

baka, a fool: *baka na,* or *baka-rashii,* foolish; *hito wo baka ni suru,* to make a fool of a person.

bakari, about, more or less (bookish); only.

bambutsu, all things, nature.

bamme, a word used to form ordinal numbers.

bam-meshi, supper, (late) dinner.

ban, a myriad, ten thousand; also used as a pluralizing prefix, as *ban-ji,* all things.

ban, a night, an evening.

ban, number (so-and-so); see page 98.

banchi, the number (of a house in a street).

banji, all things, everything.

bankoku, all countries, international: *bankoku kōhō,* international law.

bantō, a head clerk or manager.

bara, a thorny bush, hence a rose-bush.

bara-bara, helter-skelter.

basha, a carriage.

bassuru, to punish.

Beikoku, America, the United States.

bengōshi, lawyer.

benkō, eloquence: *benkō no yoi,* eloquent, glib.

benkyō, diligence.

benri, convenience: *benri no yoi* or *benri* (*na*), convenient; *benri no warui,* inconvenient.

bentō, food carried with one, *e.g.*, luncheon for a picnic.

beppin, a superior article, a pretty girl.

berabō(-me), a scoundrel.

betsu, a difference; *betsu ni,* differently, specially; *betsu no,* different, other.

betsudan (no), special.
bettō, a groom.
biiru, beer (from English).
bijin, a belle.
bijutsu, the fine arts.
bimbō, poverty : *bimbō na,* poor.
bin, a bottle.
bōeki, trade.
bōenkyō, a telescope.
bōfū, typhoon.
boku, a servant, (hence) I.
bon, a tray.
bon-yari, an onomatope for obscurity, tedium, dullness: *bon-yari suru,* to feel dull or dazed.
bōsan, a Buddhist priest.
bōshi, a hat.
botan, a button (from English).
botchan, a little boy.
boy, a house-servant, a valet (from English).
bōzu, a Buddhist priest (rude).
bu, a copy of a book.
budō, grapes : *budō-shu,* wine.
buji, no accident, safe and sound.
Bukkyō, Buddhism.
bummei, enlightenment, civilization : *bummei na,* civilized, cultured.
bumpō, grammar.
bun, a part.
bunshō, sentence.
bura-bura, in a sauntering manner.
burei, rudeness : *burei na,* rude ; *go burei.*
busata, failure to give notice, remissness in paying a visit.
bushi, a warrior.
buta, a pig.
butsu, to beat, to strike : *buchi-korosu,* to beat to death ; *buchi-taosu,* to knock down.
byōin, a hospital.
byōki, a disease : *byōki (na),* ill, sick.
byōnin, an invalid, a patient.

C

cha, tea ; *cha-nomi-jawan,* a tea-cup ; *cha-ya,* a tea-house ; *cha wo ireru,* to make tea.
chakŭsuru, (irreg.) to arrive.
chanto, quietly : *chanto shĭta,* quiet.
chawan, a tea-cup, a bowl.
chaya, a tea-house.
chi, blood : *chi ga deru,* to bleed (intrans.).
chichi, a father.
chichi, milk.
chie, intelligence, cleverness.
chigai, a difference, a mistake : *chigai nai,* there is no doubt.
chigau, to differ, to be mistaken, to be the wrong one.
chihō, a direction, a district, a locality.
chiisai or **chiisa na,** small : *chiisaku naru,* to crouch.
chikagoro, recently.
chikai, near : *chikai uchi,* soon.
chikara, strength : *chikara wo tsŭkusu,* to do one's best, to endeavor.
chikŭshō, a brute animal, a beast.
chikyū, the earth.
chira-chira, flutteringly.
chirasu, to scatter.

chiri, dust.
chiru, to fall (as leaves or as the petals of flowers).
chishĭki, talent, wisdom.
chishitsu-gaku, geology.
chisō, (generally with the honorific *go* prefixed), a feast.
chō, an auxiliary numeral.
chō, a measure of distance equivalent to about 120 yards English. *Chō* also means street or ward.
chō, a million.
chōdai suru, to receive respectfully.
chōdo, just, exactly.
chōhō, convenience: *chōhō na,* convenient, useful.
choito, choto, chotto, chito, or **chitto,** just a little, a trifle: *choito shĭta,* slight, trifling.
chokusetsu na, direct.
Chōsen, Korea.
cho(t)to, see *choito.*
chōzu, water to wash the hands with: *chōzu-ba,* a water-closet.
chū, in.
chū, loyalty (to a superior): *chū wo tsukŭsu,* to behave with perfect loyalty.
chūgi, loyalty.
chūi, attention, care: *chūi suru,* to pay attention.
chūjō, a general or admiral of the second rank.
chūmon, an order.
chūtō, second class, middling.

D

dai, great, big, very.
dai, a word used to form ordinal numbers.
dai, the auxiliary numeral for vehicles.
dai, a reign, a generation.
daibu, a good deal.
daidokoro, a kitchen.
daigakkō, } a university.
daigaku, }
daiji, importance: *daiji na,* important; *daiji ni suru,* to take great care of.
daijin, a minister of state.
daijōbu (na), all right, safe and sound.
daikon, a large species of radish.
daiku, a carpenter.
daimyō, the title of a class of nobles in feudal times.
dairi, a substitute.
dai-sŭki, very fond.
daitai, the general character of a thing, its main features.
daitōryō, a president,—of the United States, etc.
dajaku (na), indolent.
dake, only, about, as . . . as.
damaru, to keep silence.
damasu, to cheat.
dampan, deliberation, consultation.
dan, a step: *dan-dan,* gradually.
danjiru, to consult.
danna, a master: *danna san* sometimes means you.
danshi, a male child, a man.

dare ? who ?
dasu, to take out, to put outside.
dashimono, something put forth, a show.
de, a postposition ; see page 112.
de-guchi, an exit, the way out.
de-kakeru, to start off.
deki, (generally with honorific prefix *o*), or **dekimono,** anything which *comes out* on the skin, as a boil, a sore.
dekiru, to come out.
dempō, a telegram.
denshin, telegraphy : *denshin-kyoku,* a telegraph-office.
deru, to come out of, to issue forth, to go out: *de-au,* to meet out of doors, to encounter ; *de-kakeru,* to go out.
deshi, a pupil, a disciple.
do, a time.
dō, same, *e.g., dōjitsu,* the same day ; *dōyō,* the same manner.
dō ? how ?
dōbutsu, an animal.
dōbutsuen, Zoo.
dochi ? or **dochira ?** where ? sometimes which ?
dōgu, a utensil ; *dōgu-ya,* a secondhand shop, a dealer in secondhand wares.
Doitsu, Germany : *Doitsu-jin,* a German ; *Doitsu no,* German.
dōka, please.
dokkoisho ! an interjection.
doko ? where ?
dokoera ? whereabouts ?
doku, poison : *doku ni naru,* to be unwholesome.
dokūshin(-mono), a bachelor.
don, bang : *don to,* with a banging noise.
donata ? who ?
donna ? what kind of ?
dono ? which ?
dono, Mr. (in Book Language).
dore ? which ? (subst.).
dōri, reason.
doro, mud.
dorobō, a thief.
dote, an embankment, a bank.
doya-doya, tumultuously.
Doyōbi, Saturday.
dozō, a mud godown.
dōzo, please.

E

e ! eh ! eh ?
e, a picture.
e, an inlet with a stream running into it.
ebi, a prawn.
eda, a branch of a tree, river, etc.
ei ! ah ! oh !
Eikoku, England.
ekaki, a painter.
empitsu, a pencil.
empō, a long way off : *empō na,* distant.
embifūku, a swallow-tail coat.
engawa, a verandah.
en-kin, distance, how far ?
enryo, diffidence : *enryo suru,* to be diffident.
entotsu, chimney.
enzetsu, a lecture : *enzetsu suru,* to lecture.
erai, wonderful, able, very.
eru, to get.

F

fū, two (in enumeration).

fuben, inconvenience : *fuben na,* inconvenient.

fudan, the ordinary routine : *fudan no,* usual, common.

fude, a writing brush.

fueru, to increase (intrans.).

fūfu, husband and wife.

fuji, the wistaria plant.

fujin, a lady.

Fuji(-san), Mt. Fuji.

fujiyū, inconvenience : *fujiyū na,* inconvenient.

fŭkai, deep.

fŭku, an auxiliary numeral.

fŭku, to blow (*e.g.,* the wind).

fŭku, to wipe.

fuku, vice, assistant : *fuku kyōju,* assistant professor.

fŭkumu, to contain, to include.

fŭkuro, a bag : *o fŭkuro,* a mother.

fŭkuzatsu, a medley, a complication : *fŭkuzatsu na,* disorderly, complicated.

fumu, to tread (on) : *fumishimeru,* to tread firmly.

fun, a fraction, a tenth part, a minute.

fune, any kind of boat or ship : *fune ni you,* to be seasick.

Fŭransu, France : *Fŭransu-jin,* a Frenchman ; *Fŭransu no,* French.

furi, a fall (of rain or snow).

furi, airs, gait, pretence.

furo, a bath : *furo-ba,* a bath-place, a tub.

furoshĭki, a cloth used to wrap up parcels in.

furu, to fall,—said only of rain, snow, hail, etc. : *furi-dasu,* to come on to rain, etc.

furu, to brandish, to wave.

furui, old (said only of things) : *furu-dōgu,* an old utensil or curio.

fŭseru, to lie down, to go to bed.

fūsetsu, rumor, report.

fŭshigi, a strange thing, a miracle : *fŭshigi na,* strange.

fŭshinsetsu (na), unkind.

fŭshōchi, dissent, objection : *fŭshōchi wo iu,* to object.

fŭta, a lid.

fŭtago, twins.

fŭtari, two persons : *fŭtari-mae,* portions for two.

fŭta(tsu), two.

fŭto, suddenly, accidentally.

fŭton, a bed-quilt.

fŭtoru, to grow fat : *fŭtotta,* fat.

fŭtsū (no), usual, general.

futsugō, inconvenience : *futsugō na,* inconvenient ; less often, improper.

futsŭka, two days, the second day of the month.

Futsŭkoku, France.

fuyasŭ, to increase (trans.).

fuyu, winter.

fuzai, not at home, absent.

fūzoku, manners, customs.

G

gake, while, during, as *kaeri-gake,* while returning, on the way back.

gakkari, a sort of onomatope for bodily exhaustion.

gakkō, a school.

gakkwa, a subject, or line of study.

gaku, science, learning.

gakuin, academy, school.

gakumon, study, learning: *gakumon suru,* to study.

gakŭsha, a learned man.

gakŭshi, a graduate.

gaman, patience: *gaman suru,* to be patient.

garasu, glass (from the Dutch).

garu, a verbal suffix.

Gasshūkoku, the United States.

gasŭ, gas.

gata, a pluralizing particle.

gaten, comprehension, acquiescence: *gaten suru,* to comprehend, to acquiesce.

geisha, a singing-girl.

gejo, a maid-servant.

genan, a man-servant.

genkwa(n), the entrance to a house, a porch.

gendai, the present time.

getsu, a month.

Getsuyōbi, Monday.

gi, duty, signification, affair.

gikwai, Parliament: Diet: *gikwaido,* House of Parliament.

gimon, a question.

gimu, duty, an obligation.

gin, silver.

ginkō, a bank (for money).

go, five.

go, an honorific prefix.

go, after: *sono go,* since then.

gobu-gobu, an onomatope for the gurgling sound made by a liquid when poured out.

gochisō, a feast.

gogo, the afternoon.

Go-gatsu, May.

gohan, rice, food.

go-jū, fifty.

goku, extremely, very.

gokuraku, paradise.

gomen, (properly **go men**), lit., august pardon: *gomen nasai,* please excuse me.

gomi, dust (on things).

goran nasaru, to deign to look.

goro, time, about.

go-roku, five or six.

gotoki, like, such as.

gozaimasŭ, gozarimasŭ, gozaru, to be.

gozen, boiled rice, (hence) a meal.

gozen, the forenoon.

gun, a district.

gunkan, a war-vessel.

gururi, around.

gutto, tightly, suddenly.

guzu-guzu, a word descriptive of the sound or act of complaining or scolding.

gwaikoku, foreign countries, abroad: *gwaikoku-jin,* a foreigner; *gwaikoku no,* foreign; *gwaikoku go,* foreign language.

gwaimushō, the foreign office.

gwaitō, an overcoat.

gwan-yaku, a pill.

gwatsu, or *gatsu*, a month.
gyō, work, business.
gyūniku, beef.

H

ha, a leaf (of a tree).
ha, a tooth: *ha-migaki*, tooth-powder; *ha ga itai*, I have a toothache.
hachi, a bee, a wasp.
hachi, a pot.
hachi, eight.
Hachi-gatsu, August.
hachi-jū, eighty.
hadaka (na), naked.
hagaki, a postcard.
hagane, steel.
haha, a mother.
ha-hā, ho! oh! I see.
hai, the auxiliary numeral for cupfuls of liquid.
hai, a fly.
hai! same as *he*!
haibyō, consumption.
haiken suru, to look respectfully at something belonging to a superior.
hairi-kūchi, an entrance, the way in.
hairu, to go in: *haitte iru*, to be inside, to be included.
ha-isha, a dentist.
haishaku suru, to borrow.
hajimari, the beginning.
hajimaru, to begin (intrans.).
hajime, the beginning.
hajimeru, to begin (trans.).
hajimete, (gerund of *hajimeru*), for the first time, never before.
hakaru, to weigh, to estimate, to plot.
haki-dame, a dust heap.
hakkiri (to), clearly.
hako, a box.
hakobu, to transport, to carry.
haku, to sweep.
haku, to wear, or put on the feet or legs.
hakubutsūkwan, a museum.
hakurai, imported from abroad: *hakurai-hin*, an imported article.
hakurankwai, an exhibition.
hambun, half.
ha-migaki, tooth-powder.
han, edition.
han, rice, a meal.
hana, a flower, a blossom.
hana, the nose.
hanabi, fire works.
hanahada, very.
hanahadashii, excessive, extreme.
hanareru, to separate from, to part with.
hanashi, a story, a talk.
hanasu, to speak, to tell.
hane, a feather, a wing.
haneru, to splash,—as mud (intrans.); to cut off,—as a head (trans.).
hanshi, a common kind of writing paper.
haori, a sort of coat worn by the upper and middle classes as half full dress.
hara, the abdomen.
harau, to clear away (trans.); hence to play.
hareru, to clear (intrans.)—said of the sky or clouds.

hari, a pin, a needle.
haru, to stick (trans.).
haru, spring(-time).
hasami, scissors.
hasamu, to cut with scissors.
hashi, chopsticks.
hashi, a bridge.
hashira, a post; also the auxiliary numeral for Shintō gods and goddesses.
hashiru, to run.
hata, a flag.
hatachi, twenty years of age.
hatake, a vegetable field.
hataraki, work, action.
hataraku, to work.
hate-na! well I never! how extraordinary!
hateru, to finish (intrans.).
hatsūka, twenty days, the twentieth day of the month.
hatsumei, an invention, a discovery, inventive genius.
hattatsu, development, progress: *hattatsu suru,* to develop (intrans.).
hatto, an onomatope for starting—as with fright or sudden recollection of something forgotten.
hau, to creep.
hayai, quick, early.
hayari, a fashion: *hayari no,* fashionable.
hayaru, to be wide-spread (*e.g.,* a disease), to be fashionable.
hayashi, a forest.
hayasu, to grow (trans.)—*e.g.,* a beard.
hazu, necessity, should, ought.
hazukashii, bashful.
hazukashisa, bashfulness.
he! hei! or **hai!** yes.
hebi, a snake.
hei! same as *he!*
hei, a hedge, a fence.
Heika, Your, His, or Her Majesty
heikin, an average.
heisotsu, a common soldier.
heitai, a soldier, troops.
hen, a change: *hen na,* odd, queer.
hen, a neighborhood, a locality.
hen, a time.
hen, a section of a book, a treatise.
henji, an answer.
henkwa, a change.
hentō, an answer: *hentō suru,* to answer.
herasu, to diminish (trans.).
heru, to diminish (intrans.).
heta (na), a bad hand at, unskillful.
heya, a room, a cabin.
hi, the sun, hence a day: *hi ga kureru,* the day is waning, darkness approaching.
hi, fire.
hī, one (in enumeration).
hibachi, a brazier.
hidari, the left (side).
hidoi, harsh, cruel: *hidoi me ni au,* to experience harsh treatment.
hieru, to be cold.
higashi, east.
hige, the beard: *hige wo hayasu,* to grow a beard.
hijō (na), unusual, extraordinary.
hīkaru, to shine, to glitter.
hīki, an auxiliary numeral.

Tokyo tower

Peace memorial park

hĭki-dashi, a drawer.
hĭki-shio, low tide.
hikkomu, to retire inside.
hĭku, to pull, to draw, hence to quote: *hĭki-dasu,* to draw out.
hĭkui, low.
hĭkyō, cowardice: *hĭkyō na,* cowardly.
hima, an interval, leisure: *hima wo yaru,* to dismiss, also to allow to go on leave.
hinkō, conduct: *hinkō no ii,* well-conducted, moral.
Hira-gana, the cursive form of the Jap. syllabary.
hirakeru, to be opened out, to become civilized.
hiraku, to open, to civilize.
hirattai, flat.
hiroi, broad.
hiroi-mono, something picked up, a find.
hirou, to pick up, hence to find.
hiru, daytime, noon: *hiru (-gozen),* the midday meal, luncheon.
hiru-sugi, afternoon.
hĭsashii, long (of time).
hisuru, to compare.
hissori to, quiet, deserted.
hĭto, a person, a human being; *hĭto-goroshi,* murder, manslaughter, a murderer; *hĭto-me,* public notice; *ano hĭto,* he, she.
hĭtoe, properly one fold; hence single.
hĭtori, one person, hence alone: *hĭtori-de ni,* of itself, spontaneously.
hĭto(tsu), one; sometimes whole, all, same: *hĭto-ban,* all night long; *hĭto-me,* one look; *hĭtotsu oki,* alternate.
hitsuyō (na), indispensable.
hiyori, the weather.
hiza, the knee.
ho, a sail: *ho-bashira,* a mast.
hō, a law, a rule, a usage.
hō, side: *hō ga yoi* (or *ii*).
hōbō, on all sides; everywhere.
hōchō, a knife.
hodo, degree, quantity, proper limit, about.
hoeru, to bark: *hoe-kakaru,* to spring at with a bark.
hōhō, manner, way, rule.
hōgozei, Protection (*versus* Free Trade).
hoka, another place, besides, except: *no hoka ni,* besides . . . . .
hombako, bookcase.
home, praise.
homeru, to praise.
hon, a book.
hon, an auxiliary numeral.
hone, a bone: *hone ga oreru* or *hone wo oru,* to take a great deal of trouble.
hongoku, one's native country.
hontō, truth: *hontō no,* true, real.
hon-ya, a bookstore, hence a bookseller.
hon-yaku, a translation: *hon-yaku suru,* to translate.
horeru, to be in love.
hori, a canal, a moat.
horimono, a carving.

hōritsu, a law: *hōritsu-gaku,* legal studies.

horobiru, to be overthrown or ruined.

horobosu, to overthrow, to ruin.

horu, to dig, to excavate, to carve

hoshi, a star.

hoshii, desirous.

hosoi, narrow: *hoso-nagai,* slender.

hossuru, to wish.

hosu, to dry (trans.).

hotoke, a Buddha.

hotondo, almost; (with a negative) hardly.

hyaku, a hundred: *hyaku-man,* a million.

hyakŭshō, a peasant, a farmer.

hyakkwazenshō, encyclopedia.

hyōban, rumor, report.

hyōgi, a conference.

hyoro-hyoro, an onomatope for staggering.

I

i, (oftener *ido*) a well.

ichi, one.

ichi(-ba), a market (-place), a fair.

ichi-ban, number one, first; hence used as a prefix to indicate the superlative.

ido, a well.

ie, a house: *ie no uchi,* indoors.

iedomo, though; sometimes even.

ifŭku, a garment.

Igirisu, England: *Igirisu-jin,* an Englishman; *Igirisu no,* English.

ii, a corruption of *yoi,* good.

ii-tsŭkeru, to order; less often, to inform.

iiye, no.

ijiru, to meddle, to tease.

ijō, from thence upwards, that and upwards (the Japanese generally reckoning inclusively).

ikaga ? how ?

ikahodo ? how much ?

ikan ? or **ikani ?** how ?

ikanimo, yes, certainly.

ikasu, to vivify, to free.

ikenai, "is no go," won't do.

iki, the act of going, the way there.

iki-gake, while going, on the way to.

ikioi, strength, force.

ikiru, to live: *ikite iru,* to be alive.

ikka ? what day ? such and such a day.

iku ? how many ?

iku, to go: *iki-kaeru,* to go and come back again; *iki-tagaru,* to want to go; *iki-todoku,* to reach, to be effectual; *itte shimau,* to go away.

ikura ? how much ?

ikŭsa, war: *ikŭsa wo suru,* to make war.

iku(tsu) ? how many ?

ima, now.

imaimashii, disagreeable.

imashimeru, to reprove, to warn.

imi, signification, meaning.

imo, a potato.

imōto, a younger sister.

inabikari, lightning.

inai, within the limits of ; towards the interior.
inaka, the country (as opposed to the town).
ine, rice (growing).
Indo, India.
inochi, life.
inori, prayer : *inori wo suru,* to pray.
inoru, to pray.
inu, a dog.
ip-pai, one cupful, full : *ip-pai na,* full.
ippan (no), general, universal.
irai, henceforth, since, after.
irasshai, or **iraserare,** imperative of *irassharu.*
irassharu, go, see, be.
ireba, an artificial tooth.
ireru, to put in, to insert ; to make (tea).
iri-kunda, complicated.
iriyō (na), needed, necessary.
iro, color : *iro-iro,* all sorts.
iru, to enter.
iru, to be.
iru, to shoot.
isha, a physician.
ishi, a stone.
ishi-bei, a stone wall.
isogashii, busy.
isogi, a hurry.
isogu, to make haste.
issakujitsu, the day before yesterday.
is-shin, one person : *jibun is-shin,* oneself only.
isshō, a whole lifetime.
issho, together.
is-sō, a pair.
isu, a chair.
itadaku, to receive.
itai, painful, hurting.
itameru, to hurt (trans.).
itamu, to hurt (intrans.).
itaru, to reach : *ni itaru made,* down to ; *ni itatte,* at.
itasu, to do.
itazura, mischief.
itatte, very.
itchi, union, unison.
ito, a string, thread.
itoko, cousin.
itoma, leave (of absence), dismissal : *mō o itoma itashimasŭ* (or *mōshimasŭ*), I must be saying goodbye.
itsu, same as *ichi,* one.
itsu ? when ?
itsŭka, five days, the fifth day of the month.
itsu(tsu), five.
itsuwari, a lie.
ittai, altogether ; but sometimes almost an expletive.
iu, to say.
iwa, a rock.
iwaku, a Classical form of *iu,* to say.
iya ! nay ! no ! *iya na,* objectionable.
iyagaru, to dislike.
iyo-iyo, more and more.
izumi, a spring, a fountain.
izure ? which ? in any case ; but often a mere expletive.

J

ja, a contraction of *de wa.*
jama, obstruction, impediment : *jama wo suru,* to be in the way.

ji, time, hour, as in *nan-ji* ? what o'clock ?
ji, a written character, specifically a Chinese ideograph.
jibiki, a dictionary.
jibun, a time, a season.
jibun, self.
jidōsha, automobile.
jigi, (generally with *o*) a bow—of the head and body.
jikan, a period of time, an hour.
jiki (ni), immediately.
jikken-shitsu, a laboratory.
jikō, temperature, the state of the weather.
jimbō, popularity.
jimen, a plot of ground.
jimusho, an office.
jin, a person, a man.
jinja, a Shintō temple.
jinkō, population.
jinrikī(sha), a *jinrikīsha.*
jinryoku suru, (irreg.) to endeavor, to do one's very best.
jinshu, a race of men.
jisatsu, suicide : *jisatsu suru,* to commit suicide.
jishin, self.
jishin, an earthquake.
jisho, a dictionary.
jissai, practice (as opposed to theory).
jiten, a dictionary.
jitensha, bicycle.
jitsu, truth : *jitsu no,* true.
jitsu-getsu, the sun and moon.
jiyū, freedom, liberty : *jiyū na,* free ; *jiyū-seido,* a free government.
jō, the auxiliary numeral for mats.
jōbu (na), sturdy, solid, strong.
jōbukuro, an envelope (for letters).
jochū, a maid-servant.
jōdan, a joke : *jōdan wo iu,* to joke.
jōkīsen, a steamer.
jōsama, (generally with *o* prefixed), a young lady, Miss, a daughter (honorific).
jōsan, short for *jōsama.*
jōtō, first-class, good society.
jōyaku, an agreement, a treaty.
jōzu (na), a good hand at, skillful.
jū, ten.
jūbako, a lacquer box.
jūbun, plenty, ample.
jū-go, fifteen.
Jū-gatsu, October.
jū-hachi, eighteen.
jū-ichi, eleven.
Jū-ichi-gatsu, November.
jū-ku, nineteen.
jumbi, preparations.
jū-ni, twelve.
Jū-ni-gatsu, December.
junsa, a policeman.
jūroku, sixteen.
jū-san, thirteen.
jū-shi, fourteen.
jū-shīchi, seventeen.

K

ka, a mosquito.
ka, an auxiliary numeral.
ka ? an interrogative postposition ; *ka mo shiran,* perhaps.
kabe, a mud wall.

kaeri, the way back: *kaeri-gake ni,* on the way back.
kaeru, a frog.
kaeru, to change (trans.).
kaeru, to return (intrans.), hence to go away.
kaesu, to give back, to send back, to return (trans.).
kaette, contrary to what one might have expected, rather.
kagami, a mirror.
kage, shade, shadow, reflection, hence influence: *no kage ni,* in the shadow of, hence behind; *o kage sama,* see page 67.
kagi, a key.
kagiri, a limit: *kagiri no nai,* boundless.
kagiru, to limit, to be limited.
kago, a kind of palanquin.
kai, floor, story.
kaigun, a navy.
kaiko, a silkworm.
kaikwa, civilization: *kaikwa suru,* to become civilized.
kaimono, a purchase, shopping.
kaisan, dispersion, adjournment: *kaisan suru,* to disperse.
kaishin reform: *kaishin suru,* to reform.
kakaru, to hang (intrans.): *o me ni kakaru,* see page 4. Sometimes *kakaru* means to cost, also to take time.
kakemono, a hanging scroll.
kakeru, to hand (trans.), to put.
kakeru, to write (intrans.).
kaki, an oyster.
kaki, a persimmon.
Kakka, Your or His Excellency.
kakkoku, all countries, foreign countries in general.
kaku, each (in compounds).
kaku, to scratch, to write.
kakubetsu (no or na), different, special.
kakujitsu, every other day.
kakumei, a revolution.
kakureru, to hide (intrans.).
kakūsu, to hide (trans.).
kamau, to have to do with, to meddle with, to matter: *kamaimasen,* it doesn't matter.
kamben, forbearance, forgiveness.
kame, a tortoise.
kami, the hair of the head: *kami-hasami,* hair-cutting.
kami, above, upper: *o kami,* the government; *o kami san,* see *okamisan.*
kami, a Shintō god or goddess.
kami (no ke), the hair of the head: *kami-yui,* a hair-dresser
kami, paper.
kami-hasami, hair-cutting.
kaminari, thunder.
kamo, a wild duck.
kamu, to bite.
kan, interval; see page 101.
Kana, the Japanese syllabic writing.
kanai, inside a house, all the members of a household; hence a humble word for wife.
kanarazu, positively, certainly.
kanau, to correspond, to agree. with.
kan-dan, cold and heat, temperature.

kandankei, a thermometer.

kane, metal, money : *kane-ire,* a purse ; *kane-mochi,* a rich man.

kane, a bell.

kaneru, to be unable.

kanete, beforehand, together.

kangae, consideration, reflection, a thought, an intention.

kangaeru, to consider, to reflect.

kani, a crab.

kanji, a feeling.

kanji, literally, China letters, ideographs.

kanjiru, to feel.

kanjō, an account, a bill.

kano, Classical for *ano,* that.

kanshin, admiration, astonishment : *kanshin suru,* to admire to be astonished at.

kantan, simple.

kanzume, tinned provisions.

kao, the face.

Kara, China.

kara, a postposition.

kara, a collar (from the English).

kara (na), empty.

karada, the body (of any living creature).

karashi, mustard.

karasu, a crow.

kare, Classical for *are,* that.

kari, (in compounds), temporary.

kariru, to borrow, to hire.

karui, light ; hence soft (in speaking of water).

kasa, a broad sun-hat, a parasol, an umbrella.

kasaneru, to pile up, to repeat.

kasanete, several times, again.

kashĭkoi, awe-inspiring ; also clever.

kashĭkomaru, to receive orders respectfully : *kashĭkomarimashĭta,* all right, Sir !

kashikomu, to reverence.

kashĭkosa, awe-inspiringness, cleverness.

kashira, the head, a chief, a superior.

kasu, to lend, to let (*e.g.*, a house).

kata, the side of anything, a direction, hence one side, one : *kata-ashi,* one foot ; *kata-te,* one hand ; (*o*) *kata,* a gentleman, a lady.

katai, hard, hence strict, honest.

Kata-kana, the square form of the Jap. syllabary.

katamaru, to grow hard.

katamichi, single fare.

katana, a sword : *katana-ya,* a sword shop, a dealer in swords.

katazukeru, to put away.

katchiri, a word expressive of the sound of clicking.

katō, low class, third class (on railways, etc.).

katsu, to conquer, to win.

katsudōshashin, cinematograph.

katte, will, choice, (hence) convenience, (hence) kitchen : *anata no go katte desŭ,* you can do as you like.

katto, an onomatope for suddenness.

kau, to buy : *kaimono* a purchase.

kau, to keep (domestic animals).

kawa, a river.

kawa, the skin, rind, or bark of anything ; leather.

kawai, pet, dear little, poor little.

kawaisō, worthy of pity, in distress.

kawaku, to get dry : *kawaite iru,* to be dry ; *nodo ga kawakimashĭta,* I am thirsty.

kawari, a change,—especially for the worse : *no kawari ni,* instead of.

kawaru, to change (intrans.).

kawazu, a frog.

kaya, a mosquito net.

kaza-kami, (to) windward.

kaze, the wind : *kaze wo hĭku,* to catch cold.

kazoeru, to count.

kazu, a number.

ke, hair.

kedamono, a quadruped.

kēga, a wound : *kega suru,* to be wounded, to hurt oneself severely.

keiba, a horse race.

keiben (na), easily to be used, convenient.

keiko, practice : *keiko wo suru,* to practice.

keisatsŭsho, a police station.

keisatsŭkwan, a police officer.

keishoku, scenery.

keizai-gaku, political economy : *keizai-gakŭsha,* a political economist.

kekkō (na), splendid, sufficient.

kembutsu, sightseeing : *kembutsu suru,* to go to see.

kempō, constitution.

kemono, a quadruped.

kemuri, smoke.

kemushi, a caterpillar.

ken, the auxiliary numeral for houses.

kenjutsu, swordsmanship.

kenkwa, a quarrel : *kenkwa suru,* to quarrel.

kenkyū, investigation, research : *kenkyū suru,* to investigate.

kennon, danger : *kennon na,* dangerous.

keredo(mo), though, but.

kesa, this morning.

keshĭkaran, outrageous, absurd.

keshĭki, a view, scenery, appearance.

kesshĭte, positively, certainly.

kessuru, to decide.

kesu, to extinguish, to put out.

ketchaku, decision, final resolve.

ketto, a rug.

ki, the spirits (of a person), sometimes intention : *ki ga tsŭku,* to have one's attention called to something ; *ki ni iru,* to be agreeable to one ; *ki no kiita,* quick-witted ; *ki wo tsukeru,* to pay attention.

ki, a tree, wood.

ki, the indefinite form of *kuru,* to come.

kichigai (no), mad.

ki-gae, a change of clothes.

kigen, the bodily feelings : *go kigen yō,* I wish you good health.

ki-iroi, yellow.

kiji, a pheasant.

ki-jōbu, of good cheer, not alarmed.

kikai, a machine.

kikaseru, to inform.

kiki-gurushii, ugly (to hear).

kikken(na), danger(ous).

kikō, climate, temperature.

kikoeru, to be audible, to be able to hear.

kikoku, (your) august country.

kiku, a chrysanthemum.

kiku, to hear, to listen ; hence to ask, to enquire.

kimari, a fixed arrangement: *kimari ga nai,* there is no rule.

kimi, a prince, a sovereign; (hence) you.

kimi, feelings: *kimi ga warui,* to feel unwell, to feel frightened.

kimono, clothes, specifically the long upper robe worn by the Japanese.

kin, gold, money.

kin, a pound.

kingyo, a goldfish.

kinjiru, to forbid.

kinjitsu, a few days hence.

kinjo, neighborhood.

kinō, yesterday.

kinodoku, (literally, poison of the spirit) regret or concern felt for others.

kinu, silk.

Kin-yōbi, Friday.

kippu, a ticket.

kirai, averse to.

kirau, to dislike.

kirei (na), pretty, neat, clean.

kireu, to cut (intrans.).

kiri, a suffix derived from *kiru,* to cut, and meaning only.

kiri, mist.

kiriritto shita, sharp, well-defined.

kiru, to cut, (hence) to kill.

kiru, to wear, to have on or put on (clothes): *ki-kaeru,* to change one's clothes.

kiryō, countenance, looks.

kisama, you.

kiresu, a pipe (for smoking).

kisha, a railway train.

kishō, spirit, temper: *kishō na,* spirited.

kisoku, a law.

kita, north.

kitanai, kitanarashii, dirty.

kitsui, strong, severe, cruel.

kitsune, a fox.

kitto, positively.

ko, an auxiliary numeral.

ko, a child, the young of any animal ; hence used as a prefix to form diminutives.

kō, thus, like this, in this way: *kō iu,* this kind of, such as this ; *kō suru to,* if one does this.

kō or **kōkō,** filial piety: *kō wo tsŭkusu,* to be very filial.

koboreru, to get spilt.

kobosu, to spill (trans.).

kobune, a boat.

kochi or **kochira,** here.

kōdai (na), gigantic, immense.

kōdan, a lecture.

kodomo, properly the plural children, but also used for the singular child: *kodomo ga dekiru,* children are born.

koe, the voice.

kōen, a public park.

ko-gatana, a penknife.

kogu, to row.

kōhō, public law.

ko-ishi, a pebble.

koitsu, a contraction of *kon o yatsu,* this fellow, this rascal.

kojiki, a beggar.

koko, here: *koko ni,* here, but sometimes thereupon, well.

kōkō, filial piety.

kokoera, hereabouts.

kōkoku, an advertisement.

kokonoka, nine days, the ninth day of the month.

kokono(tsu), nine.

kokoro, the heart (metaph.): *kokoro-mochi,* the feelings (especially the bodily ones); *kokoro-yasui* intimate, great friends: *ko-koro-yoi,* comfortable, well.

koku, a country; used only in compounds, as *kikoku,* (your) august country.

kokumin, the people of a country.

komakai or **komaka (na),** minute, small: *komaka ni,* in detail.

kōman, pride, conceit.

komaru, to be in a quandary, to be in trouble.

komban, tonight.

kome, hulled rice.

kōmori, a bat (animal): *kōmori-gasa,* a European umbrella.

komu, to stuff into.

komugi, wheat.

kōmuru, to receive from a superior.

kona, fine powder, flour.

konaida, a short while ago, recently.

konata, hither.

kondate, a bill of fare.

kondo, this time.

kon-i, intimacy; friendly feelings: *kon-i na,* intimate.

kon-in, marriage.

konna, this kind of, such as this.

konnichi, today.

kono, this (adj.).

konrei, a wedding.

konzatsu, confusion.

koppu, a glass (from the Dutch *kop,* a cup).

koraeru, to endure, to bear.

kore, this (subst.): *kore kara* or *kore yori,* henceforward.

kōri, ice.

koro, a period of time.

korosu, to kill.

kōru, to freeze (intrans.).

kōseki, efficiency, merit: *kōseki no aru,* efficient.

kōshaku, a lecture.

koshi, the loins: *koshi wo kakeru,* to sit down.

koshiraeru, to prepare.

koshō, pepper.

kōshō, (na), exalted, sublime.

kosu, to cross (a mountain).

kosui, a lake.

kotaeru, to answer,

kotchi, vulgar for *kochi,* here.

kōtei, an emperor.

koto, an (abstract) thing.

kōtō, higher: *kōtōgakkō,* high school.

kotoba, a word, a language.

kotogotoku, all, completely.

ko-tori, a small bird.

kotoshi, this year.

kotowari, a refusal, an excuse.

kotowaru, to refuse; less often, to explain, to mention.

kowagaru, to be frightened.

kowai, afraid, also frightful.

kowareru, to break (intrans.).

kowasu, to break (trans.).

koya, a hut.

koyomi, an almanac.

ko-zashĭki, a small room.
ku, nine.
ku, the indefinite or adverbial termination of adjectives.
kubetsu, a difference: *kubetsu suru,* to discriminate.
kubi, the neck, the head.
kŭchi, the mouth, an opening.
kudaru, to descend.
kudasai or **kudasare,** imperative of *kudasaru.*
kudasaru, to condescend.
kugi, a nail (to fasten things with)
Ku-gatsu, September.
kujira, a whale.
ku-jū, ninety.
kūki, the air, the atmosphere.
kuma, a bear.
kumi, a set, a clique: also an auxiliary numeral.
kumo, a spider: *kumo no su,* a spider's web (literally, nest).
kumo, a cloud.
kumoru, to get cloudy; *kumotte iru,* to be cloudy.
kun, a prince, also Mr.
kuni, a country, a province: *o kuni,* your (honorable) country.
kura, a godown.
kurai, rank, hence quantity, about, such as to: *dono kurai*? how much?
kurai, dark,
kurasa, darkness.
kurashi, a livelihood: *kurashi wo tateru* (or *tsŭkeru*), to gain a livelihood.
kurasu, to spend time, to live.
kureru, to give.
kureru, to grow dark: *hi ga kureru,* the daylight is waning, it is getting dark.
kurō, trouble, pains: *go kurō sama.*
kuroi, black.
kuro-megane, black goggles.
kuroto, professional.
kuku, (irreg.) to come: *motte kuru,* to bring; *totte kuru,* to fetch.
kuruma, a wheel, anything moved by a wheel, specifically a *jinrikĭsha*: *kuruma-ya,* a *jinrikĭsha*-man.
kurushii, painful, in pain.
kŭsa, a plant, a herb.
kŭsai, stinking.
kŭsari, a chain.
kŭshi, a comb.
kŭsuri, medicine: *kŭsuri ni naru* to be good for one's health.
kŭtabireru, to get tired: *kŭtabirete iru,* to be tired.
kutsu, a boot, a shoe: *kutsu-ya,* a bootmaker's shop, hence a bootmaker.
kuttsŭku, to stick close to.
kuu, to eat: *kui-tsŭku,* to bite (as a dog, etc.).
kuwaeru, to add.
kuwashii, minute, exact.
kwai, an association, a society, a meeting, a church (metaph.).
kwaisha, company: *kabushi-kwaisha,* joint stock company; *gōmei kwaisha,* limited partnership.
kwaiwa or **kaiwa,** conversation.
kwaji, a conflagration, a fire.

kwan-in, an official.
kwankei, connection, relation, having to do with something else : *kwankei suru,* to depend.
kwashi, any sweetmeat, cake.
Kwayōbi or **Kayōbi,** Tuesday.
kwazan, a volcano.
kyaku, a guest, a customer, a fare : *kyakuma,* a drawing-room.
kyaku, the auxiliary numeral for chairs and tables.
kyan-kyan, the sound which dogs make in yelping.
kyō, today : *kyō-jū,* during to-day, by tonight.
kyōdai, brothers ; hence sometimes brothers and sisters.
kyō-iku, education.
kyōju, teacher, professor.
kyoku, a bureau or subdivision of a government department an office.
kyokŭtan, the acme.
kyōkwai, a church (metaph.).
kyōkwaidō, a church, a chapel, a meeting-house.
kyonen, last year.
kyōshi, a teacher, a missionary, a clergyman.
kyū, rare for *ku,* nine.
kyū (na), sudden.
kyūji, waiting at table, a waiter.
kyūjitsu, a holiday.
kyūkin, wages.

M

ma, space, interval, hence a room : *ma ni au,* to be in time.
mā ! an interjection.
mabushii, dazzling.
machi, the mercantile quarter of a town, a street.
machi-dōi, long to wait, tediously long of coming : *o machidō sama.*
machigai, a mistake, a misunderstanding : *machigai-rashii,* apparently a mistake.
machigau, to make a mistake, to mistake.
mada, still ; (with a negative) not yet.
made, a postposition.
mado, a window.
mae, in front, before : *mae kara,* beforehand.
magaru, to bend (intrans.) : *magatte iru,* to be bent, crooked
mageru, to bend (trans.).
mago, a grandchild.
mai, an auxiliary numeral.
mai, a verbal termination.
mai, each, every, as in *mai-do,* each time, always ; *mai-nichi,* every day.
mairu, to come, to go.
majiwaru, to mix with, to associate.
makaru, to go down in price (intrans.).
make-oshimi, unwillingness to give way.
makeru, to lose, to be beaten ; to lower a price.

maki-tabako, a cigarette.
makka, very red.
makoto, truth: *makoto no,* true.
makura, a pillow.
mama, way, manner.
mame, beans.
mamoru, to guard, to keep, to watch.
man, a myriad, ten thousand.
manabu, to practice, to study.
mane, imitation: *mane wo suru,* to imitate, hence sometimes to do (in a bad sense).
maneku, to invite.
mannaka, the middle.
manzoku, contentment: *manzoku suru,* to be content.
maru de, quite.
marui, round.
massao, perfectly green, livid.
massugu (na), straight.
masŭ, an honorific verbal suffix.
masu, to increase (trans.).
masu-masu, more and more.
mata, again, (with a negative) no more.
matsu, a pine tree.
matsu, to wait.
matsuri, a festival.
mattaku, quite.
mawaru, to turn (intrans.).
mawasu, to turn (trans.).
mazaru, to be mixed.
mazeru, to mix (trans.).
mazu, in the first place, well, anyhow, at all events.
mazui, nasty to eat.
me, the eyes, space: *me ga sameru,* to wake (intrans.); *o me ni kakaru,* to have the honor to meet you; *o me ni kakeru,* to have the honor to show you; *me no chikai,* shortsighted; *me ni tsŭkanai,* not to notice; *me no tama,* the eyeballs. *Me* is also used to form ordinal numbers.
me, a feminine prefix.
medetai, auspicious: *o medetō gozaimasŭ,* I beg to congratulate you.
megane, spectacles.
meguru, to go round: *meguri-au,* to come across after many adventures.
mei, a name.
meibutsu, the production for which a locality is specially noted.
meijiru, to command.
meisho, a celebrated place.
meiwaku, perplexity, trouble: *meiwaku suru,* to be in perplexity or trouble.
mekata, weight.
mekki, plated—*e.g.,* with gold.
mekura, blind.
memboku, the countenance (metaph.): *memboku ga nai,* to feel ashamed.
memma, a mare.
men, (generally *go men*), permission, excuse.
men, a surface.
mendō, trouble: *mendō na,* troublesome.
mendokŭsai, troublesome.
mendori, a hen bird.
menjō, a diploma, a passport.
meshi, boiled rice, a meal.
meshi-tsŭkai, a servant.
mesu, female.

mesu, to employ (honorific): *meshi-agaru,* to eat or drink (honorific).

metta ni, (with a negative), rarely, hardly ever.

mezurashigaru, to think strange, to lionize.

mezurashii, strange, wonderful.

mi, three.

mi, three (in enumeration).

mi, a suffix used to form nouns.

michi, a road, a way.

midori, a lightish green.

mieru, to be visible, to appear, to seem; hence sometimes to come: *mienaku naru,* to disappear.

migi, the right (side): *migi-(t)te* the right hand.

migurushii, ugly (to look at).

mihon, a sample.

mijikai, short.

mikan, an orange.

mikka, three days, the third day of the month.

mimi, the ears: *mimi ni mo kakenai,* won't listen to it; *mimi no tōi,* hard of hearing.

mina, all: *mina san,* all of you, all your people.

minami, south.

minato, a harbor, a port.

minken, popular rights, democracy.

miru, to see, to look, sometimes to try.

mise, a shop.

miseru, to show.

misoka, the last day of the month, whether the 30th or 31st.

mi(tsu), three.

miya, a Shintō shrine.

miyako, a capital city.

mizu, water.

mo, a postposition.

mo, mourning.

mō, already, still, yet, more, (with a negative verb) no more: *mō hĭtotsu,* one more.

mochiiru, to employ.

mochimashite, polite for *motte.* both as gerund of *motsu* and as postposition.

mochiron, of course.

mohaya, same as *mō.*

moji, or **monji,** a written character, specifically a Chinese ideograph.

mōkaru, to be earned or made, —said of money.

mōke, profits, gains.

mōkeru, to make (money).

mokuroku, a list.

mokŭteki, an object, a motive.

Mokuyōbi, Thursday.

momen, cotton.

momiji, maple tree.

momo, a peach.

mon, a "cash" (a small copper coin).

mon, a gate.

mon., short for *mono,* a thing.

mondai, a problem, a question.

mono, a (concrete) thing.

mono-oki, an outhouse.

moppara, chiefly.

morau, to have given one, to receive.

mōshi, an initial exclamation answering to our phrase excuse me.

mōshi-wake, an excuse, an apology.
mōsu, to say: *mōshi-ageru,* to say to a superior.
moto, origin, originally, cause.
motsu, to hold, (hence) to have: *mochi-ageru,* to lift.
motte, a postposition: *motte iku,* to carry away; *motte kuru* to bring (things).
motto, still, more.
mottomo, quite, very, (hence) quite right or reasonable, of course.
mu, six.
mū, six (in enumeration).
muchū, (as) in a dream.
muda (na), useless.
mugaku, ignorance: *mugaku na* or *no,* ignorant.
mugi, a general name for wheat and barley.
muika, six days, the sixth day of the month.
mukade, a centipede.
mukashi, antiquity, old days.
mukatte, (preceded by *ni*), turning to, towards, to.
mukau, to be opposite to: *ni mukatte,* confronting, towards, to.
muko, a bridegroom, a son-in-law.
mukō, the opposite side, opposite, the other party, he she, they, there: *no mukō ni,* on the other side, opposite, beyond.
mumei (no), anonymous.
mune, the chest.
mune, a roof-ridge.
mura, a village.
murasaki, lilac.
muri, unreasonable: *go muri desŭ,* what you say is unreasonable.
muron, of course, needless to say.
muryō, incalculable, infinite.
mushi, an insect.
musŭko, a boy, a son.
musŭme, a girl, a daughter.
mu(tsu), six.
muyami (na), reckless, helter-skelter: *muyami ni,* recklessly, wholesale.
muyō (no), useless.
muzukashii, difficult.
myōchō, tomorrow morning.
myō (na), wonderful, strange.
myōgonichi, the day after tomorrow.
myōji, a family name.
myōnichi, tomorrow.

N

n', short for *no,* of.
na, name.
na, termination of the positive imperative.
na, termination of the negative imperative.
na, a particle used to form quasi-adjectives.
nā ! an interjection.
nabe, a saucepan.
nada, a reach or stretch of sea along a limited portion of the coast.
nadakai, famous.

nadameru, to pacify.
naderu, to stroke.
nado, etc.
nagai, long.
naga-iki, long life.
nagameru, to gaze.
nagara, while.
nagare, a flow.
nagareru, to flow.
nageru, to throw.
nai, the "negative adjective."
naka, inside: *no naka ni,* inside; *o naka,* a person's inside; *o naka ga sŭkimashĭta,* I feel hungry.
nakagoro, a middle or intermediate time.
nakama, a mate, a comrade.
naka-naka, very, more than you might think.
nakereba narimasen, must.
nakōdo, a middleman, a matchmaker.
naku, to cry, to sing.
naku naru, to die (literally, to become non-existent).
nama, raw, crude.
namakeru, to be lazy.
Nambei, South America.
namae, a (person's) name.
nami, a wave.
nami (no), ordinary, average.
namida, tears: *namida wo kobosu,* to shed tears.
nan? abbrev. of *nani*? what?
nana(tsu), seven.
nani? what?
nanni, popular for *nani*: *nanni mo nai,* there is nothing at all.
nan-nyo, men and women, sex.
nansen, a shipwreck: *nansen ni au,* to be shipwrecked.
nanuka, seven days, the seventh day of the month.
nanzo, something, how? what?
nao, still, more.
naoru, to get well, to recover (intrans.).
naosu, to amend, to rectify, to cure, to change.
nara, short for *naraba.*
naraba, if, but.
naraberu, to place in a row
narabu, to be in a row, to be parallel.
narai, a habit, a usage.
narasu, to ring (trans.).
narau, to learn.
nareru, to get accustomed: *narete iru,* to be accustomed.
naru, to ring (intrans.).
naru, to be.
naru, to become, sometimes to ripen.
naruhodo!
narutake, as . . . as possible, if possible.
nasai or **nasare,** imperative of *nasaru.*
nasaru.
nasasō na, apparently non-existent.
nashi, (there) is not.
nashi, a pear.
nasu, to do.
natsu, summer.
nawa, a rope.
naze? why?
ne, a root.
ne, price.

ne or **nē !** an important interjection.
nebeya, a bedroom.
nedai, a (European) bed.
nedan, a price.
nedoko, a bed.
negai, a request, a desire.
negau, to request, to beg.
negi, an onion.
neko, a cat.
nema, a bedroom.
nemaki, night-clothes.
nemui, sleepy.
nen, a year.
nengō, a "year-name."
nenrei, age, years.
neru, to go to bed, to down, to sleep: *nete iru,* to be asleep.
nēsan, literally, Miss, elder sister (*ane san*), and hence used as an address in talking to girls.
nesshin, zeal.
netsu, fever.
nezumi, a rat.
ni, a postposition.
ni, two.
nichi, a day.
Nichiyōbi, Sunday.
nigai, bitter.
nigeru to run away: *nige-dasu,* to begin to run away.
nigiru, to grasp.
nigiyaka (na), lively.
Ni-gatsu, February.
Nihon, (less elegantly **Nippon**), Japan: *Nihon-go,* the Japanese language; *Nihon-jin,* a Japanese; *Nihon-koku,* Japan; *Nihon no,* Japanese (adj.).
ni-jū, twenty.
ni-jū-yokka, twenty four days, the twenty-fourth day of the month.
nikai, a second story, upstairs.
niku, flesh, meat.
nimben, the ideographic radical for man.
ni(-motsu), luggage, cargo.
nin, a person.
ningen, a human being.
ningyō, a doll.
ninjin, a carrot.
nintai, patience.
nioi, a smell.
Nippon, Japan; see **Nihonl**
niru, to boil (food, not water.).
nishi, west.
niwa, a courtyard, a garden.
niwatori, the barndoor fowl.
no, a postposition.
nobasu, to stretch (trans.), to put off.
noberu, to narrate.
noboru, to go up, to climb.
nochi, after, afterwards: *nochi-hodo,* afterwards, by and by.
nodo, the neck, the throat: *nodo ga kawaku,* to be thirsty.
nokorazu, without exception, all.
nokori, a remainder.
nokoru, to remain over, to be left.
nokosu, to leave behind.
nomi, a flea.
nomu, to drink: *tabako wo nomu,* to smoke.
nonoshiru, to revile.
norite, one who rides (on a horse, in a carriage, etc.).
noru, to ride—on a horse, in a vehicle, in a boat, etc.

noshi-kakaru, to spring upon.
nozomi, a wish: *nozomi-dōri,* according to one's wish.
nuguu, to wipe.
nuibari, a needle.
nuimono, needlework.
nukeru, to slip out, to get pulled out, to get out of joint.
nuku, to pull out (*e.g.*, a cork).
nureru, to get wet: *nurete iru,* to be wet.
nurui, lukewarm.
nusumu, to steal.
nuu, to sew.
nyōbō, a wife.
nyūhi, expenses.

O

o a tail.
o, an honorific prefix.
o, a masculine prefix; see page 76.
ō, a king.
ō, an augmentative prefix.
oba, an aunt.
obāsan, an old lady, granny.
Ō-Bei, Europe and America.
obi, a sash, a belt.
oboeru, to remember, to feel, to learn.
ōchaku (na), villainous: *ōchaku-mono,* a rascal.
ochiru, to fall.
odayaka (na), calm, quiet.
odokasu, to frighten.
odoroku, to be astonished, to be afraid.
odoru, to dance.
ōfŭku, going and returning: *ō-fŭku-gippu,* a return ticket.
ohayō (better *o hayō*), good morning.
ōi, plentiful: *ōi ni,* very, chiefly.
oi-oi, gradually.
oira, a very vulgar word for we.
oishii, nice to eat, tasty.
oite, in.
oji, an uncle.
ojiisan, an old gentleman, grandpapa.
ōjiru, to correspond, to answer, to suit.
oka, land (as opposed to water).
oka, a mound.
okamisan, a married woman of the lower or lower middle class, Mrs. It might also be written *o kami san.*
okashii or **okashi na,** absurd, laughable.
ōkata, for the most part, probably.
oki, the offing, out at sea.
ōkii or **ōki na,** large: *ōki ni,* very.
okiru, to rise, to get up.
ōkisa, size.
okkasan, mamma, a mother.
okonai, conduct, behavior.
okonau, to practise (*e.g.*, virtue).
okoru, to arise, to take place.
okoru, to get angry.
okosu, to rouse, to raise.
oku, to put, sometimes to lay aside.
oku, a hundred thousand.
oku, the inner part or recesses of anything.
okureru, to be too late, not to be in time.

okuru, to send, to give, to accompany, to see off.

okŭsama, okŭsan, a married woman of the upper class, my lady, Lady, Mrs.

omae, you.

omma, a stallion.

omocha, a toy.

omoi, heavy, serious, severe.

omoi, thought, (hence) affection.

omoshiroi, amusing, interesting.

omoshiromi, (a certain amount of) fun, or interest.

omoshirosa, amusement, fun, interest, the amount or degree of amusement.

omotai, heavy.

omote, the front, out-of-doors.

omou, to think: *omoi-dasu,* to call to mind.

omowareru, to venture to think.

ōmugi, barley.

on, kindness: *on wo shiranai,* to be ungrateful.

on, an honorific prefix.

onaji, the same.

ondori, a cock bird.

onna, a woman: *onna no ko,* a girl.

onore, self; also you (insulting).

onsen, a hot spring.

orā, I.

ōrai, going and coming, a thoroughfare: *ōrai-dome,* no thoroughfare.

oreru, to break (intrans.).

ori, an occasion, a time: *ori-ori,* from time to time.

orifŭshi, on a certain occasion, just then.

oriru, to descend.

orosoka (na), remiss.

orosu, to lower, hence to launch.

oru, to be.

oru, to break (trans.), to pluck.

osameru, to pacify, hence to govern, to guide; also to put away.

ō-sawagi, confusion, a hubbub.

ōserareru, honorific for to say.

oshie, instruction doctrine, a religion.

oshiekata, mode of teaching.

oshieru, to teach, to show how, to inform.

oshii, regrettable: *oshii koto desŭ ne!* what a pity!

oshimu, to regret, to grudge.

osoi, late.

osoreru, to fear: *osore-iru,* to be filled with dread.

osoroshii, frightful.

ossharu, to say (honorific).

osu, male.

osu, to push.

oto, a sound, a noise: *oto ga suru,* there is a noise.

otoko, a man: *otoko-buri,* a manly air; *otoko no ko,* a boy.

otona, a grown-up person.

otonashii, good (of a child), quiet in behavior.

otosu, to let fall.

ototoi, the day before yesterday. ototoshi, the year before last.

otōto, a younger brother.

otōsan, father.

otto, a husband.

ou, to pursue.

ō-warai, a good laugh.

owari, the end.

owaru, to end (intrans. and trans.).
oya, a parent: *oya-ko*, parents and children.
oyaji, a father.
oya(-oya) ! an interjection.
oyobosu, to cause to reach, to extend to (trans.).
oyobu, to reach (intrans.).
oyogu, to swim.
oyoso, or **ōyoso,** altogether, on the whole, in the main.
ōzara, a dish (large plate).
ōzei, a crowd.

P

pan, bread: *pan-ya*, a bakery, hence a baker.
pata(t)to, flop, bang.
pika-pika, pikatto, with a flash, glitteringly.

R

ra, a particle of vagueness or plurality.
rai, next (in composition), as *rai-nen*, next year.
rambō, disorderly conduct: *rambō na*, wild riotous; *rambō-nin*, a turbulent fellow.
rampu, a lamp (from the English word): *rampu wo tsŭkeru*, to light a lamp.
rashii, a suffix.
rei, ceremonies, politeness, thanks: *o rei wo iu*, to thank.
rei, a precedent, an example.
reifŭku, full dress, dress clothes.
rekĭshi, history.
rieki, profit, advantage.
rigaku, physical science, physics.
rikken-seiji, constitutional government.
rikō (na), 'cute, intelligent.
riku, rare for *roku*, six.
riku, land.
rikugun, an army.
rikutsu, a reason.
ringo, an apple.
rippa (na), splendid.
ro, an imperative termination.
rōjin, an old man.
rōka, a passage (in a house), a corridor.
roku, six.
Roku-gatsu, June.
roku-jū, sixty.
Rōmaji, the Roman alphabet.
ron, argument, opinion.
rōnjiru, to argue: *ronji-tateru*, to start an idea.
ronrigaku, logic.
rōsoku, a candle.
ro(ya), prison.
rusu, absent: *rusu-ban*, a caretaker; *rusu-chū*, while absent.
ryō, both, as in *ryō-hō*, both (sides); *ryō-nin*, both people; *ryō-te*, both hands.
ryohi, travelling expenses.
ryōji, a consul: *ryōjikwan*, a consulate.
ryōken, judgment, opinion, intention, sometimes excuse.

ryokō, a journey: *ryokō-suru,* to travel.

ryōri, cooking: *ryōri-nin,* a cook; *ryōri-ya,* a restaurant; *ryōri wo suru,* to cook.

ryōshin, both parents.

S

sa, a suffix used to form abstract nouns.

sa! or **sā!** an interjection.

sabishii, lonely, dull.

sadamaru, to be fixed, settled.

sadameru, to fix, to settle.

sadameshi or **sadamete,** positive-ly, surely.

sae, even (adverb), if only.

sagaru, to descend (hence) to go away.

sagasu, to seek, to look for.

sageru, to lower, to hang down (trans.).

sai, a humble word for wife: *sai-shi,* wife and children.

saikun, an honorific word for wife.

saisho, the beginning.

saiwai, good luck, happiness.

saji, a spoon.

saka, the hilly part of a road, an ascent.

sakan (na), prosperous: *sakan ni,* greatly.

sakana, anything taken with *sake,* hence more especially fish.

saka-ya, a grog-shop.

sakazuki, a *sake* cup.

sake, rice-beer, also alcoholic liquors in general: *sake ni you,* to get tipsy.

saki, front, before, on ahead, further, a cape.

saki-hodo, previously, a short while ago.

saku, to blossom.

saku, to tear (trans.).

saku, last (in composition), as *sakuban,* last night; *sakujitsu,* yesterday; *sakunen,* last year.

sakura, a cherry tree.

sama, way, fashion; also Mr., Mrs., Miss.

samasu, to cool (trans.).

sam-bai, treble.

sameru, to cool (intrans.). to fade: *me ga sameru,* to wake.

samisen, a kind of banjo.

samui, cold; —said only of the weather, or of one's own feel-ings.

samurai, a gentleman of the military casre under the feudal system, a warrior.

samusa, coldness, the degree of cold.

samushii, lonely, dull.

san, three.

san short for *sama.*

san, a mountain, (in composition) as *Fuji-san,* Mount Fuji.

San-gatsu, March.

san-jū, thirty.

sansei suru to approve, to second (a motion).

sappari, quite (with a negative) not at all.

sara, a plate.

Thanksgiving celebration

Playing the five-string biwa

saru, a monkey.
saru, to leave (a place), hence to be distant from.
sasayaku, to whisper.
saseru, to cause to do, to let.
sashimi, raw fish.
sashitsukai, engagement.
sassoku, at once.
sasu, to thrust, to sting ; to carry (*e.g.*, a sword) : *sashi-ageru*, to present (to a superior).
sate, well ! (at the beginning of a sentence.)
sato, a village.
satō, sugar.
satsu, a volume.
satsu, paper-money : *satsu-ire*, a pocketbook.
Satsuma-imo, a sweet potato.
sawagasu, to disturb, to make turbulent.
sawagi, a fuss, a row.
sawaru, to strike or clash against, to touch.
sayō, (a contraction of *sono yō*, that way) so : *sayō de gozaimasŭ*, that is so, yes ; *sayō de gozaimasen*, no.
sayōnara, goodbye.
sazo, indeed, surely, doubtless.
segare, a humble word for son.
sei, stature : *sei no hĭkui*, short (of stature) ; *sei no takai*, tall.
sei, make, manufacture : *seisuru*, to manufacture.
seibanjin, savage, aborigine.
seibutsu, a living being.
seifu, seiji, a government.
seijin, a sage, a philosopher.
seinen the prime of life, youth.
seiryoku, strength.
sei-shitsu, character, disposition, nature.
Seiyō, Western or European countries generally, Europe, America : *Seiyō-jin*, a European, an American ; *Seiyō-zŭkuri*, foreign-built.
seji, compliments, flattery.
sekai, the world : *seken narete iru*, to be used to the ways of the world.
seki, a cough : *seki ga deru*, to cough.
sekitan, coal.
sekkaku, special pains, signal kindness, on purpose.
sekkyō, a sermon : *sekkyō suru*, to preach.
semai, narrow, small.
semete, at any rate, at least, at most.
semeru, to treat with rigor, to press upon.
semmon, a speciality (in learning).
sen, a thousand.
sen, a cent.
senaka, the back (of the body).
sendō, the master of a junk, hence a boatman.
senjitsu, the other day.
senkyōshi, a clergyman, a missionary.
sensei, an elder, a teacher, hence you, he.
senshū, last week.
sensō, war.
sentaku, the washing of clothes : *sentaku-ya*, a washerman ; *sentaku suru*, to wash (clothes).
senzo, an ancestor

seppuku, the same as *hara-kiri,*
seshimeru, to cause to do.
sessha, I, literally, the awkward person.
setsu, an opinion.
setsumei, an explanation : *setsumei suru,* to explain.
sewa, help, work : *sewa ni naru,* to be helped by ; *sewa ga yakeru,* to be busy and anxious ; *sewa wo suru* (or *yaku*), to help.
sha, a company, a society, a firm.
shaberi, chatter, a chatter-box.
shaberu, to chatter.
shabon, soap (from the Spanish *jabon*).
shafu, a *jinrikĭsha*-man.
shain, a partner in a firm, a member of society.
shake, (properly *sake*) a salmon.
shakkin, a debt.
shaku, a foot (measurement).
shakwai, (a) society ; also in such phrases as *gakŭsha shakwai,* the learned world.
shashin, a photograph : *shashin-ya,* a photographer ; *shashinki,* a camera.
shatsu, a shirt (from the English word).
shi, death.
shi, four.
shi, Mr. (in the Written Language).
shi, a postposition.
shi, the indefinite form of *suru,* to do.
shi-awase, good fortune, lucky.
shiba, turf, grass.
shibaraku, some time (whether short or long) : *makoto ni shibaraku,* "It has been a long time (since I saw you.)"
shibaru, to tie.
shibashi, a short while.
shi-bun no ichi, a quarter ($\frac{1}{4}$).
shĭchi, seven
Shĭchi-gatsu, July.
shĭchi-jū, seventy.
shidai, arrangement, state, (hence) according to : *shidai nĭ* according to, gradually.
shi-go, four or five.
shigoku, extremely, very.
Shi-gatsu, April.
shihainin, the manager of a commercial house.
shijū, constantly.
shi-jū, forty.
shĭka, (with a negative), nothing but, only.
shĭka, a deer, a stag.
shĭkaku, four sides : *shĭkaku na* or *no,* square.
shĭkaru, to scold.
shĭkashi, but.
shĭkata, a way of doing : *shĭkata ga nai,* there is nothing to be done, no help for it.
shĭken, an examination, an experiment.
shĭki, a ceremony.
shĭki-mono, literally, a spread thing, hence a carpet, a table-cloth, etc.
shĭkiri (ni), perpetually.
shikkari, firm, tight : *shikkari shĭta,* firm.
shikkei, rudeness : *shikkei na,* rude, impolite.

shikwan, an official, an officer.
shima, an island.
shimai, the end: *mō shimai,* its finished.
shimatsu, the beginning and end, the whole of any affair.
shimau, to finish.
shimbun, news, a newspaper: *shimbun-ya,* a newspaper man.
shimbunshi, a newspaper.
shimeppoi, damp,
shimeru, to fasten, to close.
shimmitsu (na), intimate.
shimo, below.
shimpai, anxiety, sorrow: *shimpai suru,* to be anxious or troubled; *shimpai ni naru,* to become anxious.
shimpo, progress: *shimpo suru,* to progress.
shimpu, a father,—by birth, not by adoption; *go shimpu (sama),* your father.
shin, new, (in composition), as *shinnen,* the new year.
shin, the heart; hence the wick of a lamp.
shin (no), true, real: *shin ni,* really.
shina, a kind, hence more frequently an article, goods: *shinamono.*
Shina, China: *Shina-jin,* a Chinaman.
shinja, a believer.
shinjiru, to believe.
shinjō suru, (irreg.), to present respectfully to a superior.
shinkō, belief: *shinkō-shin,* a believing heart; *shinkō suru,* to believe.
shinkwa, evolution: *shinkwa-ron,* the doctrine of evolution.
shinnen, the new year.
shinri, truth.
shinrui, a relation, a kinsman
shinsetsu, kindness: *shinsetsu na,* kind.
shinshi, a gentleman.
Shintō, the name of the aboriginal religion of the Japanese.
shinuru, to die.
shinzu-beki, credible.
shio, salt, salt water, the tide.
shirase, an intimation, an announcement.
shiraseru, to inform.
shireta, self-evident.
shira, familiar for *shiran,* don't know.
shira-ga, white hair.
shiro, a castle.
shiro, imperative of *suru,* to do: *nani shiro.*
shiroi, white.
shiromi, a tinge of whiteness.
shiromono, merchandise.
shiroto, amateur.
shirosa, whiteness, the degree of whiteness.
shiru, to know: *shirenai,* can't tell.
shirushi, a sign, a mark.
shishi, lion.
shisō, a thought.
shisoku, (with honorific prefix *go*) your son.
shison, a descendant.
shita, the under or lower part of anything, downstairs: *no shita ni,* below, underneath; *shita no hō,* the bottom, beneath.

shĭta, the tongue.
shĭtagau, to follow, to conform, to obey: *ni shĭtagatte,* according to.
shĭtaku, preparations: *shĭtaku wo suru,* to prepare.
shitateya, tailor.
shitsu, a room, a cabin.
shitsurei, rudeness: *shitsurei na,* rude, impolite.
shiyō, a way of doing: *shiyō ga nai,* there is no help for it, nothing to be done.
shizen, spontaneity: *shizen no,* spontaneous, natural.
shizuka (na), quiet.
shizumaru, to quiet down (intrans.).
shizumu, to sink (intrans.).
sho, all; —used only in composition, as *shokoku,* all countries.
shōbai, trade.
shōchi, consent, assent, comprehension: *shōchi suru,* to consent etc.
Shō-gatsu, January.
shōji, the wood and paper or glass slides which enclose a Japanese room.
shōjiki, honesty: *shōjiki na,* honest.
shoki, a secretary.
shōko, a proof.
shokubutsu, a plant.
shokugyō, occupation.
shokuma, a dining room.
shokumotsu, food.
shokun, gentlemen, Sirs, all of you.
shomotsu, a book.
shōnin, a merchant, a dealer.
shosei, a student.
shōsei, I, literally, junior.
shōsetsu, a novel.
shōsho, a certificate.
shōshō, a little.
shōshō, a general or admiral of the third rank.
shōyu, soy (our word comes from the Japanese).
shu, a master.
shu, the auxiliary numeral for poems.
shu, Chinese for *sake,* strong liquor.
shu, rarely **shū,** also **shi,** a pluralising suffix.
shū, a province, a country.
shujin, the master of a household.
shūkan, a week.
shūkyō, religion, a sect: *shūkyō-tetsŭgaku,* religious philosophy.
shurui, a sort.
shuttatsu, starting, departure: *shuttatsu suru,* to start.
sō, like that, in that way, so: *sō iu,* that kind of, such as that.
sō, the auxiliary numeral for boats and ships.
sō (na), a termination of quasi-adjectives; also used separately, as "it would seem that."
soba, alongside, beside.
sōba, the market price, the current rate.
sochi, or *sochira,* there.
sōdan, consultation: *sōdan suru,* to hold a consultation.
sōji, cleansing: *sōji wo suru,* to cleanse.

sōken (**na**), healthy, vigorous.
soko, there.
soko, the bottom (*e.g.*, of a lake) : *soko-bie*, an under-chill.
sokoera, thereabouts.
soku, the auxiliary numeral for all sorts of foot-gear.
somatsu, coarseness : *somatsu na*, coarse, rude.
someru, to dye.
sōmoku, herbs and trees, vegetation.
son, loss, especially pecuniary loss.
son, a village,—the auxiliary numeral for *mura*, village.
sonaeru, to provide ; (sometimes) to be provided with.
sonata, you.
sonna, that kind of, such as that : *sonna ni*, so (much).
sonnara, (for *sō nara*), if that is so, well then.
sono, that (adj.) : *sono hō*, you (in legal parlance).
sora, the sky : *sora-iro*, sky-blue.
sore, that (subst.) : *sore de wa*, that being so, then ; *sore kara*, after that, and then, next.
soroban, an abacus.
soroe, a match, a set.
soroeru, to put in order, to arrange.
sorou, to be in order, to be all in their places.
soro-soro, leisurely, slowly.
soru, to shave.
sorya ! there now !
sōryō, an eldest son.
sōshĭki, a funeral.
soshiru, to blame, to revile.
sōshĭte, having done so, and (then).
sōtai, (**no**), whole.
soto, the exterior, out-of-doors : *no soto ni*, outside of.
sotsŭgyō, graduation : *sotsŭgyō suru*, to graduate.
sotto, gently ; also used for *chotto*, a little.
sōzō, a fancy : *sōzō-tetsŭgaku*, metaphysics.
sū, a number.
suberu, to slide, to slip.
suberu, to unite in one.
subete, altogether, all.
sude ni, already.
sue, the end or tip of a thing.
sueru, to set, to place.
sugi, past, after.
sugiru, to exceed. Suffixed to an adjective or verb, it may be rendered by too or too much, as *yo-sugiru*, to be too good ; *nomi-sugiru*, to drink too much.
sugu (**ni** or **to**), immediately.
suidō, an aqueduct.
suifu, a seaman, a common sailor.
suishō, a crystal.
Suiyōbi, Wednesday.
suji, a line.
sŭki, fond.
sukkari, quite, completely ; (with a negative) not at all.
sŭkoburu, very.
sŭkoshi, a little.
sŭku, to be empty.
sŭkunai, few, scarce.
sumai, a residence.
sumau, to reside.
sumasu, to conclude (trans.).

sumō, wrestling: *sumo wo toru,* to wrestle.
sumu, to dwell.
sumu, to finish.
sumu, to be clear.
sun, an inch.
sŭna, sand.
sunawachi, namely, forthwith.
sūnen or **sunen,** many years.
suppai, sour.
surari to, sura-sura to, smoothly, without more ado.
surippa, slipper.
suru, to do, to make.
susumeru, to urge, to offer, to recommend.
susumu, to advance, to progress (intrans.).
sŭteru, to throw away.
suu, to suck.
suwaru, to squat (Japanese fashion).
suzume, a sparrow.
suzushii, cool.

T

ta, a suffix denoting past time.
ta, other: *sono ta,* besides that.
ta, a rice-field.
tabako, tobacco (from the European word): *tabako-ire,* a tobacco-pouch; *tabako wo nomu,* to smoke.
taberu, to eat.
tabemono, food.
tabi, a time: *tabi-tabi,* often; *iku tabi?* how many times?
tabi, a journey; *tabi ye deru,* to go on a journey.
tabi-bito, a traveller.
tabun, a good deal, most; hence probably.
tachi, a pluralizing suffix.
tada, only, simply.
tadaima, immediately.
tagai (ni), mutually.
tagaru, a verbal suffix.
tai, termination of desiderative adjectives.
taiboku, a large tree.
taigai, for the most part, probably.
taihen, literally, a great change, hence very, awfully.
taihō, a cannon.
taika, a famous man.
taikutsu, tedium, ennui: *taikutsu suru,* to feel bored.
taira (na), flat.
taisa, a colonel, a post-captain.
taisetsu, importance: *taisetsu na,* important.
taishi, ambassador.
taishĭta, important.
taishō, a general or admiral of the first rank.
taisō, greatly, much, very.
tasshiru, to reach.
taisuru, to be opposite to: *ni taishite,* vis-a-vis, to.
taitei, for the most part, generally, average.
taiyō, the sun.
taka, a quantity.
takai, high, hence dear (in price).
takara, a treasure.
take, a bamboo.
take, a mountain peak.
taki, a waterfall.

tako a kite (toy).
taku, a house, hence a humble term for husband: *o taku de,* at home.
taku, to light (the fire), to cook (rice).
takŭsan, much, many, plenty: *mō takŭsan,* that is plenty, I don't want any more.
tama, a ball, a bead, a jewel.
tamago, an egg.
tamaru, (intrans.). to collect (as water in a puddle).
tamaru, (trans.), to endure: *tamaranai* sometimes means too.
tamashii, the soul.
tamau, to deign.
tame, sake: *no tame ni,* for the sake of, because of, in order to; *tame ni naru,* to be profitable.
tamotsu, to keep (trans.).
tana, a shelf.
tane, a seed.
tani, a valley.
tanin, another person, a stranger.
tanjun (na), simple.
tanomu, to rely on, to apply to, to ask.
tanoshimi, joy, pleasure.
tansu, a cabinet, a chest of drawers.
taoreru, to fall over.
tara, a cod-fish.
tara (ba), termination of the conditional past.
taredo(mo), termination of the concessive past.
tari, termination of the frequentative form.
tariru, to suffice, to be enough.
tarō, termination of the probable past.
tashika ni, certainly.
tashō, more or less, hence amount degree.
tasŭkaru, to be saved.
tasŭkeru, to save, to help.
tataku, to knock.
tatami, a mat.
tatamu, to pile up.
tatemono, building.
tateru, to set up, to build.
tateru, to be able to stand (intrans.).
tatoe, a comparison, a metaphor.
tatoeba for instance.
tatoeru, to compare.
tatsu, to stand up, to rise, to depart.
tatta, vulgar and emphatic for *tada.*
tattobu, to honor, to venerate.
tattoi, venerable, worshipful.
tazuneru, to ask, to enquire, to visit.
te, the termination of the gerund.
te, the hand, the arm.
tebukuro, a glove.
techō, a notebook.
tegami, a letter.
tegarui, easy, slight, not troublesome.
teikoku, an empire, specifically Japan.
teinei (na), polite.
teishaba, station (railroad).
teishu, the master of a house, a husband.
teki, an enemy (public).

teki, a drop.
teki suru, to be appropriate.
teki, of.
temae, front; hence you, also I.
temmongaku, astronomy.
ten, the sky, heaven.
ten, a point.
ten-chi, heaven and earth.
tenjō, a ceiling.
tenki, the weather.
tentaku, changing houses: *tentakŭ suru,* to change houses.
tentō, (*o tentō sama*), the sun.
tenugui, a towel.
teppō, a gun: *teppō wo utsu,* to fire a gun.
tera, a Buddhist temple.
teru, to shine.
tesŭki, leisure, nothing to do.
tetsu, iron: *tetsubin,* a kettle; *tetsudō,* a railroad.
tetsŭgaku, philosophy: *tetsŭgakŭsha,* a philosopher.
to, a door.
tō, ten.
to, a postposition.
tō, a pagoda.
tō, an auxiliary numeral for animals.
tō, etcetera.
tobu, to jump, to fly: *tobi-agaru,* to fly up; *tobi-komu,* to jump or fly in; *tobi-kosu,* to jump across.
tōchaku, arrival: *tōchaku suru,* to arrive.
tochi, a locality, a place, soil,
tochū, on the road, by the way.
todana, a cupboard.
todoke, a report.
todokeru, to send to destination, to give notice, to report.
todoku, to reach (intrans.).
todomaru, to stop, to stay (intrans.).
todome, a stop, a pause, the coup de grace.
todomeru, to stop (trans.).
tōfu, bean-curd: *tōfu-ya,* a shop for, or seller of, bean-curd.
tōgarashi, cayenne pepper.
tōge, a mountain pass.
tōgetsu, this month.
tohōmonai, outrageous, extortionate.
tōi, far, distant.
toji, the binding of a book.
tōji, the present time.
tōka, ten days, the tenth day of the month.
tokei, a clock, a watch.
tokeru, to melt (intrans.).
toki, time, hence when; *toki-doki,* often.
to(k)kuri, a bottle.
toko, an abbreviation of *tokoro,* place.
tokonoma, an alcove.
tokoro, a place.
toku, to loosen, to unfasten, to explain: *toki-akasu,* to explain
toku, profit, advantage, efficacy.
toku, to melt (trans.).
tokuhon, a reading book.
tokusho suru, to read.
tomai, the auxiliary numeral for godowns.
tomaru, to stop, to stay (intrans.)
tombi, a kite (bird).
tombo, a dragonfly.
tō-megane, a telescope.

tomeru, to stop, to stay (trans.).
tomo, a companion, a follower: *o tomo suru,* to accompany.
tomodachi, a companion, a friend.
tomokaku(**mo**), in any case, be that as it may, somehow or other.
tonaeru, to recite, to proclaim (*e.g.*, opinions).
tonari, next door.
tonda, tondemonai, absurd, awful, excessive.
tōnen, this year.
tonikaku, same as *tomokaku.*
tōnin, the person in question.
tonto (**mo**), altogether; (with a negative) not at all. *Ton to* sometimes means thud.
tora, a tiger.
toraeru, to seize, to arrest.
toreru, to take (intrans.), to be able to take.
tori, a bird, especially the barn-door fowl.
tōri, a thoroughfare, a street, a way.
tori-atsŭkai, management, treatment.
tori-ire, ingathering, harvest.
toru, to take, but sometimes merely expletive in compounds: *tori ni iku,* to go for; *tori ni kuru,* to come for; *tori ni yaru,* to send for; *tori-atsŭkau,* to undertake, to manage; *tori-shiraberu,* investigate.
tōru, to pass through, to pass by.
tosan, the ascent of a mountain: *tosan suru,* to ascend a mountain.
toshi, a year, hence age: *toshi wo toru,* to grow old; *toshi no yotta,* elderly, aged.
toshiyori (**no**), old (said only of people).
tōsu, to put or let through, to admit (*e.g.*, a guest).
tote, a postposition.
totemo, anyhow, at any price (metaph.); (with a negative) not at all, by no means.
tōtō, at last.
Tōyō, the Orient.
tsŭchi, the earth: *tsŭchi-yaki,* earthenware.
tsue, a stick, a staff: *tsue wo tsŭku,* to lean on a staff.
tsugi (**no**), the next: *sono tsugi ni,* next (adverb).
tsugō, the sum total, altogether; also convenience, certain reasons: *tsugō no yoi,* convenient; *tsugō no warui,* inconvenient; *go tsugō shidai,* according to your convenience.
tsugu, to join (trans.), to follow, to succeed to (a patrimony); also to pour into.
tsui (**ni**), at last.
tsuide, occasion, apropos: *no tsuide ni,* apropos of.
tsuitachi, the first day of the month.
tsuite, (preceded by *ni*) according to, owing to, about.
tsŭkaeru to serve.
tsŭkai, a message, a messenger *tsŭka no mono,* a messenger.
tsŭkai-michi, a means of employing.
tsŭkasadoru, to control, to direct.

tsukai, messenger.
tsŭkau, to use, to employ.
tsŭkawasu, to give to send.
tsŭkeru, to fix, to affix, (hence) to set down in writing, to add.
tsŭki, the moon, a month: *tsŭki-zue,* the end of the month; *tsŭki ga agaru,* the moon rises.
tsŭki-ai, association.
tsūkō, passing through a thoroughfare; *tsūkō suru,* to pass through or along.
tsŭku, to push, to shove.
tsŭku, to stick (intrans.), sometimes to result.
tsŭkue, a table, specifically a very low Japanese writing-table.
tsŭkuru, to make, to compose; to grow (trans.): *tsŭkuri-dasu,* to produce.
tsŭkusu, to exhaust, to do to the utmost.
tsŭku-tsŭku, attentively.
tsuma, a wife.
tsumaran(ai), worthless, trifling.
tsumari, at last, in the long run.
tsume, a finger or toe nail, a claw.
tsumeru, to stuff, pack, or squeeze into.
tsumetai, cold (to the touch).
tsumi, a sin, a crime: *tsumi no nai,* innocent; *tsumi suru,* to punish.
tsumori, an intention.
tsumoru, to be heaped up.
tsune (ni), generally.
tsuno, a horn.
tsunoru, to collect (trans.), to levy, to increase or grow violent.
tsurai, disagreeable, unsympathetic.
tsure, a companion.
tsureru, to take with one: *tsurete kuru,* to bring (a person).
tsūrei, the general precedent, the usual plan.
tsuru, a stork.
tsuru, to hang (*e.g.*, a mosquito-net).
tsuru, to angle, to catch fish with a line and hook.
tsutsumi, a parcel.
tsutsumu, to wrap up.
tsūyō, circulation: *tsūyō suru,* to circulate (as money).
tsuyoi, strong.
tsūzoku, colloquial, common.

U

ubau, to steal.
uchi, the inside, hence a house, etc.
uchiwa, a fan of the kind that does not open and shut.
ude, the arm.
uderu, to boil,—*e.g.*, an egg.
ue, the top of anything: *no ue ni,* above, on, after.
ueki, a garden plant: *ueki-ya,* a gardener.
ueru, to plant.
ugokasu, to move (trans.).
ugoku, to move (intrans.).
ukagau, to enquire, to ask, to listen to, to visit.
ukeru, to receive: *uke-toru,* to take delivery, to receive.
uketori, a receipt.

ŭma, a horse.
ŭmai, nice to eat, tasty.
ŭmareru, to be born.
ŭmare-tsŭki, by birth ; hence the character or disposition.
ŭme, a plum tree.
umi, the sea.
umu, to give birth to, to bear.
umitate, fresh.
un, luck : *un no yoi,* lucky ; *un no warui,* unlucky.
unazuku, to nod.
unchin, freight (-money).
undō, bodily exercise : *undō suru* to take exercise.
ura, the back or reverse side of anything.
ureru, to sell (intrans.), to be able to sell.
ureshii, joyful,
ureshigaru, to feel joyful.
uri, a melon.
uru, to sell (trans.).
urusai, troublesome, a bother.
urusagaru, to find troublesome.
uruwashii, beautiful, lovely.
usagi, a hare.
ushi, a cow, a bull, an ox, beef.
ushinau, to lose.
ushiro, the back or hinder part of anything : *no ushiro ni,* at the back of, behind.
uso, a lie, a falsehood : *uso wo iu,* to lie ; *uso-tsŭki,* a liar.
usui, light, thin : *usu-akai,* pink ; *usu-gurai,* dusk.
utagai, a doubt.
utsu, to strike, to hit.
uwagi, an overcoat, a coat.
uwo, a fish.

W

wa, a postposition.
wa, an auxiliary numeral.
wa, a wheel.
wabiru, to lament, to apologize.
waga, my own, one's own : *waga mi,* myself.
waka-danna, the son of the master of the house.
wakai, young.
wakari, understanding : *o wakari ni naru,* to understand (honorific) ; *wakari no hayai,* quick-witted, sharp.
wakari-nikui, hard to understand.
wakari-yasui, easy to understand.
wakaru, to understand.
wakasu, to boil (trans.) ; said of water.
wakatsu, to discern.
wake, a reason, a cause : *dō iu wake de* ? why ?
wakeru, to divide : *wake-ataeru,* to distribute in appropriate shares.
wakete, specially.
wakimaeru, to discriminate, to comprehend.
waku, to boil (intrans.).
wampaku (na), naughty.
wan, a bowl.
wan-wan, bow-bow. Children call dogs so.
wara, straw.
warai, laughter.
waraji, a kind of straw sandals used only out-of-doors.

warau, to laugh.
ware, I (in Book Language): *ware-ware,* people like me, we.
wari-ai, proportion.
warui, bad (hence sometimes) ugly: *waruku iu,* to blame.
waru-kŭchi, bad language.
waru-mono, a worthless fellow, a ruffian.
Wasei, made in Japan.
washi, a vulgar contraction of *watakŭshi,* I.
wasure-mono, something forgotten.
wasureru, to forget.
watakŭshi, selfishness, (hence) I: *watakŭshi-domo,* we, people like me, I.
wataru, to cross (a river).
watashi, a somewhat vulgar contraction of *watakŭshi,* I.
watasu, to hand over.
wazawai, a calamity.
waza-waza, on purpose.
wazuka, a trifle: *wazuka ni,* only, nothing but.
wo, a postposition.

Y

ya, a termination signifying house.
ya, a postposition.
yā, eight (in enumeration).
yaban, a barbarian: *yaban no* or *na,* barbarous.
yachin, house-rent.
yado, a dwelling-place, a hotel; hence a humble word for husband: *yadoya,* a hotel.
yagate, forthwith, by and bye.
yahari, also.
yai! halloa!
yakamashii, noisy.
yakedo, a burn.
yakeru to burn (intrans.).
yaki, burning, roasting, annealing.
yakkai, assistance.
yaku, to burn (trans.), to roast, to toast, to bake.
yaku, usefulness, service: *yaku ni tatsu,* to be of use.
yakunin, an official.
yakŭsha, an actor.
yakŭsho, a public office.
yakŭsoku, an agreement, a promise, an engagement.
yama, a mountain, a hill: *yama-michi,* a mountain path.
Yamato, the name of one of the central provinces of Japan; hence by extension Japan itself
yameru, to put a stop to.
yami, total darkness.
yane, a roof:
yappari, emphatic for *yahari.*
yaru, to send, to give: *yatte miru,* to try (one's hand at). *Yaru* is sometimes used instead of *suru,* to do.
yasai(-mono), vegetables.
yasashii, easy, gentle.
yaseru, to grow thin: *yasete iru,* to be thin; *yaseta,* thin.
yashĭki, a nobleman's mansion.
yashiro, a Shintō temple.
yashoku, supper, (late) dinner.

Yaso, Jesus: *Yasokyō* or *Yasoshū* (Protestant) Christianity; *Yasokyōshi,* a (Protestant) missionary or clergyman.

yasui, cheap, easy.

yasumi, a holiday.

yasumu, to rest, to go to bed: *oyasumi nasai,* goodnight.

yatou, to hire, to engage.

yatsu, a (low) fellow; rarely a thing.

ya(tsu), eight.

yatte, a meaningless expletive.

yawarakai or **yawaraka na,** soft.

ye, a postposition.

yo! an interjection.

yo, the night: *yo ni iru,* to become dark.

yo, the world.

yō, four (in enumeration).

yō, business, use.

yo, appearance, way kind: *yō ni* to, so that.

yobō, a precaution.

yobu, to call: *yobi-dasu,* to summon; *yobi-kaesu,* to call back.

yōfūku, European clothes.

yohodo, plenty, a lot, very.

yoi, good, (hence) handsome.

yō-i (na), easy.

yōka, eight days, the eighth day of the month.

yōkan, a kind of sweetmeat made of beans and sugar.

yokei, superfluity; (with a negative) not very, not much.

yokka, four days, the fourth day of the month.

yoko, cross athwart: *yoko-chō,* a side street (whether cross or parallel).

yokomoji, European written characters, Roman letters.

yokosu, to send hither.

yoku, well, (hence) often.

yome, a bride, a daughter-in-law: *yome ni yaru,* to give (a girl) in marriage; *yome wo morau,* to marry (a wife).

yomeru, to read (intrans.), can read.

yomu to read (trans.).

yone, hulled rice.

yo (no naka), the world.

yopparai, a drunkard.

yopparatte iru, to be intoxicated.

yoppodo, emphatic for *yohodo.*

yori, a postposition.

yorokeru, to reel.

yorokobi, joy.

yorokobu, to rejoice.

yōroppa, Europe.

yoroshii, good.

yoru, the night.

yoru, to lean on, to rely, to depend; hence to look in at, to stop at for a short time: *ni yotte,* owing to.

yoru, to select: *yori-dasu,* do.

yoru, to assemble.

yosasō (na), having a good appearance.

yose, music hall, variety theater.

yoseru, to collect (trans.).

yoshi, good, all right: *yoshi,* adopted child.

yoso, elsewhere.

yosu, to leave off, to abstain from to put an end to.

yōsu, appearance, circumstances.

yo-sugiru, to be too good.

yo(tsu), four.
yottari, four persons.
yotte, for that reason : *ni yotte,* owing to.
you, to become drunk.
yowai, weak.
yōyaku, yōyō, barely, at last, with difficulty.
yu, hot water, a hot bath *yu wo sasu,* to pour in hot water.
yūbe, last night.
yubi, a finger, a toe.
yūbin, the post : *yūbin-kyoku,* a post office ; *yūbin-zei,* postage.
yūgata, twilight, evening.
yuka, the floor.
yuki, snow.
yukkuri, leisurely, slowly.
yume, a dream : *yume wo miru,* to dream.
yūmei na, famous.
yūmeshi, supper, (late) dinner.
yumi, a bow (for shooting).
yunyū suru, to import.
yūrei, a ghost.
yuri, a lily.
yurui, loose.
yururi (to), leisurely.
yurusu, to allow.
yūsei, a planet.
yūshoku, supper, (late) dinner.
yūyū to, nonchalantly.

Z

zannen, regret : *zannen-garu,* to regret.
zashiki, a room.
zasshi, a magazine, a review.
zehi, right and/or wrong ; (hence) positively.
zen, before ; (in compounds), as *shi-go-nen-zen,* four or five years ago.
zen-aku, good and/or evil.
zentai, properly the whole body ; more often usually, generally.
zetchō, the summit of a mountain.
zo, an interjection.
zōkin, rag.
zoku, commonplace, vulgarity.
zokugo, a colloquial word, the spoken dialect.
zonji, knowledge ; used in such phrases as *go zonji desŭ ka ?* do you know ?
zonjiru, to know.
zōri, a kind of straw sandals worn indoors.
zōsa, difficulty : always with a negative, as *zōsa mo nai,* there is no difficulty.
zotto suru, to start with surprise; also to be natural or pleasant.
zuibun, a good deal, pretty (adverb), very.
zutsu, (one, etc.) at a time, apiece, each, as *mitsu-zutsu,* three at a time.
zutsu, a headache : *zutsū ga suru,* to have a headache.
zutto, straight, quite, a great deal.

APPENDIX

Japanese Writing System & Pronunciation

Written language came to Japan in the third century CE, when the Chinese ideographic script, or *kanji* was adopted. While the acquisition of a written language was a major boon to Japanese culture, the transition was a difficult one for many reasons. The primary challenge emerged from the fact that Chinese is a monosyllabic, inflected language, meaning that a single syllable can have many different meanings depending on how it is spoken. Japanese, like English, is a polysyllabic language in which inflection does not affect meaning. In addition, kanji ideograms are very complex, some being comprised of twenty strokes or more with clear standards for both stroke form and stroke order.

Because of these challenges, the written language of Japan evolved into a mixture of forms, each with a specific role in written expression. These forms are:

Kanji: The Japanese form of the Chinese written language described above. Ideograms number in the thousands, and each one is linked to an idea rather than a sound. Kanji is most often used to express place names, people's names and many other nouns, along with verb and adjective stems.

Katakaná: An angular script, katakaná is a phonetic syllabary, comprised of 46 basic characters. Each character corresponds to one sound in the Japanese language. It is most often used to express non-Japanese names, words borrowed from other languages, names of companies, and recent entrants into the Japanese language.

Hiraganá: A smoother, more flowing script, hiragana is a phonetic syllabary, like katakaná. There are 46 basic characters, each corresponding to a sound. Hiraganá shares most of the rules of katakaná and is the first writing system taught in Japanese schools. Therefore, most children's books are written in hiraganá. As students learn kanji, difficult or complex ideograms may be supplemented by hiraganá pronunciations in textbooks. Hiraganá is most often used to express simple words, verb conjugations, and particles of speech.

Katakaná and hiraganá are known collectively as *kaná*, and evolved out of the kanji system roughly five centuries after its adoption.

Romaji: Romaji is the "Romanized" version of Japanese, or the use of the Latin alphabet with which we are all familiar to write out Japanese sounds. There are numerous systems used to make Japanese easier for Westerners to learn, including the *Kunrei-Shiki* and the *Nippon* systems. By far the most popular is the Hepburn system, which is the one used in this text. While romaji will be invaluable in early study, and can be essential to business travelers or others who wish only to "get around" in Japan, students should not become too reliant on it. It is not a perfect system, and obscures some connections between words in which the same kana characters are used. In Japan, romaji appears in the popular press and in tourist information. Most Japanese have a working knowledge of romaji, can spell their names, sound out romjai words, etc.

The mix of these systems can be confusing for the beginning student, but it adds to the richness of the Japanese written language. While the two kana systems cannot be mixed in a single word, there is otherwise a great deal of freedom of expression provided by blending systems. Experienced students and native speakers will often blend systems to suit their purpose and audience.

In the first of the following tables are given the *katakana* characters arranged in the Japanese order of the ***go-jū-on*** 五十音 "the fifty sounds." Under each *katakana* is given the corresponding *hiragana*, and under that the equivalent in roman letters.

Katakaná and ***Hiraganá*** Table I

	ワ わ wa	ラ ら ra	ヤ や ya	マ ま ma	ハ は ha	ナ な na	タ た ta	サ さ sa	カ か ka	ア あ a
	ヰ ゐ i	リ り ri	イ い i	ミ み mi	ヒ ひ hi	ニ に ni	チ ち chi	シ し shi	キ き ki	イ い i
	ウ う u	ル る ru	ユ ゆ yu	ム む mu	フ ふ fu	ヌ ぬ nu	ツ つ tsu	ス す su	ク く ku	ウ う u
	ヱ ゑ e	レ れ re	エ え e	メ め me	ヘ へ he	ネ ね ne	テ て te	セ せ se	ケ け ke	エ え e
ン ん n	ヲ を wo	ロ ろ ro	ヨ よ yo	モ も mo	ホ ほ ho	ノ の no	ト と to	ソ そ so	コ こ ko	オ お o

By putting two small marks or a small circle on the right side of the upper part of certain syllables, their sound is modified.

The two small marks are called ***nigori*** **濁**, and the small circle is called ***maru*** 丸 or ***handaku*** 半濁.

Table II

ヴァ va	パ ぱ pa	バ ば ba	ダ だ da	ザ ざ za	ガ が ga
ヴィ vi	ピ ぴ p	ビ び bi	ヂ ぢ ji	ジ じ ji	ギ ぎ gi
ヴ vu	プ ぷ pu	ブ ぶ bu	ヅ づ zu	ズ ず zu	グ ぐ gu
ヴェ ve	ペ ぺ pe	ベ べ be	デ で de	ゼ ぜ ze	ゲ げ ge
ヴォ vo	ポ ぽ po	ボ ぼ bo	ド ど do	ゾ ぞ zo	ゴ ご go

N. B. The separate column on the left includes four combinations of characters representing the sounds of the consonant ***v*** with the four vowels ***a, i, e,*** and ***o,*** and one single character to represent the sound of ***v*** and ***u,*** all of which are used only to write foreign words.

In writing words of foreign derivation, the sound of **di,** as in the word *dictation*, may be represented by the symbol **チ** or **ティ.**

birudingu ビルヂング or ビルディング building

By the combination of certain syllables with ***ya*** ャ, ***yu*** ュ, and ***yo*** ョ, other sounds are obtained. In this case the characters corresponding to *ya, yu*, and *yo* are written in a smaller size than the characters with which they are combined.

Table III

リャ りゃ rya	ミャ みゃ mya	ヒャ ひゃ hya	ニャ にゃ nya	チャ ちゃ cha	シャ しゃ sha	キャ きゃ kya
リュ りゅ ryu	ミュ みゅ myu	ヒュ ひゅ hyu	ニュ にゅ nyu	チュ ちゅ chu	シュ しゅ shu	キュ きゅ kyu
リョ りょ ryo	ミョ みょ myo	ヒョ ひょ hyo	ニョ にょ nyo	チョ ちょ cho	ショ しょ sho	キョ きょ kyo
	ピャ ぴゃ pya	ビャ びゃ bya	ヂャ ぢゃ ja	ジャ じゃ ja	ギャ ぎゃ gya	
	ピュ ぴゅ pyu	ビュ びゅ byu	ヂュ ぢゅ ju	ジュ じゅ ju	ギュ ぎゅ gyu	
	ピョ ぴょ pyo	ビョ びょ byo	ヂョ ぢょ jo	ジョ じょ jo	ギョ ぎょ gyo	

Note that all the Japanese characters transliterated with roman letters and containing ***y*** in the body of the syllable, have diphthongal sounds

Short Vowels

A, a is pronounced as **a** in *father.*
E, e as in the first syllable of the words *enamel, enemy, edge, melody.*
I, i as **e** in *me, be.*
O, o as in *oasis, opinion, original.*
U, u as in *put, push, pull, full.*

The ***u*** of the syllable ***su*** is almost silent when followed by a syllable beginning with ***k,*** and the ***u*** of the syllable ***ku*** is, in certain words, almost silent when followed by a syllable beginning with ***s.***

U is almost silent also in the verbal suffix *masu* マス, as in *tabemasu* (*tabemas'*) 食ベマス I eat, *ikimasu* (*ikimas'*) 行キマス I go.

sukoshi (*s'koshi*) 少シ little *suki* (*s'ki*) 好キ I like
takusan (*tak'san*) 沢山 much *okusan* (*ok'san*) 奥サン Madam

In such cases the almost silent ***u*** will be, in this book, distinguished by a curve placed above, as shown below:

sŭkóshi 少シ little ***sŭkí*** 好キ I like
takŭsán 沢山 much ***ókŭsan*** 奥サン Mrs., Madam
ikimásŭ 行キマス I go
kakimásŭ 書キマス I write

In certain words, and invariably in the suffix ***máshĭta*** マシタ, also the vowel ***i*** is almost silent, as in ***shĭtá*** (*sh'ta*) 下 *under,* in which case the ***i*** will similarly be distinguished by a curve, as in the following examples:

ikimáshĭta 行キマシタ I went ***mimáshĭta*** 見マシタ I saw

The graphic accent placed on one of the vowels of each of the above words given as phonetic examples, indicates the force of utterance to be laid on their stressed syllables.

Long Vowels

The long vowels are characterized by a line placed above them.

Ā, ā as in *park, lark, spark.*
Ē, ē as the sound of **a** in *ape, fame, same* or ***ay*** in *day, may, say.*
Ō, ō as in *so, old,* and as **oa** in *oats, oath.*
Ū, ū as **oo** in *boom, soon, broom, spoon.*

The long vowel ***e*** is often written ***ei.***

The long sound of ***i*** (pron. **ee,** as in **beer**) is generally written ***ii.***

okāsan	オ母サン	mother	***ōkii***	大キイ	big, large
obāsan	オバアサン	grandmother	***kōsan***	降参	surrender
nēsan	姉サン	elder sister	***ureshii***	ウレシイ	glad, happy
kēsan	ケーサン	paper weight	***kanashii***	カナシイ	sad
eikō	栄光	glory	***joyū***	女優	actress
heitai	兵隊	soldier	***kūshū***	空襲	air raid
kōhei	公平	impartiality	***mōbaku***	盲爆	blind bombing
kōkei	光景	a scene	***sabishii***	淋シイ	lonesome
sōkei	総計	total amount	***niisan***	兄サン	elder brother

Note that it is essential to distinguish long from short vowel sounds, if one wishes to speak the Japanese language intelligibly. Many words written with short vowels have a different meaning when written with long vowels.

koshí	腰	the waist	***kōshi***	孝子	dutiful child
kósei	個性	personality	***kōsei***	校正	proof reading
súji	筋	muscle	***sūji***	数字	a numeral, a figure
bóshi	拇指	thumb	***bōshi***	帽子	hat
kukí	茎	a stalk	***kūki***	空気	air
kosúi	湖水	a lake	***kōsui***	香水	perfume
kúro	黒	black	***kurō***	苦労	suffering
tóru	取ル	to take	***tōru***	通ル	to go through
toshí	年	year	***tōshi***	投資	investment

When writing Japanese with *kaná*, the sound of the long vowel ***a*** may be represented by the symbol **ア,** placed after the character containing the long vowel, as in the following examples:

obāsan	オバアサン	grandmother
okāsan	オカアサン	mother

The sound of the long vowel ***o*** may be represented in five ways, as shown in Table IV and Table V, and the long vowel ***u*** in two ways, as given in Table VIII.

The different ways of representing the sound of thelong vowels *o* and *u* are indiscriminately used by the Japanese, both in writing and in printing. However, to avoid confusion, the sound of the long vowel *o* and *u* has been represented in this book in one way only, as given in the upper division of each of the following tables.

Katakaná

Table IV

rō	yō	mō	pō	bō	hō	nō	dō	tō	zō	sō	gō	kō	ō
ロオ	ヨオ	モオ	ポオ	ボオ	ホオ	ノオ	ドオ	トオ	ゾオ	ソオ	ゴオ	コオ	オオ
ロウ	ヨウ	モウ	ポウ	ボウ	ホウ	ノウ	ドウ	トウ	ゾウ	ソウ	ゴウ	コウ	オウ
ラウ	ヤウ	マウ	パウ	バウ	ハウ	ナウ	ダウ	タウ	ザウ	サウ	ガウ	カウ	アウ
ラフ	ヤフ	マフ	パフ	バフ	ハフ	ナフ	ダフ	タフ	ザフ	サフ	ガフ	カフ	アフ
ロフ	ヨフ	モフ	ポフ	ボフ	ホフ	ノフ	ドフ	トフ	ゾフ	ソフ	ゴフ	コフ	オフ

	ō
OBSOLETE SPELLING	ヲウ
	ワウ
	ワフ
	ヲフ

Hiraganá

Table V

rō	yō	mō	pō	bō	hō	nō	dō	tō	zō	sō	gō	kō	ō
ろお	よお	もお	ぽお	ぼお	ほお	のお	どお	とお	ぞお	そお	ごお	こお	おお
ろう	よう	もう	ぽう	ぼう	ほう	のう	どう	とう	ぞう	そう	ごう	こう	おう
らう	やう	まう	ぱう	ばう	はう	なう	だう	たう	ざう	さう	がう	かう	あう
らふ	やふ	まふ	ぱふ	ばふ	はふ	なふ	だふ	たふ	ざふ	さふ	がふ	かふ	あふ
ろふ	よふ	もふ	ぽふ	ぼふ	ほふ	のふ	どふ	とふ	ぞふ	そふ	ごふ	こふ	おふ

	ō
OBSOLETE SPELLING	をう
	わう
	わふ
	をふ

Katakaná

Table VI

ryō	myō	pyō	byō	hyō	nyō	chō	shō	gyō	kyō	jō	OBSOLETE SPELLING jō
リョウ	ミョウ	ピョウ	ビョウ	ヒョウ	ニョウ	チョウ	ショウ	ギョウ	キョウ	ジョウ	ヂョウ
リャウ	ミャウ	ピャウ	ビャウ	ヒャウ	ニャウ	チャウ	シャウ	ギャウ	キャウ	ジャウ	ヂャウ
レウ	メウ	ペウ	ベウ	ヘウ	ネウ	テウ	セウ	ゲウ	ケウ	ゼウ	デウ
レフ	ミフ	ペフ	ベフ	ヘフ	ネフ	テフ	セフ	ゲフ	ケフ	ゼフ	デフ

Hiraganá

Table VII

ryō	myō	pyō	byō	hyō	nyō	chō	shō	gyo	kyō	jō	OBSOLETE SPELLING jō
りょう	みょう	ぴょう	びょう	ひょう	にょう	ちょう	しょう	ぎょう	きょう	じょう	ぢょう
りゃう	みゃう	ぴゃう	びゃう	ひゃう	にゃう	ちゃう	しゃう	ぎゃう	きゃう	じゃう	ぢゃう
れう	めう	ぺう	べう	べう	ねう	てう	せう	げう	けう	ぜう	でう
れふ	みふ	ぺふ	べふ	へふ	ねふ	てふ	せふ	げふ	けふ	ぜふ	でふ

Table VIII

ryū	myū	pyū	byū	hyū	nyū	jū	chū	jū	shū	gyū	kyū	yū
リュウ	ミュウ	ピュウ	ビュウ	ヒュウ	ニュウ	ヂュウ	チュウ	ジュウ	シュウ	ギュウ	キュウ	ユウ
リフ	ミフ	ピフ	ビフ	ヒフ	ニフ	ヂフ	チフ	ジフ	シフ	ギフ	キフ	ユフ

The sound of all long vowels may also be represented, when writing in *kana*, by a bar placed immediately after the syllable containing the long vowel, especially when writing certain words of foreign derivation, as shown in the following examples:

bīru	ビール	beer
erebētā	エレベーター	elevator
kōhī	コーヒー	coffee
sūtēshon	ステーション	station
taipūraitā	タイプライター	typewriter
tēburu	テーブル	table

Note that words of foreign derivation generally maintain the accent upon the syllable corresponding to the one stressed in the original foreign word.

When a *kaná* character is repeated in succession in the same word, the duplicated character is represented by the symbol ヽ.

háha ハヽ mother ***chichí*** チヽ father

When writing Japanese in horizontal lines, a word written in *kaná* may be regularly repeated with syllabic characters, as for instance ***iró-iró*** イロイロ *various*, ***kutá-kutá*** クタクタ *worn out*, but when writing Japanese in vertical lines, the repetition is indicated by a long mark resembing the character く (ku) of the *hiraganá* syllabary, as shown on the right side of this explanation.

イロ〳〵 クタ〳〵

The symbol ヽ takes the *nigori* when it is used to indicate that the sound of the duplicated character is altered according to Table III.

Ex: *kagamí* カヾミ mirror *kogotó* コヾト a scolding

Also the symbol used to indicate the repetition of a word takes the *nigori* when the sound of the first character of the duplicated word is altered according to Table III. The words vertically written on the right of this explanation correspond to the ones given below.

トキ〱 クニ〱

kuníguni クニグニ countries *tokidokí* トキドキ now and then

The repetition of a *kanji* is indicated by the symbol **々**.

iró-iró 色々 various ***tabí-tabí*** 度々 often

Consonants

The consonants ***b, d, j, k, m, n, p,*** and ***t,*** are pronounced as they are in English.

G is always pronounced hard as in *garland*. Ex. *gakú* 額 framed picture, *géki* 劇 a drama, *gímu* 義務 duty, *gógo* 午後 afternoon. When ***g*** is in the body of a word, it is generally pronounced as if it were preceded by a faint sound of **n.** Ex. *kagó* (*ka$_n$go*) 籠 cage, *kagamí* (*ka$_n$gami*) 鏡 mirror.

F is pronounced with the two lips a little apart, and one's lower and upper teeth almost in contact, not with the lower lip and the upper teeth as Western people pronounce it.

H is always pronounced aspirated as in *hope*.

The symbol **ン,** corresponding to the sound of ***n,*** is pronounced ***m*** before ***b, p*** and ***m.***

シンブン *shi**m**bún* newspaper ワンパクナ *wá**m**paku-na* naughty
センモンカ *se**mm**onká* specialist ホンモノ *ho**mm**onó* genuine article

R is not pronounced as distinctly as it is in English; it approaches the sound of **l,** but until one hears it from a Japanese, it is better not to try to pronounce it differently from the natural way one is accustomed to.

The sound of **l** does not exist in the Japanese language, and when foreign words containing this consonant are to be written with *kana* characters, the **r** symbols are used.

Labrador	*Rabŭradorú*	ラブラドル	lamp	*rámpu*	ランプ
London	*Róndon*	ロンドン	lemonade	*remonēdo*	レモネード

S before a vowel, is always pronounced as in *salmon, self, solar.*

Sh is pronounced as in *shaft, sheep.*

Ch is pronounced as in *cherry, chief, choice.*

The syllable ***wa*** is pronounced as in *waft*, and the syllable ***wo***, which is used to indicate the accusative case, is pronounced as **wo** in *worship*, when it follows a word ending in ***n***, but when it follows a word ending in a vowel, the ***w*** is almost silent.

wakái	ワカイ	young	*waraú*	ワラウ	to laugh
hon wo	ホンヲ	the book	*umá wo*	ウマヲ	the horse

Y is pronounced as in English in the words *yacht*, *yell*, *yonder*, *you*. When **y** is preceded by **i**, both letters should be pronounced distinctly to avoid mistaking their combined sound for that of some of the diphtongs given in Table IV.

biyōin	美ビ容ヨウ院イン	beauty parlour	***byōin***	病ビョウ院イン	hospital
kiyō	器キ用ヨウ	skilful	***kyō***	今日(キョウ)	to-day

Z is pronounced as in *zeal*, *zodiac*, *zone*.

Double Consonants

Care must be taken to distinguish single from double consonants, as many words that have single consonants change meaning when these are pronounced double. The double consonants are pronounced in Japanese as they are in Italian, that is, they are stressed by holding for a moment the vocal organs in the position required to pronounce them.

kóka	古コ歌カ	an old song	***kokká***	国コッ歌カ	national anthem
isó	磯イソ	beach	***issō***	一イッ層ソウ	more
sóto	外ソト	outside	***sottó***	ソット	softly
tokú	徳トク	virtue	***tokkú***	トック	already
hikakú	比ヒ較カク	comparison	***hikkáku***	引ヒッ掻カク	to scratch

The small *katakaná* on the right side of the above *kanji* indicate the pronunciation of the latter.

The phonetic syllables attached to ideograms, whether written with *katakaná* or *hiraganá*, are called *furiganá* 振フリ仮ガ名ナ. Use of furiganá was once frowned upon in Japan. But today, in the age of the Internet an international commerce, furiganá is viewed as a "necessary evil," since, essentially the writer is using the same sound twice.

Katakaná and *hiraganá* cannot be mixed in the same composition, so that the *furiganá* must be written with the characters of the same syllabary used with the ideograms.

The double consonants are indicated by having the affected character preceded by a small ッ (*tsu*), as shown in the above five words on the right.

The double pronunciation of **ch** is represented in roman characters by ***tch*** and in *kaná* characters by ッ placed before the affected syllable.

kotchí	コッチ	here	***dótchi***	ドッチ	which
atchí	アッチ	there	***mátchi***	マッチ	matches

Accentuation

Some of the early studies of the Japanese language expressed the view that the syllables of Japanese words bear scarcely any accentuation. This error concerning Japanese accentuation has been carried over into later studies, mainly because of inadequate research into this important aspect of the language.

The fact is that syllabic stresses vary in any words containing two or more syllables, no matter what the language may be.

To the untrained Western ear, the comparatively unemotional manner of speaking of the Japanese may appear to lack syllabic stress. When their emotions are aroused, however, the Japanese stress their syllables clearly and specifically.

If Japanese words are not correctly accented, they sound as oddly foreign to Japanese ears as, say, the English language sounds to English ears when spoken by French students who may tend to stress the last syllables of English words according to French usage.

The correct stress on Japanese syllables is the more important in that the Japanese language contains numerous words which, although spelled with the same letters, have different meaning according to the position of the stressed syllable.

The examples given below, which represent only a very small number of words spelled with the same letters but having different meaning according to the position of their stressed syllable, will demonstrate how necessary it is to know the right accentuation of Japanese words.

ása	朝	morning	***asá***	麻	flax, hemp
haná	花	flower	***hána***	端	the outset, beginning
hashí	橋	a bridge	***háshi***	箸	chopsticks
ippái	いっぱい	full, up to the brim	***íppai***	一杯	one cupful
kagú	嗅ぐ	to smell	***kágu***	家具	furniture
karasu	枯らす	to let wither	***kárasu***	烏	a crow
kashí	貸し	loan	***káshi***	樫	oak tree

kaú	買う	to buy	***káu***	飼う	to keep (animals)
kiji	雉子	a pheasant	***kiji***	記事	article (of newspaper)
kirú	着る	to wear put on	***kíru***	切る	to cut
nashi	梨	a pear	***náshi***	無し	without
magó	孫	grandchild	***mágo***	馬子	pack-horseman
omoi	重い	heavy	***omói***	思い	emotion, feeling
séki	席	seat, pew	***seki***	咳	cough
shímai	姉妹	sisters	***shimai***	仕舞	end, close
tátsu	立つ	to stand up	***tatsú***	竜	dragon
úji	氏	family stock	***uji***	蛆	larva
yói	良い	good	***yoi***	宵	early evening

To provide the student with the essential approach to correct pronunciation, the authors have had a graphic accent printed on the stressed syllable of the Japanese words given throughout the book.

This new and unique feature will prove to be of great benefit to the student, as he will be able, from the very beginning of his study, and without mental effort, to pronounce the words he gradually learns, correctly and intelligibly to Japanese ears.

Romanization of the Language

There are three systems of romanization of the Japanese language. Of the three, however, the Hepburn system is by far the most widley used, both in Japan as well as abroad, for which the reason it has been adopted by this volume.

Below, the syllables of the three systems that are differently spelled are given for comparison:

Hepburn Spelling	Nippon Spelling	Kunrei Spelling
cha	tya	tya
chi	ti	ti
chu	tyu	tyu
cho	tyo	tyo
fu	hu	hu
ja	dya	zya
ji	di	zi
ju	dyu	zyu
jo	dyo	zyo
sha	sya	sya
shi	si	si
shu	syu	syu
sho	syo	syo
tsu	tu	tu

How to use this CD-ROM for Japanese

This CD-ROM includes **games, tutors, and utilities** that will enrich the experience of learning about Japanese language and culture. Most of the applications included on the CD-ROM focus on learning the Japanese writing systems, kanji, katakana, and hiragana. As you begin your study of the Japanese language, these applications will help you deepen your understanding of written and spoken Japanese, as well as assist you in tracking your progress. As your fluidity with the language increases, you will find new challenges in the software, complementing your study of the text.

To begin, open the file entitled OPENME.HTML in your favorite Web browser, such as Microsoft Internet Explorer or Netscape Navigator. This file will provide an overview of the applications included on the CD-ROM.

Microsoft Internet Explorer users may install the applications by simply clicking on their icons. This will initiate the installation process. When prompted, choose to open the file from its current location.

Netscape Navigator users may view the HTML file to get more information about each application. When you have chosen the applications you would like to install, follow the steps below:

1. Double-click on the My Computer icon on your desktop

2. Right-click on the CD-ROM icon in the My Computer window, and choose "Explore."

3. Double-click on the shortcut that corresponds to the program you would like to install.

For more information about the developers of each application, view the "Links" page in your favorite Web browser. Please note that a browser is not required to install the applications on the CD-ROM. If you prefer not to use a Web browser, you can install any or all of the applications included by following the steps above.